D1276671

Praise for Paul Raffaele:

"Raffaele might just be the last of the great old-fashioned adventure writers."

—Peter Carlson, *Washington Post.*

"Raffaele is one of the great journalists of our time."

—Bernard Ohanian, former deputy editor, *National Geographic* magazine.

"Raffaele is the last of a breed. He is a throwback to such nineteenth-century British explorer-writers as Richard Burton and John Hanning Speke."

—Carey Winfrey, editor-in-chief, *Smithsonian* magazine.

"Paul Raffaele is nothing less than a one-of-a-kind world treasure. Travelling via camel back and canoe, wrapping an anaconda around his neck, dancing with tribesmen, uncovering supposedly non-existent pockets of slavery—Raffaele brings back accurate, colorful stories from the remotest regions on earth. He reveals just how diverse human beings can be. His writing will not only grip readers but provide invaluable material for the historians of tomorrow."

—Alvin Toffler, best-selling author of *Future Shock* and *The Third Wave.*

"In breathtaking dispatches from forest front lines around the world, Paul Raffaele documents the fascinating richness and alarming future of the lives of our close cousins."

—Professor Richard Wrangham, world-renowned primatologist, Harvard University.

THE RAINFOREST SURVIVORS

THE
RAINFOREST
SURVIVORS

ADVENTURES AMONG TODAY'S STONE AGE JUNGLE TRIBES

PAUL RAFFAELE

Skyhorse Publishing

For Cecilia, Cathy, Andrew, Bobby, and Bear

Skyhorse Publishing books may be purchased in bulk at special discounts for sales promotion, corporate gifts, fund-raising, or educational purposes. Special editions can also be created to specifications. For details, contact the Special Sales Department, Skyhorse Publishing, 307 West 36th Street, 11th Floor, New York, NY 10018 or info@skyhorsepublishing.com.

Skyhorse® and Skyhorse Publishing® are registered trademarks of Skyhorse Publishing, Inc.®, a Delaware corporation.

Visit our website at www.skyhorsepublishing.com.

10 9 8 7 6 5 4 3 2 1

Library of Congress Cataloging-in-Publication Data is available on file.

Cover design by Tom Lau

Print ISBN: 978-1-5107-3711-2
Ebook ISBN: 978-1-5107-3713-6

Printed in the United States of America

CONTENTS

"One of the gladdest moments in human life is the departure upon a distant journey into unknown lands." —Sir Richard Burton

PROLOGUE

For much of my life I have wandered all the continents as a foreign correspondent seeking the most extraordinary peoples on Earth to witness and relate their compelling exploits. I especially seek the tribal survivors of the rainforests, those tens of thousands of indigenous peoples such as the Congo Pygmies, New Guinea's Korowai cannibals, and the Amazon Korubo who still live traditionally in remote and often dangerous jungles with an annual rainfall of at least sixty inches. Their roots remain in the Stone Age even as the early years of the twenty-first century threaten to demolish forever their unique ways of life.

All over the world I have seen ancient civilizations discarding much of what made them unique for centuries, even millennia. Their youngsters have led the charge to modernize, clad in jeans, T-shirts, and sneakers, lining up to see the latest superhero movie on the big screen and mesmerized by the celebrities of Instagram and the taste of the latest McDonalds' fare. But it is not just food, music, movies, and flashy clothes that have seduced them.

At the forefront of our Western ways is the compelling message to the young that they no longer need to obey ancient time-tested moral codes and behavior administered, sometimes harshly, by their elders. Our Western ways have undergone a profound cultural revolution, beginning in the 1960s based on the strident rights of the individual rather than traditional obligations to the community, and the world's youth have enthusiastically flocked to it.

However, there are a few dozen tribes that remain living in the Stone Age, cut off from the rest of the world and knowing little or nothing about us and our very different ways. These rainforest survivor tribes, by their presence, are protecting many millions of square miles of virgin rainforest, the lungs of the earth.

I have journeyed many times to such peoples to witness how they live in admirable harmony with their environments, to hunt with them in their rainforests, to listen to their ancient stories, and to witness and attempt to understand their wisdom and mysterious rites forged over many millennia.

What are their similarities and differences, and what habitat and spiritual forces forged their unique natures? Soon enough their cultures will disappear, swamped by the lure of our modern ways—fast food, satellite TV, and the tourist dollar that have turned many of their kin into sideshow acts in their own lands.

In this book I have relived my most recent memorable and meaningful adventures with these people from a distant time.

Mention of Pygmies evokes an alien world in deepest Africa humming with mystery and adventure. The ancients were dazzled by wanderers' tales of a mysterious race of tiny Africans. Pharaohs and emperors of Rome were captivated by the world's smallest people. Modern moguls, Hollywood movie directors, cast them as exotic extras in tales of primitive Africa.

And yet they are among the most modern of humans today, living traditionally in complete harmony with nature in their rainforests. For many thousands of years they have taken only what they needed from the forests—all their food, clothing, tools, and the saplings and mud they use to build their domed huts. All of it is biodegradable, disintegrating into forest mulch when abandoned.

In contrast, over the past centuries the Bantu, taller Africans, have invaded their homelands, burning and chopping down the forests to provide living space for themselves and grazing land for their cattle. The Pygmies lived side by side with their forests' wildlife for millennia but Bantu poachers are stripping many of the forests of their wild creatures for marketplace meat. This is plunging the gorillas, rainforest elephants, and many other creatures to the edge of endangerment.

Many Pygmy clans by force or by necessity now live almost as diminutive Bantu, well outside of their beloved rainforests. The Bantu commonly marginalize, mock, brutalize, and enslave them. But the Bayaka clan in the tumultuous Central African Republic have retained most of their traditional practices even though they too are under daily threat from the Bantu.

I spent much time with the Bayaka in their vast rainforest during three journeys there. The clan's greatest hunter, who barely came up to my shoulder (I'm a mere 5'7") took me deep into the rainforest to track lowland gorillas and the rarely seen mysterious forest elephants. Our bond grew stronger when I saved the life of his baby boy.

Pygmy clans have no chief. The young Pygmies practice free love with their parents' blessing, but once they marry infidelity is taboo. On my final night with them their most powerful rainforest spirit, Ejengi, emerged from a cluster of tall trees to greet the stranger from far away and dance for many hours in a frenzy of chanting and drumming with his people.

Halfway across the world, in another rainforest in Indonesian New Guinea, the Korowai are the last cannibal tribe on earth. Cannibal—it is one of the most repelling and yet compelling words in our language. The Korowai build their straw huts high in the trees and live in the Stone Age, hunting with bows and arrows, using axes hacked from rock, and having limited or no contact with the outside world. In an eerie ritual that could date back millennia, they seek out witch-men to kill and eat them.

My journey to be with the Korowai was long and hazardous. Like the Pygmies, they have no chiefs, though in their frequent battles with other clans' warriors they follow the lead of their best fighter, honored with the title "fierce man." I stayed in the tree house of Agoos, a "fierce man," even though the Korowai call outsiders *laleo*, or ghost demon. He yearned to see the outside world, what he called my "village." When I tried to describe skyscrapers, cars, movies, and whales to him, it was like relating fairy tales. With considerable common sense, he would only believe me if he saw them with his own eyes. In one of the most moving and memorable experiences of my life, I gave Agoos that chance.

For countless millennia many human tribes were cannibalistic, even in Europe, but the Korowai are the last survivors of a time beyond time.

In Brazil, Sydney Possuelo, a modern-day explorer and one of history's greatest, took me into a no-man's-land, a stretch of dense rainforest the size of South Carolina, to visit a naked Stone Age tribe, the ferocious club-wielding Korubo. Under Possuelo's prompting, the Brazilian government quarantined their traditional territory from outsiders to protect the ancient lifestyles of about 1,400 tribal people still living as their ancestors did many thousands of years ago.

The Korubo have little or no contact with outsiders. I was the first journalist Possuelo had ever taken to meet them, a tribe so aggressive that even Possuelo dared not enter their village at night and on day visits was always accompanied by a pair of armed guards in case the warriors attacked him.

The threat was real. Ta'van, the clan's war chief, had caved in the head of Possuelo's colleague with his fighting pole, and not long before our visit had led a war party to murder three white men when they blundered into the Korubo territory, smashing their heads to pulp and gutting them.

Making friends with the warriors and their chieftain, Maya, a powerful middle-aged woman, was an adventure as thrilling as any undertaken by Indiana Jones, that escapade-loving professor of archaeology. And, like Indy in *Raiders of the Lost Ark*, there was much meaning in the journey. Using the living example of the Korubo, as if taking me time-traveling back to the Stone Age, Possuelo shared with me his ground-breaking philosophy of ensuring that remote Amazon tribes retain as much as possible of their ancient ways for as long as possible.

SECTION ONE:

WITH THE PYGMIES IN THE CONGO

CHAPTER 1

The Congo Pygmies beckon.

There are not many books devoted to the Pygmies, but there are enough references to sharpen my desire to find out more. They are believed to be the world's second oldest race, just behind the Bushmen of southern Africa. The earliest known mention of Pygmies came in a letter written in 2276 BC by Pharaoh Pepi II to a general who brought a Pygmy back to Egypt from a jungle expedition in Central Africa. The Pharaoh called him "the dancing dwarf of the god from the land of the spirits."

Homer pitched Pygmies into a mythical fight to the death against a flock of cranes in his epic *Iliad* to invoke the intensity of the charge of the Trojan army. In the fifth century BC, the Greek historian Herodotus wrote of a Persian explorer seeing from a distance "dwarfish men who used clothing made from the palm tree" at a remote spot along the West African coast.

The secretive Pygmies spawned countless colorful tales far away in their jungle encampments, but they were so elusive that it took another two millennia before the French-American explorer Paul du Chaillu published the first modern account of Pygmies. "Their eyes had an unmistakable wildness about them that struck me as very remarkable," he wrote in 1867.

And in 1890, renowned Welsh explorer Sir Henry Morton Stanley described meeting a Pygmy couple in the Congo in his epic book, *In Darkest Africa*. "In him was a mimicked dignity, as of Adam; in her the womanliness of a miniature Eve."

The Pygmies took such a hold on the outside world's imagination that some were captured and displayed in the US and Europe in circuses, sideshows, and even in zoos, disgracefully portrayed as the missing link between apes and humans. In 1904, several Pygmies were brought from the Congo to live in the anthropology exhibit at the St. Louis World's Fair. Two years later, one of them, Ota Benga, was displayed temporarily at the American Museum of Natural History in New York City and then exhibited, briefly and controversially, in a cage at the Bronx Zoo.

It is not only Caucasians in the past who believed the Pygmies to be sub-human. In 2007 the Republic of the Congo organized a festival of pan-African music in the capital, Brazzaville. The government put all other participants, including the other African performers in the city's hotels, but the organizers housed the twenty-two Pygmy performers in tents at the local zoo.

Today, almost all traditional Pygmy clans are under severe threat from their neighbors, the taller Africans known as the Bantu, and the destruction of their homelands, the rainforests, by corrupt politicians across Central Africa who fatten their bank accounts with the loot from the sale of hundreds of thousands of high-value logs. Within a generation or two, most Pygmy clans will have abandoned or been forced out of their rainforests, primarily because of the deforestation and because their ancient lifestyle cannot compete with the more aggressive Bantu and increasing Westernization. The Bantu population all over Central Africa is surging, while the Pygmies, still living largely in the rainforests, are in steep decline.

Anthropologist Jerome Lewis, who lived with a Pygmy clan, wrote: "Everywhere they have great difficulty with their dispossession (of their land) because their numbers are small and because their egalitarian social organization undermines anyone who emerges as a leader, rejects their authority and generally favors avoidance over confrontation, sharing over private property, individual freedom over organized representation and immediate over delayed returns on labor."

The United Nations spotlighted the consequences of dispossession. "Expulsion of Rwanda's Batwa (Pygmy) people from their rainforest habitat forced them to live as beggars and put them in danger of extinction."

For many thousands of years the Pygmies, unknown to the outside world, were nomads in Equatorial Africa's immense rainforests. They inhabit a narrow band of tropical rainforest about four degrees above and four degrees below the Equator, stretching from the Atlantic coast eastward to Lake Victoria. Pygmies live in the Central African Republic, Uganda, Gabon, Cameroon, Equatorial Guinea, Burundi, Rwanda, the Republic of the Congo, and the Democratic Republic of Congo. With about 500,000 remaining, Pygmies are the largest group of hunter-gatherers left on Earth.

The World Wide Fund for Nature (WWF) has an office in Bangui, capital of the Central African Republic (CAR), whose rainforests are home to thousands of Pygmies. "You'd better come soon because many Pygmies have had to abandon life in the jungles to live as crop growers," a woman in the Bangui office tells me by phone. "The loggers are already in their forests, devastating them."

"Bring me back a poison arrow," my daughter Cathy says cheekily as I board a taxi to take me from my home in Sydney, Australia, to the airport. "But take care you don't sit on it."

A few days later, taking off at midnight from Paris, I jet over North Africa's deserts, bound for the Pygmy homelands. Sitting next to me is an American diplomatic courier, a bulging briefcase never out of her grip. I'm disappointed that it is not handcuffed to her wrist, as in the movies. She has the earnest look of a mid-level official on a mission far more important than herself.

She keeps silent for almost all of the journey, a policy I suppose that could be set out in the courier handbook. You never know who you can trust sitting next to you on an overnight flight. But just before the jet descends at her destination, N'Djamena, capital of Chad, she notices that I am reading a travel handbook devoted to my destination. "You're going to Bangui and the Central African Republic?" she asks. "Be careful, there's a civil war going on with a lot of fighting. It's so dangerous that our government bans all non-essential travel there."

No wonder. The US State Department advisory offers a blunt warning to US citizens to stay away from the CAR, "due to an unpredictable security situation subject to rapid deterioration, activities of armed groups and violent crime. In the event of unrest, airport, and border, and road closure may occur with little or no notice."

To survive in my profession, a foreign correspondent for decades focusing on Africa, Asia, and South America, all you can do is shrug when reading or being given such dire warnings. And I have shrugged countless times over the many years of wandering the dangerous lands. I cannot count the number of times people have told me, sometimes sneeringly and often concerned for my safety, that I have a death wish and should give it up.

My reply is always much the same. "On the contrary, I have an intense life wish," a compelling curiosity to see and experience the best and worst, the most extreme, the happiest and saddest, the most beautiful and even the most tyrannical aspects of human nature in places where Rambo himself might hunger to base his latest adventure movie.

The Central African Republic has much wealth–gold, oil, uranium, cobalt, lumber, hydropower, and diamonds–but hardly any of the wealth trickles down to the common people, who are among the world's poorest. Welcome to Africa. The spoils of victory, military and political, have prompted many civil wars and the extreme poverty impels the horrendous rate of urban and rural crime across the continent.

On the United Nations Human Development Index, a statistic that mercilessly measures a nation's life expectancy, education, and per capita income, the CAR comes 187th out of 188 countries. Norway heads the list and the US comes in at fourteenth.

The country has a long history of utter misery that continues to this day. At 240,535 square miles, it is more than twice as big as many US states and yet its population is just over five million. The slave trade was a major reason for the country's depopulation, one of the hardest hit from the sixteenth through the nineteenth centuries. In *Central African Republic, The Failure of Decolonization,* Pierre Kalck wrote: "For several centuries the fate of many Central Africans was to be bought, or captured and then deported to distant lands."

Slave ports and markets known as *barracoons* were set up along its great river, the Ubangi, with African chieftains financing ruthless slave hunts across Central Africa. They sold uncountable unfortunates to slave traders, who shipped them in millions to the Mediterranean coast, Europe, Arabia, and the Americas. The CAR's ravaged population has yet to recover.

The French added to the misery. Kalck wrote: "The first years during which France took responsibility for Central Africa can be divided into several periods: exploration (before 1900; brutal exploitation (1900-20); attempts at colonization (1920-45; emancipation (1945-60); and the achievement of independence (after 1960)."

The Pygmies, far away in the southwest corner of Central Africa, were spared the slave traders' horrors. Their diminutive size also could not be compared with that of the tall, muscular Bantu. However, as I was to discover, many Pygmies in their own homeland were and still are forced by the Bantu to endure another form of slavery. The following thought might send the politically correct into a fit of social media anger but from what I have witnessed in several continents and through my reading of history across the millennia, humans enslaving other humans is a trait entrenched deep within the common DNA of humankind.

Bangui is the jet's next stop. The jet climbs back into a darkened sky but a couple of hours later, as daylight filters through the gloom, dense forests and winding rivers appear below, shimmering with ribbons of drifting mist. We land at Bangui airport, a ramshackle huddle of sheds. Sullen barefoot porters in torn shorts and T-shirts dump the bags on a concrete floor under a tin roof. When all the bags are taken off the plane, there are still ten of us waiting empty-handed. I recognise them as fellow business-class passengers.

"Your bags must have been left in Paris," says a stocky manager from the airline. "They'll arrive in a couple of days on the next flight."

"How come it's just the business class luggage that's missing?" I ask.

"It's obvious, they were in the same container," he shrugs, all lips, shoulders, and hands. The region that is now known as the Central African Republic was colonised by the French in 1894, and although the CAR gained independence in 1960, it is still tied to Paris by economic, defense, and cultural links. During the colonial rule the locals obviously took a liking to the emotive Gallic body language.

A tall, square-shouldered Frenchman in an elegantly cut dark suit, blue silk tie, and polished black shoes mutters something to the official. Though clad in the uniform of an international businessman, he has the merciless eyes of a battle-hardened soldier.

The airline official shrugs once more. The Frenchman peppers him with a machine-gun clatter of short sharp words. This time the official nervously pulls at his collar and nods.

I may be lucky but in what must be almost one thousand flights over the decades across the globe, my suitcase has only been "lost" once. That was in Colombo, capital of Sri Lanka, and I was the last passenger at the baggage carousel. Just one suitcase made its lonely journey around and around the carousel but it was not mine. It was the wrong color.

I dutifully filled out a lost baggage form and then, through the fog of jet lag, the truth hit me. The suitcase on the carousel was mine. I had discarded my previous, much battered bag, and purchased a new one a day before I flew to Colombo. I explained my mistake but the airline clerk was not convinced because it sounded feeble even to me. He tore up the form when I described the suitcase contents and then opened it, followed by a sheepish grin. The clerk waved me off with a cynical smirk.

Bangui, swathed with tropical trees and flowers, overlooks a broad muddy river, the Ubangi, notorious for its essential role in the former slave trade. The city must have once been a delightful place, but many of its buildings are pockmarked by bullets from the ongoing civil war. "This place is hell on earth," the taxi driver says in English with a soupy French accent when I ask about the visible evidence of mayhem. He surprises me by not suggesting a tour of Bangui's delights, usually the opening offer by airport taxi drivers I have encountered around the developing world. Perhaps there are no delights.

At the Kilometre 5 intersection, the checkpoint for entry into the city, amid a snarl of honking minibuses, the taxi inches forward at a roadblock manned by tough-faced French Foreign Legionnaires standing by an armored personnel carrier (APC). A lieutenant, ignoring my "bonjour," inspects my passport and waves the taxi on.

Bangui looks as if it is about to explode into warfare. More APCs manned by Legionnaires roar through the streets, a watchful soldier gripping a machine gun mounted on each carrier. We pass grim-faced soldiers from an African peacekeeping force patrolling in single file and carrying assault rifles, their nervous eyes swivelling from side to side. Other peacekeepers crouch behind sandbag positions piled up at street intersections, rifles at the ready.

The multi-story Bangui Hotel perches on the riverbank with a view across the wide, fast-flowing Ubangi River to the fields of the Democratic Republic of Congo (DRC). A large jagged hole with scorch marks mars the front wall. "The rebels fired a rocket at the hotel a few months ago," the taxi driver says.

Two army trucks painted with camouflage patterns are parked in the hotel driveway. The twenty soldiers they brought here cradle assault rifles as they sit on stools behind two piles of sandbags. "They're here to protect hotel guests," the desk clerk tells me. After checking in, I thank him for warning me to remain in the hotel, then I take a stroll up a steep hill to the town, just over a mile away.

Much later at home in Sydney, when I recalled that perilous behavior, it prompted a knowing smile. Repeatedly over the decades I have strolled or flown or driven into dangerous places, willingly facing down rebels bristling with assault rifles pointed at me. I've also walked up to silverback gorillas thumping their barrel chests as warnings that they were going to charge me, and was once stalked by a massive Siberian tiger through a snowfield in the Russian Far East. It seemed at the time as everyday normal behavior as having coffee at the local café or strolling up the road to buy the daily newspaper.

But when I get home each time and read through my location notes and look at the photos I had taken, I often shake my head in wonder. Who is this crazy man? I think. What on earth prompted him to do things most people would regard as insanely risky and death-defying? To this day I have no idea of the genesis of my bisected personality. Mild-mannered Paul and Mad Dog Raffaele.

Bangui's streets still have stirring French names: Avenue de l'Independence, Avenue des Martyrs, Route de la Grand Corniche, and even a Boulevard General de Gaulle, but their grandiloquent titles are not matched by the crumbling concrete buildings that line them. It is mid-morning, but apart from the patrolling soldiers, the APCs, and the peacekeepers peering from behind sandbags, the boulevards are largely deserted. Bangui is eerily quiet.

By the Place de la Republique, marked by a moldy triumphal arch celebrating the coronation of a bloodthirsty dictator, a young man with molten dark eyes, jet-black hair, hooked nose, and olive skin beckons me into his dimly lit trade store. The shelves are largely empty and his stock consists of a few cans of corned beef, some packets of washing powder, and a stack of cheaply printed school exercise books. "My name is Ali, my family come from Yemen," he says. "But I was born here."

Ali is one of thousands of ethnic Middle Eastern traders, mostly Yemenis and Lebanese, who run the small trade stores throughout Africa. "You better leave Bangui as soon as possible," he warns. "Trouble is on its way, I can smell it in the air." He points to a beefy African sitting on a chair by the door at the entrance. A pistol is strapped to his waist. "My bodyguard can escort you back to your hotel."

I turn down his offer, but heed his warning and walk quickly back to the hotel after slipping my watch into my pocket. I will be a couple of days at the most in Bangui waiting for my luggage, I hope, and will then head south to the Dzanga-Sangha rainforest in search of the Pygmies. It should be more peaceful down there.

At the hotel the Frenchman from the plane is eating lunch outdoors at a table overlooking the river. Dining with him are several middle-aged men clad in French army uniforms and their demeanour, age, and lapel decorations show them to be senior officers.

"Legionnaires," murmurs the waiter who serves me a salad and grilled river fish.

"Ah, the brave warriors who smashed the Tuareg warlords of the Sahara."

"Look at their stomachs," he says, lowering his voice. "They're more likely to demolish a crème brulee or attack a bowl of onion soup."

"But your city is the hotspot in a civil war and the officers surely have to lead their men on the front line."

He snorts in disgust. "These bastards are French, the officers, and you won't see them in the fighting. But we're truly scared of the

Legion's real fighters. They're mostly Germans and they show us no mercy."

That may be so, but the officer who was on the same flight from Paris looked to be a man who would not only lead his troops into battle but relish the fighting. The French Foreign Legion's long and valiant history is white-hot with such men.

At mid-afternoon, the phone rings in my room. It is the airline advising that my bag has been found. At the airport, the Frenchman is waiting in the baggage hall with several other passengers. "They were here all the time," he says as the still sullen porters carry our bags into the hall.

"How did they discover them?" I ask.

The Frenchman smiles, but his eyes do not soften. "I told the airline manager that friends of mine would apply persuasion to him if he didn't find our bags quickly," he says. "The bastards had put them aside and were going to loot them once they finished work today."

Back in my room, the phone rings just after dinner. "Hello, Paul, my name is Sophie. Would you like to come dancing with me tonight?"

Night-bird invitations are common in Third World countries. The girl had been alerted by the front desk clerk that there was a single male in room such and such. Experience has taught me that a polite refusal is usually enough to discourage further calls.

"Thanks, but I don't need a girl tonight."

Her laughter flows sweet and throaty. "Silly boy. I'm not a whore. I'm employed by the company hiring you the driver and vehicle to go to the Pygmies. I've arranged for you to leave tomorrow morning and I thought you might like to see Bangui's night-life."

"Is it dangerous?"

"Sure, but you must be the kind of man who seeks it. Why else would you come here in the middle of our civil war?"

Standing by the front desk, Sophie is a spectacular sight. Tall and willowy, she wears a yellow print dress cut in the West African style. It clings low to her bosom, sweeps down to shape her waist, and then flows tightly along her thighs to her ankles. Her slim brown face boasts high cheekbones, full lips, almond eyes, and smooth skin. She has the languid manner of a supermodel, or a cat, seemingly oblivious to her beauty and yet standing by the front desk in such a way that highlights it.

"Welcome to Bangui," she says.

"I'm like a hippo on the dance floor," I warn her.

She laughs once more, deep and bubbly, and the delight is trebled by the dazzle of her dark eyes and flash of white teeth. She pushes a finger into my ample stomach. "African girls like their men hefty," she says with a wry smile.

"You're kidding me?"

"Maybe not," she smiles. "All the chiefs here have big stomachs. It signals wealth and power."

"Well, I have neither."

She waggles a finger playfully in front of my nose. "As a Westerner you're halfway there. The average family income in Bangui is a dollar a day. In the rural areas it's even less than that."

At 5-foot-7, I feel like a dwarf beside Sophie. "My tribe, the Sara, are among the tallest people on earth," she explains.

"How tall are you," I ask, glancing up at her.

"I'm about average for a Sara female. 1.82 metres (6'0"). Our men average 1.93 metres (6'4"). We make up about 10 percent of the CAR's population."

"That's amazing. The CAR has one of the world's tallest races and the world's smallest. How come?"

"We're Nilotic, a very tall race. My ancestors migrated from the Nile a thousand years ago. But the Pygmies have been in their rainforests for tens of thousands of years. That's the way they evolved."

A taxi takes us back to Kilometer 5. A Legionnaire corporal with an assault rifle strung over his shoulder peers inside and frowns, but waves us through the roadblock. *"Guten abend"* is on the tip of my tongue but I hold it there so that it goes no farther in case he is not a German.

The intersection is thronged with the ubiquitous minibuses and people eating chicken and drinking beer at food stalls illuminated by dim lights. A few hundred yards down the street, the taxi pulls up outside a nightclub, Bar ABC. Sophie grips my hand and pulls me inside. "It's not safe to stand on the street," she says. "We're a poor country, and there are many robbers."

A DJ plays the latest CDs from Paris, and the dance floor is crowded with sturdy men and slim women dancing to the thumping beat with sinuous rhythm. A lumbering hippopotamus in the midst of graceful cheetahs is not a pretty sight. From the men I get plenty of mocking smiles and comments in Sango, the local dialect, that are probably humorously insulting. Sophie, alert to the reaction, leads me to sit at the bar to drink chilled bottles of Mocaf, local beer, and talk. In case it embarrasses her, I do not ask for a translation of the dance-floor taunts.

"I grew up in Paris, my father was a diplomat at our embassy," she says with a wistful expression. "It was a wonderful life, I went to school with French girls, and that's where I learned English. I dreamed of going to the Sorbonne. But when the government changed some years ago, my father lost his job and we had to return home. I don't like it here, it's too violent, but I'm trapped because we're not paid well in Bangui, and so I can't save enough to return to Paris."

The music throbs, the dance floor trembles, and the malty beer slips deliciously down my throat as Sophie gives me a potted history of the Central African Republic. All I know is that a former dictator, Jean-Bedel Bokassa, was mocked by the world media in 1977 when he crowned himself Emperor in a grandiose stadium ceremony. The spectacle cost $15 million, which just about rivalled the country's GDP at the time. I vaguely remembered he was rumored to be a cannibal, eating the flesh of some of his enemies.

"Bokassa was a monster," Sophie says. "He was very cruel; he'd go to the prison and personally execute criminals for the fun of it. He spent about $3 million just on his crown, and his coronation robe was stitched with thousands of pearls. He even placed the crown on his own head, just like his hero Napoleon."

Sophie stops for a few moments, eyes closed, breathing deeply, affected by the horror. "That was an outrage in such a poor country, but he controlled the army and the French President, Giscard d'Estaing, supported him. Bokassa had given him diamonds on a state visit here. But Bokassa went too far a couple of years later when he ordered all the schoolchildren to buy uniforms made by his wife's factory. Most families couldn't afford them. The students rushed into the streets to protest, and the troops shot and killed more than a hundred. Many more were taken to jail. Bokassa went there and helped beat to death another two hundred children."

"How did you get rid of him?"

"Well, the slaughter was too much even for Giscard d'Estaing, and when Bokassa went overseas soon after in 1979, the French organized a coup that overthrew him. He settled in Paris. Can you believe that? The French knew he'd murdered hundreds of innocent children, but they protected him. A few years later he grew homesick and came back to Bangui in '87. He was put on trial for eating some of his enemies and throwing others to the crocodiles he kept as pets at his farm. He was jailed for life and died in 1996."

"And the problem you face now with the streets full of soldiers?"

Having had plenty of practice in Paris, Sophie shrugs eloquently. "The usual thing. A bunch of soldiers rebelled against the government hoping to win power, and they battled it out in the streets while we hid in our homes. The French sent in the Legionnaires. The government troops and rebels fought a battle at the broadcasting station to win control of it, and the Legionnaires went there and killed most of them from both sides. That stopped the fighting. Then the peacekeepers arrived, but they aren't much use. They're only here to give it an African face. Our soldiers fear only the Legionnaires and while they are in the streets, it will be quiet."

The jet lag from journeying halfway around the world snaps in and exhaustion dims my eyes. "I'll take you back now, you need a good sleep," Sophie says. As we near the hotel, she orders the driver to stop the taxi right by the entrance where a soldier stands armed with an assault rifle. "Can't be too careful," she explains. "See you tomorrow."

Accusations of tyranny take many forms, I think, while getting ready for bed. In Sydney it can be the local council refusing permission for a swimming pool to be built in someone's backyard. I had seen how the people of the Pacific Island nation of Tonga believed their king to be a tyrant because he banned democracy and enriched his grown children. But Bokassa and some other African rulers are far more sinister. I cannot imagine the depth of pain and terror of parents who wave their children to school in the morning and then collect their bullet-shattered bodies from the street in the afternoon, or retrieve their mutilated bodies from the Bangui prison that night.

At nine the next morning Sophie has breakfast with me by the river and then introduces Jacob, the driver who will take me to the distant rainforest. He is standing by an ancient Land Rover covered with dents and scratches. The windshield is cracked. He is short and stocky with a broad open face that hints at a kind nature. "Jacob speaks excellent English," Sophie says.

"Good morning, Mister Paul," he says. "I worked for several years in Nairobi and that's where I learned English. Where are you from?"

"It's Paul, mate. We Australians don't like to be called Mister."

A look of delight brightens his face. "Australian? Gooodaayy, maaaate."

"You've seen the movie *Crocodile Dundee?*"

This is about the hundredth time I have been greeted like this abroad when someone learns I am an Australian, but I am always amused and even pleased by the reaction. Crocodile Dundee was what we Aussies call a "larrikin," which used to be the archetype of an Australian male. One of Australia's most eminent historians, Manning Clarke, described the larrikin thus:

He is "witty rather than humorous, exceeding limits, bending rules and sailing close to the wind, avoiding rather than evading responsibility, mocking pomposity and smugness, taking the piss out of people, cutting down tall poppies, larger than life, sceptical, iconoclastic, egalitarian yet suffering fools badly, and, above all, defiant."

And brave as a bull, just like Crocodile Dundee. When I was younger, most Australian males were larrikins, or yearned to be but, regretfully, the rise of the "ME" generation at home is steadily making the larrikin extinct. It is impossible to imagine Crocodile Dundee's eyes glued to an iphone or an electronic tablet all day as if it were the modern equivalent of Mao's *Little Red Book*, the alleged font of all wisdom.

"Of course I saw the movie. Mister Paul Hogan was very famous in Nairobi," Jacob booms. "Ever since I saw his film many years ago I've wanted to visit Australia." He grabs a red feather duster from the back seat of the Land Rover and, with a beefy laugh, flourishes it in front of my nose and mimics a famous scene from the movie. "That's not a knife, maaate. *This* is a knife."

The Land Rover wheezes, groans, and rattles as we head south along a winding road dotted with potholes. The farther we travel from Bangui, the worse the road gets. "Jacob, are you sure this car won't fall apart before we get to the Pygmies?" I ask.

"Hah! You Australians are jokers, just like Crocodile Dundee," he beams as he yanks the steering wheel to the left to miss a hole as wide as the top of a garbage can in the road filled with muddy water. The hole would have snapped our axle as easily as I can snap a matchstick.

"I like Australians, though you're the first one I've ever met."

"Well, I meant it as a joke, Jacob, but is there any truth in it?"

He pats the steering wheel, as if patting the bottom of his lover. "Never worry, Mister Paul. I've driven my beautiful car for thousands of kilometers from here to there and everywhere, and she never fails me."

"I'm Paul, Jacob. Paul! We Australians don't like to be called Mister."

"Of course, Paul. It's the Kenyan businessmen who like you to call them Mister. Yes sir, no sir, I snap to attention as you enter the car, sir. I learned that in Nairobi. Paul, it's the name of the Apostle. Are you a Christian?"

"I was born a Catholic, and probably still am, though I don't often go to church."

He waves a finger at me. "That is very naughty, Paul. My country is a dangerous place and it's always best to be friendly with God every day in case you get shot."

"Then, while I'm here I'll say my prayers every night before I go to bed, and before all my meals, I swear to God."

He looks at me, puzzled for a few moments, and then roars with laughter. "Hah! You Australians, always making the joke."

Jacob is clearly not a Sara. He has the build of a Rugby hooker, an inch or two taller than me and with a stocky body, broad shoulders, and a bull neck. "I'm a Manja," he says. "We have many tribes in the CAR. The Gabya, Bambari, Kaga, Bossangoa, Zande, Mondjombo, Carnot, and of course the Pygmies."

On the outskirts of Bangui we encounter the former farm of Bokassa the monster. A crumbling wall surrounds a weed-strewn compound, and the one gate is padlocked. "You know about Bokassa feeding his enemies to the crocodiles?" Jacob asks.

"Yes."

"We should have asked Crocodile Dundee to come here. He would have cleaned up the crocodiles, and Bokassa."

We pause for a few minutes to see if there is a caretaker who can unlock the gate and let us in for a look around. The response to our shouts is an eerie silence, as if only the ghosts of cannibal feasts past now wander unseen among the ruins. Perhaps no one around here wants to visit the house of horrors.

When the foreign correspondents, those birds of a feather, flocked to Bangui for the coronation, some picked up talk that Bokassa was a cannibal whose favorite meal, when he could not get young girls, was fricassee of political opponent.

When Bokassa's former cook was questioned about the macabre rumors, he confirmed them. "Yes, Bokassa liked eating human flesh. It was no secret in the palace, we all knew, and he'd boast to us that there was no better way of triumphing over an opponent than by eating him."

Bokassa was a cannibal with a demonic sense of humor. William Dale, the US Ambassador in Bangui from 1973 to 1975, wrote that during his time there, "young girls began to disappear, one by one." One Sunday morning in 1975, the Swiss pastor at Bangui's Lutheran church asked to speak in private with Dale. While visiting Bokassa's farm, he told the ambassador, he saw two schoolgirls roped to a tree in the compound.

Aware of the persistent rumors of Bokassa's taste for human flesh, Dale remembered that when he first met Bokassa to present his credentials, the ruler remarked that, "his grandfather had been a cannibal and sometimes he believed he had tendencies in that direction." Dale says Bokassa also told ambassadors at a palace dinner that, "he sometimes wondered whether his ambassadorial guests realized exactly what they were eating."

Dale made a gruesome conclusion. "The ghastly thought occurred to me that perhaps Bokassa was actually dining on parts of the schoolgirls and was possibly serving them as a routine matter to his dinner guests."

The rumors of his cannibalism turned out to be true. French investigators called in by the military leaders who overthrew Bokassa found identifiable human parts, identified as chunks of butchered missing schoolgirls hanging in Bokassa's huge meat locker at his farm.

After a few minutes outside the farm, when no one appears, we walk back to the Land Rover. Luckily, there is little traffic on the road, just the occasional truck loaded with hardwood logs, because Jacob must weave constantly to avoid the many potholes. Sometimes he has to drive along the dirt fringes to miss them. "If this is the road to the Pygmies, I truly doubt the car will get there in one piece."

"Hah! You joke again," he smiles. "This is still the highway. Soon, we'll reach the jungle path that's the shortest way to the Pygmies. This way I'll get you to the Pygmies much quicker."

Every ten miles or so we are stopped by a roadblock manned by soldiers. Each time I hide my flashy sunglasses in the glove box in case they catch their eye. Hidden within the pages of a magazine in my lap is a bundle of banknotes, each one five hundred Central African Francs (CFA), or about $1 US. Sophie warned that it was the standard bribe to smooth a quick passage through the roadblocks.

The soldiers manning them are aggressive and unfriendly. In Asia, in surviving years of roadblocks, I honed a way of easing the tension by joking with the soldiers. Usually they broke into smiles and joked back, even where there had been recent fighting nearby. But when I try to get the African soldiers to smile, it makes them nervous. They aim their rifles at me and stare with undisguised hostility.

"The soldiers are not joking people," Jacob warns. "If you make them angry, they'll shoot you."

No one asks for a bribe. "Maybe they think you're French," Jacob says. "They're very afraid of the Legionnaires."

As we pass through yet another roadblock bristling with soldiers poking their gun barrels at us, I am struck by a cruel irony. The Pygmies, reputedly among the most peaceful people on earth, live in one of the world's most dangerous places, a true heart of darkness. Joseph Conrad set his epic novel in a country he knew well, now known as the Democratic Republic of Congo, which shares a border and a savage reputation with the CAR.

I am wary and uncomfortable as the soldiers at the roadblocks peer at us with grim eyes above their tight lips. But Jacob welcomes their menacing presence. "There are many bandits along this road, they hide in the bushes and ambush anyone passing by. When they see you're a foreigner, they'd probably kill us just to get whatever money you're carrying."

Between the roadblocks Jacob buoys his confidence singing Anglican hymns at the top of his very loud voice. After finishing three verses, he asks if I know the hymn. I shake my head.

"It's 'Guide me Oh God, Thou Great Redeemer'," he explains. "It's my favorite hymn when I'm driving to Bayanga near where the Pygmies live."

Jacob begins once more:

> Guide me Thou Great Redeemer,
> A pilgrim through this barren land.
> I am weak and Thou art mighty.
> Hold me with Thy powerful hand.

The hymn has a tub-thumping martial beat, appropriate for where we are. It is at the other end of the liturgical music spectrum from the gentle, meditative ninth- and tenth-century Catholic Gregorian chants I sang during my youth and still listen to on headphones on long-distance flights. Now I listen, entranced, to Jacob, the effect intensified because of the danger as we journey through the Congo Basin, one of the planet's most verdant, fertile, and perilous places. He teaches me the words of the first and second verses and when I join him it evokes a grateful glance. Singing an Anglican hymn when I was young would have been considered as seeking union with the Devil but we now live in more tolerant times.

"Here we are, Paul, the jungle," Jacob announces.

I have been dozing and rub the sleep from my eyes. We have turned onto a dirt track that cuts a thin brown line through dense green jungle. Towering over us are trees thrust together and so thickly leafed that I cannot see beyond their frontline. The windows are down and the dank smell of the wildly promiscuous vegetation is intoxicating. I love the raw earthy smell of jungles and I have found the steamy odor to be much the same whether it be Borneo's rainforests, Brazil's remote wilds, or this jungle deep in the Central African Republic.

The going is much smoother on the dirt, the Land Rover glad to escape the bumpy and torn bitumen road. "We'll reach the Pygmies around dawn tomorrow," Jacob says.

The track narrows into a two-lane pathway hacked through the jungle, which often presses so closely on either side that the bushes brush against the Land Rover. For most of the afternoon there is no sign of human life. The jungle is cut in many places by creeks and Jacob edges the Land Rover over makeshift bridges made from half-rotten logs. His lips move constantly as we inch across each rickety bridge and I suspect he is praying that the logs do not break.

In mid-afternoon we begin passing isolated villages threaded together with long stretches of jungles. Most of the rectangular wooden huts each have a small, dome-shaped hut made from a latticework of bent branches covered with leaves and set a few paces away. "Are they toilets?" I ask Jacob.

"No, they're the huts of the Pygmy slaves," he replies. "Each Bantu family owns a Pygmy family, who are their hereditary slaves. The Bantu fathers pass on their Pygmy family to their eldest son. The Pygmies grow the cassava crops and are given a small share but no money. Cassava to us is like bread for you Westerners."

The villages are dotted with Bantu men and women but no Pygmies. "The men and women will be working in the fields and their children playing nearby," he explains.

"How can the Bantu keep the Pygmies as slaves? You're supposed to be a democratic country?"

Jacob smiles grimly. "For many centuries Bantu have believed the Pygmies to be *bambinga*. It means someone who is halfway between a human and a forest animal. So the Bantu feel no shame and regard them as their possessions, just like their goats and chickens. The government looks the other way."

The United Nations, so vocal in denouncing racial discrimination elsewhere, has rarely spotlighted this slavery. A decade ago a UNICEF report noted: "Pygmy people are the indigenous hunter-gatherers of Central African forests. Because of their short stature and distinct culture they are marginalized, exploited for cheap labor, and even considered to be slaves." Despite this damning expose, there was no follow-up.

"Pygmy families must stay close by their Bantu owners," Jacob says. "They must seek their permission even if they want to go into the forest nearby."

I feel a sudden sadness for the thousands of Pygmy families held in bondage by the Bantu across Equatorial Africa. "Where we're going, are the Pygmies living like this?"

"You'll see tomorrow. Most of our country's Pygmies live as slaves of the Bantu villagers."

I later learned that all throughout the Congo Basin the Bantu regarded the Pygmies as sub-humans, *bambinga*. The most horrific consequence of this belief came during the Congo Civil War (1998-2003) in the Democratic Republic of Congo. There, United Nations investigators and foreign correspondents verified many disturbing reports of Bantu soldiers butchering and eating Pygmies.

In 2003, the British newspaper *The Scotsman,* in reporting from the Congo, quoted a UN official as stating: "Cannibalism is the latest atrocity taking place." The rebels routinely enslaved Pygmies to forage for forest food for them. "Any hunters returning empty-handed are killed and eaten. We hear reports of enemy commanders feeding on sexual organs of Pygmies, apparently believing this would give them strength."

A UN investigation team journeyed to eastern Congo and took testimony from 368 victims and witnesses of the cannibalism. One Pygmy told the investigators that a soldier murdered his father, hacking open his chest, taking out the heart, cooking and eating it in front of him.

Sinafasi Makelo, a Congo Pygmy delegate to a UN forum in New York, said that, "Pygmies are being pursued in the forests . . . People have been eaten."

The most convincing truth of these reports came from eyewitness accounts in locations often hundreds of miles from each other. Most Pygmies are illiterate and had no way of knowing what other Pygmies were experiencing far away. Yet all the reports followed a similar pattern of cannibalism by the Bantu soldiers.

To confirm the cannibalism, Daniel Bergner, a *New York Times* correspondent, traveled to the town of Beni in the DRC. He met many

Pygmies there and heard similar horror stories. Amuzati Ndjoki, an Ituri Pygmy, told him how he crouched on a hill overlooking an army camp and on a patch of bare ground "saw the bodies of his mother, his brother, his sister. Soldiers wielding machetes were cutting the bodies into pieces. A latticework of branches had been built to grill the bodies, which also included his six-year-old nephew.

"I am remembering so many things," he told Bergner.

His mother's body was being butchered, Bergner wrote. "They were eating pieces of his brother's corpse. After a time he fled, and now he seemed to wish again for flight. He covered his face with the pink denim hat. There was the sound of unrestrained, muted weeping, a single strangulated treble note."

Was there any other explanation for the cannibalism beyond the belief that the Pygmies were somehow subhuman? In their report, the UN investigators wrote: "Particularly concerning the Pygmies' internal body parts such as the heart and liver, it can be considered to be pure fetishism aimed at helping the perpetrators to acquire the capacity and ability of the victims to hunt and live in the forest."

However, the UN Human Rights Council which dispatches investigators, termed special rapporteurs, to several countries each year to examine their human rights violations, has never sent investigators to the CAR to spotlight the Bantus' cruel slavery of tens of thousands of Pygmies. The most recent UNHRC investigation of human rights violations in the CAR, published in September 2013, contained 8,000 words and yet there was not a single mention of one of the world's worst human rights violations, the life-long slavery of the Pygmies by the Bantu.

What else would you expect when the Council has among its members many tyrannical, undemocratic regimes such as Cuba, Venezuela, Kyrgyzstan, and Saudi Arabia, where many basic human rights are banned and suppressed with imprisonment in overcrowded jails. The stench of this hypocrisy soaks the UN headquarters in New York.

CHAPTER 2

Jacob nudges me from sleep. I look at my watch; it is just after 5 a.m. With a merciful consideration for me, through the night he had not bolstered his courage with any more hymns. Seventeen hours have passed since we left Bangui and I have been dozing for most of the night. "Pygmies," he says.

My back twinges with cramp from sleeping upright but I hardly notice the pain. A childhood ambition, to be in the jungle with Pygmies, is about to come true. Don't forget to bring back a poison arrow for Cathy, I remind myself. And don't sit on it.

The dirt track has widened and the cleared land leading up to the jungle is lined with domed huts. They are waist-high and I wonder how entire families can fit inside. No creature stirs, even the camp dogs are still asleep. There are no Bantu huts.

"The Pygmies will wake soon," Jacob says with a smile. "They're Africa's greatest hunters. You can see that these Pygmies do not live as Bantu slaves."

We have reached the Dzanga-Sangha rainforest at the southwest edge of the country, about 350 miles from Bangui. It is one of Africa's greatest game reserves, a swath of pristine jungle nestled against the Sangha River. The huge river snakes through the massive rainforest forming a triangular border with Cameroon and the Republic of the Congo not far downstream.

At a bend in the river, about four miles on from the Pygmy encampment, we come upon Bayanga, a Bantu settlement. As the sun rises over the treetops, people emerge from their huts yawning and rubbing sleep from their eyes, and begin to set up market stalls, gossip, or fetch river water in basins balanced on their heads. They are a tall, well-built people, immigrants who flocked here when a French timber company set up a sawmill to cull the rainforest of its valuable tropical hardwood logs three decades earlier.

Jacob takes me to a small hotel, just three wooden bungalows and an open-air straw hut restaurant perched on poles dug into the riverbank. My bungalow has a comfortable bed protected by an opaque mosquito net and a small balcony over the broad fast-flowing Sangha, whose banks are lined with high trees and dense green vegetation. Even at this early hour, pirogues, canoes carved out of single large logs, slip by silently, poled by wiry Bantu who wave angrily when I aim a camera at them. The air drips with humidity and dozens of mosquitoes spin about me in a frenzy, unable to penetrate the protective lotion I sprayed on my exposed flesh before going onto the balcony.

Once I have showered and changed to fresh clothes, Jacob drives me up a hill to a sparsely furnished bungalow overlooking the river. It is the home and office of Allard Blom, a slim, stiff-limbed Belgian whose one visible extravagance is a mustache. A high-ranking executive with the World Wide Fund for Nature, he has been in Africa for a decade and is director of the Dzanga-Sangha National Park.

Belgians are reputed to be a dour people, lacking passion, inhospitable to foreigners, close-minded, more in the mold of money-counting merchants than fun-loving free spirits. It is no wonder that the European Union headquarters is in Brussels in a series of vast buildings with little character and populated by head-down, hard-working bureaucrats.

On my visits to Brussels, however, I have sometimes wondered how its people got such a reputation. Perhaps it has come from the British, who have long had a creaky relationship with them. Surely a people who developed and enjoy around 1,150 original Belgium beers, brewed and sold by 146 breweries and forty-four beer companies, must be party lovers, and I found to my great pleasure that they were. My favorite is a beer the color of white chocolate, a whimsical extravagance. The Belgians even have a beef stew with its gravy made from, yes, beer. It is delicious.

Blom has on khaki slacks and a comfortable, open-neck white cotton shirt, the uniform of the tens of thousands of Westerners working in Africa for non-government charity organizations such as the WWF. They swarm across the continent like locusts. He pours cups of coffee and offers me a freshly baked crusty baguette from the marketplace in Bayanga. "You're lucky to be here, because the Bangui airport reopened four weeks ago after being closed for more than a year," he says.

"Why?"

Blom shows his ancestry by shrugging with flair. "The fighting. As you probably know, Bangui is split in three, with the government troops holding one chunk of the city, the rebels another, and the peacekeeping forces there to keep them apart. Fighting could break out any time."

"Could it reach here?"

"Yes, and very quickly, but if that happens I'd radio the French Foreign Legion to rescue us. They have a base 140 kilometers north of here, but if all their troops were needed in Bangui, we have a speedboat on standby at all times by the riverbank. We'd escape to the Congo, about forty kilometers along the river."

He pauses for a few moments, allowing me to find comfort in that revelation. "Of course, we'd be escaping into another war because that area is held by Congo rebels who've taken over that part of the country."

"Well, at least it's peaceful here for the moment."

"Ah yes, so it seems, but we also have a problem because poachers from southern Sudan have recently slipped into the park in search of bush meat, gorilla, elephant, anything they can kill, as well as the ivory tusks. They sell it for high prices in their markets. They're armed with AK-47s and are ruthless."

"Do they get involved with the Pygmies?"

"Some track game for them, but most of the park's Pygmies know the poachers are breaking the law and stay clear of them. In fact, we employ Pygmies as park rangers to protect the animals. They've helped us catch many poachers. This is a very important wildlife reserve with some of the continent's densest concentrations of forest elephants and lowland gorillas. It's also home to the bongo, a rare antelope. So we don't allow any hunting in the park except for the Pygmies using traditional methods."

"How many Pygmies live here?"

"Within the park's 1,200 square kilometers, there are about 2,000, along with about 1,500 Bantu. We'd like most of the Bantu to leave—they're recent arrivals—but that's not politically possible. American Peace Corps volunteers started the park and American aid money still funds it, a major aim being to give the Pygmies the chance to continue their traditional rainforest lifestyle. Even though many live near Bayanga, they still spend months at a time in the rainforest."

Blom proves to be the model of the eternal Belgian. He only speaks the bare minimum necessary in what is a swift breakfast and sends me off with nary a word of social patter, the glue that cements relationships between people at their first meeting. It is the first and only meeting I have with him until not long before my departure for Bangui several weeks later.

Back at the bungalow, a slim dark-skinned Bantu in his twenties greets me with a firm handshake. "I'm William Bienvenu, your translator," he says. The temperature is relentlessly gathering its strength from a blazing sun on the way to reaching 35°C before midday but William has on a black suit and a red tie. I appreciate his good manners but I would swelter in such garb. Yet there is not a drop of perspiration on his face.

He must be like my wife from sub-tropical China, I think. Raised in the daily humid, oppressive heat in her homeland, during the hot Sydney summer she is always puzzled whenever I wander around the house and garden in just a pair of shorts. She claims she would shiver from the cold in such undress. Over hundreds of generations, her people had adapted their bodies to the heat, as had the Bantu and the Pygmies.

At the opposite end of the human scale, when I spent some weeks among the Inuit at Hudson Bay in the Arctic, to escape the minus

20°C cold I had to swath myself in a fur hat, fur coat with fur ear flaps, and three sets of warm pants that had me waddling in the snow like a penguin, as well as fur gloves and fur-lined boots. Aikime, the clan chieftain, smiled with good humor at my needs. He walked through the snow in a pair of cotton pants and a loose cotton shirt. His head was uncovered and his hands were bare.

One morning, as we unchained several huskies for a sled run, I took off the gloves to make it easier and the freezing air immediately stabbed my fingers. I had to put the gloves back on straight away to avoid frost-bite. I was puzzled by how Aikime's bare hands withstood the extreme cold. He put a hand against my cheek and I was astonished to feel that his fingers and palm were as warm as freshly grilled toast. "We Inuit have evolved over thousands of years here to have much larger blood vessels in our hands than yours, with the extra blood heating our hands." Going by that, William's people and also my wife's must have evolved in the heat to have narrower blood vessels than Caucasians and Inuit so that the lower blood flow counteracted the atmospheric heat.

William's handsome face is marred by a smug expression. "I'll take you to the Pygmies," he says. "Jacob says you're a Catholic. I spent five years in the seminary, but I had to leave in the final year because I liked girls too much."

"That was probably a good thing, William. A good-looking priest with an eye for the girls can be quite a devil."

Jacob roars with laughter. "See, I told you he's like Crocodile Dundee, always telling the jokes."

William stares at me with a wary, hurtful look. "It was no joke. I suffered terribly for more than a year before I gave in to temptation and had to leave. My friends at the seminary are now priests. I envy them."

I feel a pang of regret at having made fun of William, but have not come all the way to the Dzanga-Sangha to hear his confession. "Okay, let's go meet the Pygmies."

We drive to the Pygmy encampment that sprawls along a rise skirt-ing the jungle, dappled with sunlight gleaming through the trees. About twenty little domed huts are scattered across the slope, made from bent branches covered with leaves and daubed with mud to hold them in place. Smoke spirals into the damp morning air from several fires.

Squatting around them are tiny women warming water and cooking food. Outside most of the huts, small men sit cross-legged on the bare earth, chatting. "The village is called Mossapola," says William. "About a hundred Pygmies live here. As you can see they are a very primitive people."

William's remark hints at that common, deep-rooted prejudice among the Bantu, but just as I begin to reply, a dozen Pygmy men run down the slope, shouting. When they reach us their laughter cascades like a waterfall as they start pulling the hairs on my bare arms and peering at them. Their own arms are smooth-skinned. I am just 5-foot-7 and the tallest Pygmy stands only as high as my shoulder. Sophie would be a giant among them.

The word Pygmy comes from the Greek, *pygmaios*, a word describing a measure that also has the sense of dwarfish. But the people at Mossapola, though tiny, like all Pygmies differ from true dwarfs in that their limbs are normally proportioned. In 1967, an Italian medical anthropologist, Luigi Luca Cavalli Sforza, spent several months measuring Pygmies in Equatorial Africa and found tribes in the Congo's Ituri Forest to be the shortest, with men averaging 145 cm (4'9") and women about 76 mm shorter (4'6"). The Dzanga-Sangha Pygmies were one or two inches taller.

Biologists believe Pygmies are stunted because in their early teens they do not experience the growth spurt that is normal in most other humans. No one knows why they suffer this genetic quirk, but the children who gather around, giggling as I play back their mellow voices on a portable tape recorder, are not much smaller than the Bantu children of the same age in nearby Bayanga. But when they reach the age of eleven or twelve, their growth comes to a full stop. According to Cavalli-Sforza, "the activity of IGF, the insulin-like growth factor, is decreased in all Pygmies tested."

Natural selection over hundreds of generations to adapt to the tropical jungle must be a vital factor for their tiny size. Scientists have discovered that, as a rule, the average body size of humans decreases with increasing environmental temperature, with shorter people at the equator and taller folk in the snow lands. Cavalli-Forza believes this effect stems from "the need to avoid excessive dispersion of heat in cold climates. Generally, smaller people tolerate wet and hot conditions better because they generate less body heat." The rule holds true not only for the Pygmies, but also in the evolution in the Americas of the Mayans and in Asia of the Philippines' Negritos.

Parting a path through the children and the adults gathered around me, a miniature man moves to my side. "I am Wasse," he says, speaking through William. He is an inch or two shorter than my shoulder.

"Wasse is the Pygmies' greatest hunter," William says.

"Tell the stranger we are called Bayaka."

William faithfully mouths his words in English. "Bayaka," I repeat.

Wasse's broad face rewards this with a gentle smile. I trust him immediately, struck by his keen intelligent eyes. Like the other Bayaka he has a child-like face, his nostrils wider and flatter than William's, Jacob's, and the other Bantu I have seen since arriving in the CAR.

A tiny woman walks down the slope and stands by Wasse. She has a pretty face, but her neck is swollen with goitre from a lack of iodine in her diet. "This is Jandu, my wife," he tells me.

Her front upper teeth have been carefully chipped and resemble shark dorsal fins. Many other Bayaka women have the same look. "They do it with machetes," William says with a shudder. "I told you they are primitive."

"It makes me look beautiful for Wasse," Jandu explains.

I have seen how tribal women of New Guinea thrust red-hot pebbles onto their stomachs and arms to produce circular beauty scar marks. The Bayaka attack their own teeth. I have seen elderly women in remote Chinese villages with bound feet smaller than my hand. Until a few decades ago, Chinese women for more than 1,000 years commonly had their feet crippled and stunted to produce a lilting walk that sent their men crazy with desire. Western women with enough money and a desire to appear younger have their faces torn apart with scalpels and yanked back into place with twine. We are all brothers and sisters under the skin.

Wasse touches my arm to regain our attention. "We've talked enough. The sun does not stop moving. William told me you want to see the *ebobo*, the gorillas. Let's go."

With Wasse is the biggest Bayaka I have seen. He is almost as tall as me and is in his forties. His face reflects his age; it does not have a

Bayaka adult's child-like appearance and I suspect he is the union of a Bayaka woman and a Bantu man.

"This is Wunga, my good friend," says Wasse. "He was once a great hunter of elephants."

"Wunga is unmarried, he finds it impossible to woo a girl because of his size," William says, openly broaching such a sensitive topic because he knows the Pygmies cannot speak English. "Wasse told me they fear Wunga is big in every way and would harm their insides when making love. Our women are very different and smarter because they prefer men with big cocks."

William seems to be inviting me to respond, and maybe he will even boast about his own masculinity. If so, I disappoint him. Must I have to endure several weeks of his overt racism, I wonder, as we walk down the hill to Jacob's trusty Land Rover with Wasse and Wunga in tow. Perhaps I should hire another translator when we return to Bayanga later in the day.

Leaving the dirt road near Mossapola, we head straight into the jungle and drive for several miles along a narrow, grassy lumber track the loggers use to haul out the massive hardwood trees they cut down. Up ahead, a large tree that had fallen across the track halts us. Jacob has a hand ax on board for such emergencies and gets out to chop the tree in half to make it easier to lift off the track.

I join him and, horror of horrors, am immediately attacked by a swarm of small bees. There must be hundreds of them. They cake onto my exposed flesh including my face and no amount of swiping them off me scares them away. It is too late to rush back into the car because they would follow me inside. *What a gruesome way to die*, I think. *Stung by hundreds of frenzied bees.*

But in just a few moments I am puzzled. They do not sting me as they crawl across my flesh. "They're sweat bees, they have no sting," Jacob explains as dozens of the little bastards crawl into up my nostrils, into my ears, and around my eyes. I pull down the flap of my baseball cap but Jacob stops me from escaping into the car. "You'd take plenty of them with you and we'd never get rid of them."

I lie down on the ground as Jacob shoos away the bees and then covers me with a blanket he keeps in the back seat The sultry heat makes it hard to breathe under the covering and sweat pours from me. The bees must smell it because I can feel them crawling all over the blanket on the outside.

Such is life on the road. I have a grim motto fashioned by decades of journeying through some of the most remote places on earth. The more it hurts, the better the story. This is not the chant of a masochist. I must often go to places reeking with disease, trek for weeks through tough jungles, and climb high mountains to get to the best stories.

The jungles are the worst. I am very allergic to sand fly bites, the Dzanga-Sangha swarms with them, and already on the first day am suffering burning itches from several swollen red lumps, each the size of dollar coins on my arms and ankles. They seem to be able to crawl inside my long sleeves and up the legs of my pants. No matter how hard I try to keep the sand flies from me, over the next few weeks I will suffer scores more bites.

So the bees, while bothersome, do not hurt. Once the log is chopped in half, Wasse, Wunga, and Jacob drag the two halves off the track. "I'm going to drive about a hundred meters along the trail," Jacob says to me. "When you hear the car stop, jump up and run as fast as you can to join us. The bees won't be able to catch you." And so it proves.

We drive for several more miles until we stop at a small clearing. "We call this place Molgambe," Wasse says. "From here we walk."

William has brought along a bag containing his jungle clothes, which consist of commando-style gray pants, a green polo shirt, and tough trekking boots. He changes into them and we plunge into Tarzan land. The jungle presses in from all sides and overhead the dense vine-woven canopy echoes with whooping monkeys and screeching parrots.

"Watch where you walk because there are many black mamba and cobra in this forest," Wasse says. The black mamba is one of the world's most poisonous snakes and if one of us is bitten we might die before we could reach the doctor at Bayanga.

"The forest elephants are just as dangerous," Wasse warns. "If we're attacked by an elephant, jump behind a large tree and hide there. The elephant will not see you."

The risk will be worth it because Africa's forest elephants are mysterious creatures that inhabit remote rainforests and are rarely seen.

Wasse peers at the ground as he and Wunga walk splayfooted over the rainforest mulch with William and me stumbling a few paces behind. He quickly reveals his tracking skills, and where I see tangles of vine and arid patches of mud that cling to my boots like glue, Wasse sees a road map of the animals that have passed by.

We trek for about an hour through the jungle gloom, then Wasse holds up a hand to halt us. His dark eyes flit from side to side and his nostrils flare as he tests the air for scent. He points ahead toward the undergrowth. I freeze. In the dim light, about ten yards away, I see a mother elephant and calf. The mother's huge head and tusks thrust defiantly through the leaves. The calf stands next to her front leg, unafraid, imitating its mother's belligerence. A lack of fear must be your birthright when your mother is one of the biggest and meanest creatures in the jungle.

The leaves rustle as the mother moves a pace forward, glaring at us. She pushes her ears out, threatening a charge. "She'll try to kill us if she decides we're after her baby," Wasse whispers.

I look around and select the nearest big tree, tensing to dash behind it. Suddenly, the elephant raises her trunk in the air and trumpets a war cry. Wasse turns in an eye-blink and runs for his life, Wunga and William close on his heels. For a few moments I stand rooted to the spot by my astonishment and then race after them, leaves and saplings slapping against me. It is amazing how fast a middle-aged, overweight city dweller can move through the undergrowth when threatened by an angry mother elephant.

I dare not look behind to see if the elephant is chasing us. Wasse calls a halt about three hundred yards later, and I slump against a tree, gasping for air. "I thought we were supposed to jump behind a tree if an elephant was about to attack," I mutter after recovering my breath. "That's what you told me to do."

Wasse is laughing so much that it takes him a few moments to stop. "I just wanted to see how fast the white man would react and follow us," he says. "No one stays around when an elephant is angry."

He starts laughing again at the thought of me trembling behind a tree as the mother elephant tries to impale me with her tusks. Bayaka daily face such danger in the jungle and Wunga and William join in the laughter, then I do too, laughing until my sides ache. If you cannot laugh at yourself, then you will not last long on the road. Self-belief is also necessary, but it has to be balanced with a keen knowledge of your failings. Those who think they can do no wrong do not last long.

A few minutes later, still smiling at my gullibility, we resume our silent quest. The dense tree canopy has plunged the rainforest into flickering shadow, but Wasse spots a trail of bent grass that weaves a path through the giant trees. He lopes through the rainforest and the sweat streams from me as I try to keep up. No jungle movie was ever so exciting.

At mid-morning, Wasse raises a hand. Ahead, the ground is strewn with an orange-like fruit. He examines the tooth marks. "*Ebobo*," he mouths. "Gorillas."

Wasse and Wunga spread out and follow pathways through the jungle only they can see, whistling like birds to keep in touch. William and I follow Wasse, and I notice that every twenty yards or so he bends a twig on a sapling, marking our way. Halting once more, he cocks his head and listens to a sound I can't pick up. I hear only the cicadas shrieking, the monkeys chattering overhead, and the birds warbling, but Wasse whispers that several gorillas are about a mile away and they are hammering termite nests with giant fists, seeking a tasty snack.

Hampered by the thick jungle, it takes us about half an hour to get close, the gorillas' presence signalled by the musky odor of an unseen silverback, a mature male. Wasse and Wunga fan out once more, communicating with hand movements, signaling the path the gorillas have taken, mouthing silent words to indicate where they are feeding.

Wasse holds up three fingers, signaling three gorillas, and then touches my arm and points through the undergrowth. Moments later two swarthy faces pop up from behind a tree wreathed in vine leaves about fifteen yards ahead. The creatures look like Neanderthals, their brown eyes glistening with intelligence.

This is one of nature's rarest sights, a young male and female lowland gorilla in the wild, among the shyest and most elusive of Africa's creatures. They seem linked to the Pygmies, who are the shyest of Africa's tribes and also the most expert trackers of the shy lowland gorillas.

Gripping a creeper wrapped around a tree trunk, the potbellied female climbs high for a better look. She stares at us and then glances at a dense patch of bamboo near a fallen log. "She's letting the silverback know where we are," Wasse whispers. "He's probably their father."

Suddenly, the silverback roars a challenge. The fearsome screech drops us to our knees in homage. We are so close to him that the sound rings in my ears. Still hidden from view, he beats his massive chest, the *thock, thock, thock* sending a clear warning. "He's telling us to leave," Wasse says.

He motions with his hand, asking if I want to get closer. The big male has signaled that he will fight to defend the youngsters, and he must worry that we are a threat. But the chance to see a silverback up close in the wild in all his charismatic glory is worth the risk. When I answer with a nod, we crawl on our bellies through the undergrowth until we are about six yards from the log. The silverback suddenly appears from behind it, his enormous face scowling as he glares at the intruders into his realm.

It might be the first time the silverback has ever seen humans and, as we glance silently at each other, my throat clenches with emotion. Millions of years separate us on the evolution chart and yet somehow I sense that the silverback is drawn to us, as I am to him, intrigued by some hint of similarity that he cannot understand.

Neither he nor I want to break off contact, and this moving experience lasts for several minutes. That is what my watch says, but time drifts without knowing during such a supreme experience and I could not have judged whether it was thirty seconds or thirty minutes.

For all this time I keep my eyes mostly averted, switching my glance to the jungle, then to the silverback, then back to the jungle. But when I finally lock eyes with him, I commit an act of defiance. Leaping up, he whacks his chest in anger. He charges from side to side, screaming as he bangs his massive fists against the trees. In a terrifying display of his great strength, he tears heavy boughs from the trees and tosses them to the side.

To mollify the huge ape, Wasse, Wunga, William, and I hug the ground, bending our heads and casting eyes downwards, a primate gesture of humility and respect that the silverback understands, indeed expects.

I know from an earlier extended visit to the mountain gorillas in Rwanda that we could provoke the silverback to attack if we try to run away. He can run much faster and might throw us to the ground and slash us with his huge canines. Steeling every nerve in my body, I keep perfectly still. The silverback glares at us for a few minutes and then, accepting that we are no threat, he lumbers away with the youngsters scurrying by his side. The jungle gloom swallows them.

Wasse hisses with relief and grins at me. "The *ebobo* are like the Bantu. We make them happy by pretending to fear them and pretending they are better than us."

William repeats this word for word without a flicker of emotion. Whatever other virtues he might have abandoned from his time at the seminary, he holds true to the monastic rule of strict obedience to his duty.

I do not begrudge the silverback's bellicose display. Life in a Congo Basin jungle can be short-lived if humans and animals alike do not take every precaution to protect themselves and their families, and the silverback showed a keen sense of preservation. This was my first sight of lowland gorillas in the wild, but later I documented in my book, *Among the Great Apes*, the many risks all the gorilla species face from we humans, with their numbers in the wild plunging.

My long-time American friend, David Greer, the head of the WWF's Africa Great Apes Project, told me as we tracked a family of mountains gorillas through dense bush in Rwanda that within half a century most of the world's gorillas in the wild might disappear, shot dead by poachers, charcoal dealers, and settlers chopping down their forests to build new villages to soak up the burgeoning population. "There may be just a few thousand mountain and lowland gorillas left in the wild, living in small forest reserves, entry forbidden to outsiders, and guarded day and night by highly-trained rangers armed with assault rifles."

In mid-afternoon we head back to the Land Rover. Thirty minutes later, in deep forest, Wasse puts up a hand to halt us. The trees are so dense that I can only see a few yards ahead. He sniffs the air. "Poachers," he says. "Very close."

William gulps. "They'll surely be armed with AK-47s," he whispers. "We should turn back."

Wasse shakes his head. He leads us through the trees into a small clearing. Thank God it's deserted, I think. Several chest-high racks made from bamboo hold many strips of meat that have been grilled over a small fire.

"*Duiker*," Wasse murmurs, referring to small antelope the size of a miniature poodle with a reputation of having tender, tasty flesh. Half a dozen sleeping bags are rolled up and placed on plastic sheeting. Wasse touches the fire's embers. They are still warm.

"They were here not long ago," he says. "We must leave because they could return soon."

I am most happy to agree. "They're probably from Sudan," William says as we leave. "Middle-class Africans like to touch their roots by eating what we call bush meat, and duiker fetches a high price in Sudanese markets. If they find us here, they'll probably kill us to stop us alerting the police in Bayanga."

"Sudan is hundreds of miles to the north. Surely they don't walk here. And how do they transport the meat?" I ask.

"The poachers come here in a lorry," William says. "It brings them deep into the forest on the same tracks we used, carved out for the trucks carrying the trees the lumbermen cut down. The poachers set up a camp, and after a few days the lorry returns, using a GPS to find them, and then takes them and the meat back to Sudan."

We have not eaten since morning and at our vehicle William, Jacob, and I eat baguettes and cold omelets, while Wasse and Wunga have the manioc they brought along in a bamboo container. Jacob roars with laughter when William tells him about our encounter with the elephants. "Crocodile Dundee would not have run," he says. "He would have stared down the mother elephant, the same way he did the buffalo."

"Yes, and pigs might fly, Jacob. Paul Hogan is a rich actor who lives in a Hollywood mansion and the closest he's probably come to a jungle over the past decade is the Africa river ride at Disneyland."

"Pigs can't fly, Paul, but you must have been close to flying when you ran away from the elephant."

William does not translate this and Wasse looks baffled by a conversation he can't understand. He slaps his hands together to get our attention. "I'll take you to see happy elephants," he says.

CHAPTER 3

We drive for about fifteen miles along a jungle path until we reach a clearing where Jacob decides to wait once more with the Land Rover. "I prefer to see elephants and black mambas in films," he says.

A stream of murky water bars our way into the jungle. We wade through it, up to our waists, and emerge dripping wet and smelling like a sewer. Wasse halts and sniffs at the air. He senses something beyond our putrid stink. "Elephant," he whispers. "A big male."

He motions with a hand patting the air for us to stay still and points ahead. A huge bull elephant has come out from the dense trees a hundred yards ahead and moves towards us along the edge of the stream. The elephant sniffs the air and smells us. He folds his ears back against his bulbous head, and brandishes a massive set of tusks, as he sways ominously from side to side.

"He's thinking about charging us," Wasse warns. "Stay here."

Armed only with his machete, he strides through the shallows towards the behemoth. He begins slapping the machete repeatedly against the water and yells something. The elephant is not intimidated and moves forward with his head lowered.

Movies and documentaries usually depict an elephant about to charge as waggling his huge ears, but David Greer told me they were mock charges, with the elephant attempting to scare away someone it perceives to be a threat. "Once a bull folds back his ears and drops his head, then he is surely going to charge and then you'll be lucky if you survive it."

Wasse refuses to be intimidated by a creature more than fifty times his weight and ready to fight. He slaps the machete harder against the water and yells louder. The elephant pauses, peers at his diminutive challenger, and then turns and ambles back into the jungle.

Wasse offers no explanation and silently leads us for more than an hour through dense rainforest until the trees thin out, revealing a clearing. It is about three football fields in size and is ringed by high jungle trees. It looks like elephant paradise. I count forty-three adults, juveniles, and calves spread across the clearing, rolling about in the many mud patches or sucking up the muddy water.

"It's a salt lick called Dzanga Bai," William explains as we crouch behind trees at the edge of the clearing. "I've brought biologists here because they say it's the best place in Africa to see the forest elephants. The elephants need minerals in their food, just like us, and that's why they come here to get the salt."

The forest elephants are smaller than the giants of the African plains, more the size of the Asian elephants you see in circuses, their stature conditioned by their habitat. Their ears are much smaller and their tusks are straight and point downwards, rather than the curved tusks of the plains elephants. In this they resemble the pygmy elephants I once saw up close in a Borneo rainforest, though because of widespread habitat destruction there, with the forest destroyed to form oil palm plantations, they have almost been wiped out. The similarity of their tusks could be an adaption to their rainforest habitats in Borneo and the Congo, because straight tusks that point down are less likely to get entangled in the jungle bushes.

The salt lick is like the local club, and as we watch elephants arrive and leave all the time. Calves scurry next to their mothers, solitary bulls plod into the clearing, and juveniles arrive in a bunch escorted by the clan matriarch.

Scattered among the elephants are several buffaloes and one antelope slurping up the salty water. "Christ, it's a bongo," William murmurs. "You rarely see them."

I peer through binoculars at the antelope, big as a horse, rust-brown with a dozen white stripes marking its flanks. "A bongo?"

"Yes, one of the rarest animals in Africa. They're very hard to find. Our government lets hunters come from overseas to kill them, but the license for one bongo is thirty thousand American dollars. Even though the license is so expensive, many foreign hunters are so eager to kill a bongo that they'd wipe them out and that's why the season lasts just three months each year."

"How do you know?"

"Because during the season I work as translator for the hunters. I don't like to see them killing bongos, I don't even know why they kill bongos, but it brings in plenty of foreign currency for our country."

"I'll bet most of it ends up in the pockets of the politicians in Bangui."

"Look," Wunga says, ending our conversation. In the middle of the clearing, two bull elephants are jostling for dominance by pitting their strength against each other, locking tusks and shoving hard. They huff and puff, forced back a step or two, thrusting forward again for about ten minutes until the weaker bull suddenly pulls away and plods back into the rainforest. The eligible females at the salt lick were probably all eyes, but in case any missed the tussle, the victor struts around the clearing showing off his enormous bulk and powerful tusks.

Angered by the antics of a pair of buffaloes rolling in the mud, another bull charges them, trumpeting his displeasure. The agile buffaloes easily evade the bull, leading him on a chase around the clearing, as if it were a game, until he tires and gives up.

Ignoring the ruckus, many of the elephants kneel in the mineral-rich mud and use their trunks to probe for holes in the substrata and then suck up the salt-laden water. Others dig fresh holes with their tusks, or stand in line waiting patiently for their turn. The calves, always by their mothers' sides, wallow merrily in the mud until they look as if they are made of dark chocolate.

Wunga's eyes gleam as he watches all this elephant flesh. Blom had told me that the Bayaka are allowed to hunt big game in the reserve in the traditional way, except for gorillas, but it is rare for the clans to go after elephants because of the danger. Wunga last killed an elephant four years earlier. He went alone into the jungle armed only with a spear dipped in traditional poison. Spotting a juvenile male, he risked his life by charging it. Evading the furious elephant's tusks, he plunged the spear deep into its side and left it there.

"The elephant was very angry, he was screaming as he chased me. He would have killed me if he caught me, but I hid in the jungle and then followed his tracks. It took the rest of the day for him to die."

Wunga led the Mossapola clan to the spot where they hacked off huge chunks of flesh and, singing with great excitement, carried it on poles back to the village.

"Wunga is the bravest Bayaka," Wasse says, his eyes warm with admiration. "He has even fought and killed leopards. But we've stopped killing elephants, gorillas, and chimpanzees because there are now much fewer because of the poachers."

We stay for more than two hours, fascinated by this rare glimpse of everyday forest elephant life. All over the Central African Republic, and across much of Africa, poachers have decimated the once-great herds of plains and forest elephants. The Dzanga-Sangha National Park has the only protected elephant population in the country.

Wasse frowns as he watches the elephants. "We shouldn't cut down the jungle trees because the elephants and all the other animals will disappear, and then we Bayaka will have no life."

As a young boy, Wasse spent almost all year in the rainforest with his Mossapola clan. "The jungle had many animals then," he tells me. "The Bantu were very few, Bayanga was a small village, and they never came into the forest. When we went to the edge of the forest and saw them through the trees, they looked like monsters to us. If they came towards us we ran deeper into the forest. We were very scared of them." His eyes grow wistful. "I'm glad my mother and father never lived to see the forest now. They would be very sad to see that so many of the animals have disappeared."

That night I sleep in my bungalow by the Sangha River with my lullaby the sound of hippos grunting.

Rainforest life is tough, but it is also exhilarating. The following morning William and I drive to Mossapola soon after breakfast. When Wasse sees us arrive, he shouts to alert the clan to get ready to leave to go deep into the rainforest for a hunt. The Bayaka swiftly gather and head in single file into the forest. The men, carrying spears, hunting nets, and crossbows armed with poison-tipped arrows, lead the way. The women and children follow carrying sleeping mats.

The women also have woven baskets resting against their backs and strapped to their foreheads, and when they see herbs or edible plants they stop to harvest them. Within an hour their baskets are overflowing. The Pygmies never took to agriculture because the rainforest provided all they needed. That included an inexhaustible supply of fresh fruits and plants as well as the meat of monkeys, birds, gorillas, chimpanzees, antelope, buffaloes, and elephants.

Men and women are equal in Bayaka society, unlike most other African tribes. Wasse had already told me that the women join the men in the hunt and that it baffled him how the Bantu treated their women as inferior.

Trotting alongside us are a dozen hunting dogs, basenjis, one of the world's oldest dog breeds. They are about twenty inches high, wiry, with red and white fur. Like wolves, they cannot bark because of a flattened larynx but instead utter an eerie howl when they are excited or communicating with other basenjis. Each dog has around its neck a bell carved from a chunk of wood and filled with small animal bones. "The noise lets us know where they are when we're hunting," Wasse tells me.

I bend to pat a puppy, but Wasse asks me to stop. They have a different approach to their dogs. "They're not our friends, they're our companions on the hunt," he tells me. "We never let them think they can control us."

I think of my beautiful female Rottweiler, Freia, back in Sydney. She is among the friendliest of all the dogs that have been with me over the decades. She likes me to sit on the floor in our lounge room so she can rest her bulky head on my lap and look up at me with soft loving eyes. But I know that Freia would leap in with excitement to join the pack when the basenjis hunt.

We know that dogs evolved through thousands of generations from wolves, and no matter their appearance and size, most relish hunting prey in a pack. I once wrote a feature in rural Australia about a plague of rabbits, with more than a hundred million blighting the continent's countryside. Locals at Colac in rural Victoria had a ferret club and took their killer-eyed ferrets out in the fields each weekend. They let them loose to scurry down the many rabbit holes and chase the terrified prey up to the surface. There, a dozen dogs licked their lips as they waited.

At their homes, they were content like infants to eat food that was slush with nary a hint of their secret desire to consume fresh bloody meat. Indeed, on the way to the hunt at Colac, the car driver's gentle little pug rested in my lap and looked as if she would not hurt even a flea.

But once the rabbits came hurtling out of their burrows, chased by the ferrets, all the dogs barked themselves into a frenzy with blood lust. They chased after the rabbits and tore them to shreds. Even the smallest joined in the slaughter, and all the dogs ended the day with blood-splattered mouths as they morphed back into beloved pets. But the basenjis, in tandem with the Pygmies, hunt in a different, more disciplined way honed over the millennia.

The basenjis originated in Central Africa and have been with the Pygmies for millennia, but at some distant time they were brought from the jungles to Egypt and became a favorite with the Pharaohs. The first engraving of a basenji that we know of appeared on a funerary stele of Sebeh-aa, an inspector of transport, in 2300 BCE.

A basenji website notes: "Among the tomb furnishings of rich Egyptians and Pharaohs were statues and illustrations of these dogs which because of its extremely cat-like nature, (it moves silently, is free from dog smells and washes itself like a cat) made it highly prized." I have seen an ancient life-like statue of a basenji in the Louvre's Egyptian section.

Basenjis were brought to Europe from Africa late in the nineteenth century and created a sensation when they first appeared at the world's largest dog show, Crufts, in the UK in 1937. They were then called the African bush dog. The basenji became popular as a small attractive dog that is extremely intelligent and social, devoted to its owners and has a highly developed instinct for hunting.

We trek through the rainforest all morning and soon after noon enter a clearing surrounded by giant trees, the canopy so dense that the sunlight has to stab its way through the layers of leaves. "The Pygmies are animists," William says. "They believe there are *mokoondi*, spirits, in all living things including trees, streams, rivers, forests, animals, and birds." As William and I watch the Bayaka burst into frenzied singing with the men whipping to and fro striplings they had snapped from trees.

The ritual lasts for half an hour. "We were appeasing the tree spirits of this place," Wasse tells me, "apologizing to them for our need to cut down boughs to construct our huts."

The women swiftly make the Pygmies' traditional waist-high domed huts, the same as I saw at Mossapola, using bent boughs, leaves, and mud. Within fifteen minutes they have erected a dozen waterproof huts. The men branch out in different directions in search of their favorite food, wild honey. The bees have their hives near the tops of the tall hardwood trees and the men, using twine ropes, must scale the vertical giants to get the honey. They return with glum faces and no honey. "The bees are somewhere else," Wasse says.

Wherever I have been with rainforest nomads, from the Congo to the Amazon, the clans generally have much more leisure time than we wage slaves in the West. Hunting and gathering usually takes a few hours each day and then they relax until nightfall, seated on fallen logs or cross-legged on the ground and gossiping as the children play nearby.

The Bayaka sit outside their little huts and hardly ever stop singing. Their babies learn to warble along even before they can speak. Around the encampment women with babies cradle them in their laps and, holding both their hands, help the babies clap in time to the songs' bouncy rhythms.

It is the most extraordinary sound I have ever heard, like angels singing. Each song is a high-pitched mélange of warbles and yodels, each Pygmy drifting in and out of the melody. The singing lulls to a murmur, surges to wild chanting, drifts into whispers, and then breaks into frenzied shouting. It is controlled musical anarchy, a tuneful reflection of the Bayaka's way of life in the rainforest.

An American musicologist, Louis Sarno, was so captivated by the Pygmies' unique form of singing that he spent several years living with the Bayaka in a village near Mossapola, and then wrote a book about them. "Bayaka music is one of the hidden glories of mankind," he told me when I met him later in Bangui. "It's a very sophisticated form of full, rich-voiced singing based on pentatonic five-note harmonies. But you'd expect that because music is at the heart of Bayaka life, much more than ours. Mothers constantly croon lullabies to their babies, and the children sing as soon as they can talk. Singing plays a vital role in their ceremonies. Pygmy songs from Gabon across to the Congo are much the same, with the singers constantly experimenting and improvising."

Although their songs are boisterous, they do not yell or scream but talk quietly among themselves when not singing. Whenever I have been with Pygmies in the Congo, Uganda, and Cameroon, I have never seen any arguments break out and never seen an adult hit a child. As we sit outside his hut, Wasse looks at me in shock that anyone could ever think of such a thing. "If you hit a child I think the child will grow up wanting to hit other people and will want to hit his children."

Jandu, his wife, nods in agreement. Wasse had told me that they have a baby son and I wonder where he is. "We left him at Mossapola with my wife's sister," Wasse says. "He is very sick."

"Why don't you take him to the doctor?"

"There is a Bantu medicine man in Bayanga but no Bayaka has ever been to him. We have no money. I fear our baby may not live."

Bayaka life is clearly communal and the family ties are very strong. Allard Blom had said they rarely flout rules of life that are as rigid as Old Testament commandments. It is this clan cooperation that ensures survival of all in the unforgiving jungle that seems to have formed their admirably passive nature.

I ask Wasse if his clan battles other Bayaka clans when they meet in the jungle. He looks bemused and shakes his head. "Sometimes we fight among ourselves in the village when we're angry, but we never fight other clans. The jungle is large and there is enough room and food for everybody."

The Pygmies have dinner of manioc and live caterpillars they found along with fungi, roots, berries, and forest fruit the women collected on the trek. They also eat snakes, lizards, frogs, termites, and nuts when they can find them. Then, a trio of men whip up their excitement when they start drumming wildly. The women respond with frenzied hand-clapping and singing. No one seems to notice that Wasse and five other men have disappeared.

Suddenly, from the darkened forest comes an unearthly scream. Then another scream, and another scream. I get goose bumps. Is it a leopard out there in the darkness killing prey, perhaps a chimpanzee?

"*Boyobi*," the woman seated next to me on the forest floor says softly.

"*Boyobi* are jungle spirits that visit the Pygmies on many of the nights when they're in the jungle," William explains. "Very few outsiders have ever seen them."

By now we are enveloped in darkness and I can barely see a few yards in front of me. The Bayaka fall silent and then the drumming and the singing resume louder and faster as the screams draw closer. Without warning a handful of strange creatures, the jungle spirits, leap into our midst. The *boyobi* are swathed in leaves speckled with phosphorescent algae that make them appear to glow in the dark and they move around us close to the ground on all fours, hopping like giant frogs. If I did not know better I would have sworn they were not humans.

In eerie, high-pitched voices the *boyobi* begin questioning the Pygmies about why they have come into the forest. The Pygmies have formed themselves into a semi-circle, sitting cross-legged, and answer as one in short, sharp chants, much like the call and response between a preacher and his congregation I witnessed in an African American Baptist church one Sunday morning in rural Alabama. The questions and answers come faster and faster until the *boyobi* demand that the Pygmies go deeper into the forest the next day to hunt. Then, in an eye-blink, the *boyobi* disappear. We hear their weird screams for a few more minutes growing fainter as they melt into the forest.

Wasse reappears about twenty minutes later and sits cross-legged with William and me outside our two-man tent. I was happy to sleep in one of the Pygmy mini-huts, but William snorted in scorn when I suggested it at Mossapola. He had brought along the tent that belonged to the bungalow hotel in Bayanga.

Wasse does not mention the *boyobi* and I take the hint.

That night I lay awake in the tent for a considerable time, deeply moved to have witnessed the ritual, one that must have thrilled Pygmies in their jungle encampments across Equatorial Africa for countless millennia. The cool night softens the itch from the many sand fly bites on my body and I fall asleep after a long, tiring, but enthralling day.

The next morning the men and women, accompanied by their hunting dogs, head deeper into the rainforest in single file, carrying nets slung over their shoulders. "Be careful where you walk," Wasse warns me once again. "There are also cobras and black mambas here. You will die if they bite you."

"We've plenty of deadly snakes in the bush in Australia," I tell William.

He looks down his nose at me. "Of course, you're Crocodile Dundee's brother. I should have known you wouldn't be afraid of deadly snakes. I'll see if Wasse can find you a mamba and you can amuse us by wrestling it."

"Look, mate, if you've got a chip on your shoulder, get rid of it quick or I'll find another translator."

"Be my guest, but you'll find I'm the only one around here who can speak English and Bayaka, as well as my own language."

With Wasse leading the way, we pass under a carpet of dense tree-top foliage that plunges day into night. We stride through the gloom in search of the tribe's favorite food, *mboloko*. It means blue duiker, the small forest antelope about as high as my knee. I thrill to the Bayaka's growing excitement. Their bell-like voices tinkle with laughter and whoop with glee. Only Wasse remains silent, focused on the hunt.

Unlike the Bantu, the Bayaka and other Pygmy clans have no traditional chiefs. Each man and woman is his or her own master and can do as they please, although on this hunt they all defer to Wasse's wisdom and skill. His coal-black eyes search the murk as he leads us deeper into the jungle. Sweat soaks my pants and shirt as I battle to keep up with the fast-moving Bayaka. William is younger and fitter than me, but even he struggles.

The smell of damp earth, rotting fruit, and heavy-scented blossoms soaks the air as I stumble through a forbidding alien world. The jungle shakes with the haunting shriek of cicadas perched in giant trees hung with vines and creepers and swathed with moss. The rainforest floor is dappled with toadstools and speckled with black-water puddles.

High overhead, a clan of chimpanzees scrambles from tree to tree, almost hidden by the foliage, while hornbills cling to branches far above us, alerting others to our presence with deep-throated cries. Wasse constantly turns to make sure I am still with the hunting party. As we climb a slope thick with trees that soar straight up to the canopy, a stocky, black-haired, pot-bellied creature about the size of Wasse appears out of the gloom. "*Ebobo!*" Wasse shouts.

It is a female gorilla about to climb a tree to get fruit. She stares at us with frightened eyes, and then scurries on all fours over the rise. "We used to hunt *ebobo*, but not any more," Wasse reminds me.

He raises an arm to signal a halt. Without a word, the Bayaka swiftly set six nets. Made from a vine called *nkusa*, the nets are knee-high and each stretches for about ten yards, with the Bayaka curling them into a giant semi-circle across the hillside. Wooden toggles hooked onto saplings hold the nets firm.

Wasse explains that when the tiny animals the Bayaka are hunting hear us coming they seek hiding places beneath the foliage. "We yell to frighten them, and send them running into the nets."

The Bayaka disappear up the slope. A few minutes later the jungle erupts in whoops, cries, yells, and yodels. Small, stocky silhouettes flit in and out of the trees as the Bayaka charge down the slope. The men carry bundles of leaves which they shake vigorously. The basenjis join in the hunt, silently dashing to and fro, instinctively knowing that they must drive any animals that break cover toward the nets. The hunting dogs are extremely agile, rapidly changing direction, and with their long legs can match a greyhound in speed.

A wild-eyed duiker escapes past me with Wasse in pursuit. A little out of breath, he gives up the chase and shrugs, flashing me a baffled smile. "Are any of you in early pregnancy?" he asks the women.

They shake their heads. The master hunter is searching for a reason why the duiker escaped. "Women at the start of pregnancy bring bad luck to the hunt," he tells me.

William prods me in the bulge I call my stomach. "You look pregnant, maybe you fooled the Bayaka hunting gods."

Is he trying to pick a fight, I wonder, or is it his way of showing me that this is his country and I am therefore by definition lower on the pecking order even though I am paying him a hefty fee? The hundred dollars a day he demanded and got would keep a Bantu family out here in the sticks for two or three months. It is basic economics, supply and demand. William can charge me what he wants and mock me from time to time because without him my time among the Pygmies would come to a sudden halt.

His arrogance does not bother me because it could signal a sense of insecurity and a feeling of great personal loss. It must have been heart-wrenching for William, in surrendering to his surging libido, to leave the seminary, probably in disgrace, and so abandon a dream that he might have nurtured since he was at the local primary school run by Catholic missionaries. He is an excellent translator and a mostly agreeable companion. Wasse clearly likes him and so I consider myself fortunate to have William by my side.

Once again we set the nets, and once again the cornered duikers flee by, skirting them and dashing into the thickets. The women have not wasted their time, gathering fruit, nuts, and mushrooms as they pass, storing them in the woven bamboo bags slung over their foreheads.

On the third try, the Bayaka frighten a little porcupine into the nets. As it struggles to get free, Jandu whacks it on the head with the blunt edge of a machete. A duiker fleeing the men crashes into the net. Wasse stabs it with a spear. I blanch at the deaths, so sudden, so brutal, but then we suburban dwellers have our prey killed just as ruthlessly. We shield ourselves from the horror of the abattoirs' bloodshed by hunting in supermarkets for our meat that comes anonymously bound in plastic wrapping.

An hour passes and the Bayaka emerge from the gloom carrying three duikers and four porcupines in jungle shopping baskets–vine strung in a loop around the prey's head and feet. "I sometimes hunt alone with bow and arrows, going after monkeys, but I prefer to hunt with Jandu and my friends," Wasse tells me. Jandu is carrying a bloodied duiker carcass and bursts into excited song. The other Bayaka immediately join in, accompanying their singing with frenetic hand clapping.

On the way back to the encampment Jandu stops by a tree whose trunk is studded with mushroom-like plants. "This stops pain in the tooth," she says. Wasse shows me what he calls "the water tree." Vines as thick as my fist hang down from the tree like streamers. When he cuts a six-foot-long length with a machete, rainwater gushes from either end of the vine.

A nearby tree bears bundles of yellow fruit. "Gorillas, chimpanzees, Bayaka, we all love to eat this," Wasse says. He shins up the tree as agilely as a chimpanzee and collects a bunch. Inside the shell is a red fruit, glistening like a lychee. It tastes very sweet.

The Bayaka's deep knowledge of the jungle is impressive, especially their understanding of the complex symbiosis of their habitat; how each plant, fruit, and animal is linked to the rest, woven into a dense tapestry of jungle life. We modern urban humans have mostly lost this gift of nature. Someone from Sydney or London or New York set down to be alone in this jungle might starve amid its abundance, whereas to Wasse and his people this is their version of a land of milk and honey.

Can't William see beyond his racial bias to understand the genius of the Pygmies' adaption to life in the Congo forests? Probably not. He would have to surmount not only his own bias in believing Pygmies to be *bambinga* but go against the deep-rooted bias of his people, the Bantu, and that could brand him as a someone who is at the same time insane and a dangerous stirrer.

The hunt had been a helter-skelter scramble among the trees to flush out the hiding animals, and gave me no chance to see the Pygmies tracking game. Jandu and the other women cut up the duikers and porcupines and share the meat with their neighbors after each of the hunters has taken a portion. The meat is soon cooking over small fires fuelled with saplings from nearby trees.

Anthropologist Colin Turnbull spent time with Pygmy clans in Central Africa and wrote in his book *The Forest People*: "In a small and tightly knit hunting band, survival can be achieved only by the closest cooperation and by an elaborate system of social associations which ensures that everyone gets some share in the day's catch."

Wasse is puzzled when I ask why the meat is shared equally among all the families. "Don't your people share whatever meat you get on a hunt?" he asks.

"Only among each family. I share the meat I get with my wife and daughter. The other people in my village find their own meat."

He shakes his head, frowns, and utters a few words that William has trouble translating. After a few moments thought, he says, "Wasse thinks Australians are very uncivilized." Seeing the unaggressive nature of the Pygmies up close, and their peaceful villages, he may be right.

On the hunt the Bayaka had typically taken only what they needed. Anthropologist Jerome Lewis tells of an obsessive hunter who ignored the repeated calls of his clan for him to stop hunting so much. "Eventually the women of his camp formed a coalition that refused to cook any meat that he killed." This was so offensive that he left to live with another clan. "In effect, the women exiled him for producing too much."

Next morning the clan treks back to Mossapola. Nearing the village, on a narrow track carved through the forest by the lumber company, a truck passes by carrying a load of freshly chopped down giant hardwood logs. "If the Bantu and the white people keep cutting down the trees, soon the jungle will disappear," Wasse says sadly.

"It's not the French we have to worry about," William explains. "Their company has been here more than a decade and still can't make a profit from the logging. So the government has sold concessions in the reserve to a company headed by Malaysians. They're much more ruthless. Wherever they go the jungle dies."

The Pygmies also have to worry about the actions of the high and mighty World Bank based in faraway Washington, DC.

In the British newspaper, *The Guardian*, environmental reporter John Vidal wrote: "The World Bank encouraged companies to destructively log the world's second largest forest (after the Amazon), endangering the lives of thousands of Congolese Pygmies, according to a report by an internal investigation of senior bank staff and out-side experts." The investigators travelled to the Congo Basin to see for themselves the vast deforestation.

Their report stated that 232,000 square miles of tropical hardwood forest was earmarked for logging companies. It added that the World Bank ignored the hundreds of thousands of Pygmies believed to be living in the Congolese forests and that it "put the Pygmies to serious harm."

This is the same World Bank that claims it is helping save our planet with projects to reduce global warming. On its website it piously proclaims that its Climate Change Action Plan aims to help developing countries accelerate efforts to tackle climate change. And yet ignored for an obvious reason by the group's large propaganda section, known these days as Media, the World Bank clearly does not give a hoot about the destruction of the Congo forests.

The moment we arrive at Mossapola, Jandu takes to her breast a tiny wizened baby about two months old. He had been left behind in the care of her teenage sister. His nose is clogged with snot and he struggles to breathe, wheezing and trembling. The infant's plight is not uncommon because Pygmy babies have one of the world's highest death rates. One Pygmy baby in five dies before its first birthday, mostly from respiratory infections, diarrhea, or malaria.

Alarmed, I usher mother, father, and babe into our Land Rover and head for Bayanga. The doctor's clinic is along a muddy lane near the market. A Bantu, he towers over Wasse and Jandu and frowns as he peers at the baby. Too weak to cry, the infant's eyes are dulled by pain.

The doctor prescribes antibiotics and a cough mixture. The cost is four hundred Central African Francs, about eighty cents US. "Without the medicine the baby would probably die," he tells me, "but with it he'll be okay by the end of the week." For the price of a Coke a life is saved.

Jandu's goiter can only be cured with expensive iodine-based medicine taken for three months. "It comes from eating too much manioc, which leaches the nutrients from other foods," the doctor explains. "It's common among the Bayaka."

Manioc, the staple carbohydrate for locals, is also known as cassava, and it helped the Bantu lure countless Pygmy tribes across Equatorial Africa into becoming their serfs, a more accurate description than Jacob's "slaves." The edible tuber was brought to Africa from Brazil about five hundred years ago, and the rainforest-dwelling Pygmies developed a taste for the manioc grown by the Bantu in fields near their villages. They bartered with the Bantu at the forest's edge, offering as a trade the meat of rainforest animals, wild honey, and mushrooms.

At first the shy Pygmies left their catch just inside the jungle, fearing a face-to-face meeting with the tall Bantu, the "monsters." This spooked the Bantu into believing that the rarely seen Pygmies were primitive sub-humans, a kind of forest animal. At lunch with Blom after the visit to the doctor, the Belgian tells me that this prejudiced impression still remains strong. "Several years ago the President of the CAR had to write into law that Pygmies were truly humans in an effort to banish the discrimination."

Another guest at lunch is Anne Kretsinger, an American who came here as a Peace Corps volunteer years earlier. She stayed on to learn the Bayaka language. "They are the poorest of the poor, one of the least protected ethnic groups on the planet," she tells me. "They aren't regarded as citizens in this country and so they don't have any identity papers. That means they can't file any complaints to the justice system if they are maltreated."

Few Pygmies are registered at birth and almost all the governments in Central Africa do not consider them citizens and deny them identity cards, passports, deeds to land, and even health care.

The Bantu belief that the Pygmies are less than human is common all over Equatorial Africa, with Pygmies in the two Congos, the CAR, Uganda, Cameroon, and Gabon still treated harshly. "Whenever there's a dispute between a Pygmy and a Bantu, the police always favor their fellow Bantu," says Kretsinger. "The Bantu feel contempt for the Pygmies, regarding them as primitive because they don't have a materialistic culture."

And yet it was the Pygmies' lust for manioc, cooking pots, metal spears, arrowheads, and machetes that lured many clans into abandoning the rainforest for months at a time to work in the Bantu fields in exchange for these treasures. "Over the centuries, Bantu landowners began to regard specific Pygmy families as their hereditary slaves, with fathers passing down to the sons Pygmies and their children," says Blom, repeating what Jacob had told me. "Even educated Bantu still believe the Pygmies to be primitives."

To test this, later in the day I ask William if he would consider marrying a Pygmy girl if he fell in love with her. He explodes in a rage. "Never, I'm not so stupid," he growls. "They are *bambinga*, not truly humans, they have no civilization."

There is contradiction of course because he regards Wasse as a good friend and bows to his wisdom whenever we are in the jungle.

The following day, as Kretsinger and I take Wasse and Jandu to the market at Bayanga, Wasse smiles when I tell him about William's use of the word *bambinga*.

Pygmy clans have never gone to war with the Bantu, preferring to slip back into the sanctuary of the rainforest when threatened. Cavalli-Sforza and other anthropologists have spotlighted this "essential non-aggressive nature of the Pygmies." They prefer to turn taunts back on the Bantu, using humor to soften their own hurt.

"We know the tall ones call us *bambinga*, and so we call them *ebobo*, the gorillas," Wasse says with a grin. "But we never tell them that."

To escape slavery, Bayaka clans like Wasse's have settled by tracks that timber companies cut through the rainforest, and they clear the land for their own manioc fields. "We spend time at Mossapola, but we still live in the jungle for about half of each year," Wasse says.

As Wasse and Jandu walk through the open-air market by the river, staring at the meat, fish, and vegetables stacked on wooden benches, I sense the Bantus' hostility. There is little mixing between the two peoples even though the Bayaka sometimes visit Bayanga. Normally ebullient and good-humored, Wasse and Jandu are quiet and watchful as they tread through enemy territory.

The stallholders, buxom Bantu ladies swathed in floral gowns and scarves, look away as Jandu inspects the food. They only make eye contact when she produces a bundle of francs I give her. Wasse uses some of the money to buy a slab of buffalo meat still dripping blood. "It will make Jandu's milk richer for the baby," he says. Bayaka mothers breastfeed their babies for the first three years of their life and the infants suffer malnutrition when their mother's diet is impoverished.

Kretsinger tells me that it is taboo for Bayaka men to have sex with their wives while they are breastfeeding. It seems a clever way of ensuring an infant gets all its mother's milk until it is strong enough to have a good chance of living into adolescence and adulthood.

"It's our way," Wasse says with a look of regret. "I have a long wait before Jandu and I can enjoy ourselves again."

Whether intended or not, it is also an effective way to limit the number of Pygmies and so put no stress on the forests' resources.

When I offer to buy a plump catfish caught that morning in the river, Wasse eagerly accepts. Though they live close to the river, the Bayaka are not fishers and rarely have the money to buy fish. "It tastes good, but monkey meat is better and gorilla meat is the best, but it's been a long time since we killed a gorilla," he says.

At Mossapola, Jandu squeezes more of the liquid antibiotic into her baby's mouth, smiling when I repeat the doctor's assurance that it will cure the illness in a few days. There are some ailments, though, that the Bayaka claim can only be cured by traditional medicine. One of them is an unwanted pregnancy. "My cousin is the *motuwanganga*, the medicine woman," Jandu says. "She's going into the jungle tomorrow to search for magic plants to help my sister who is in trouble. You can go with her."

Night falls swiftly in the tropics. Sipping coffee on the bungalow balcony overlooking the Sangha River, I watch the sun in its last moments devour the sky with flame, sending a wildfire racing across the heavens, burning the many clouds scarlet, orange, and pink. As the moments pass, the colors darken. The pirogues drift by silently. The Bantu at one moment glow ebony and gold with the sun's last rays as they pole back to Bayanga; at the next moment they are silhouettes etched against the swirling charcoal of the river; then in an eye-blink they are lost in the darkness.

"They are palm wine collectors," William had told me earlier in the day. "They harvest it to sell in Bayanga." He has promised to take me to see them at work early in the morning.

I eat dinner alone in an open hut at the river's edge. Grilled fish, fried potatoes, beans, and a bread roll. Another lonely meal in paradise shared with just my thoughts. My mind returns to the Bayaka's jungle encampment and their sharing of the meat from the hunt. In four decades of travelling many times around the world I had never seen anything like it. Could this be the clue to why the Pygmies are so peaceful–the lack of competition for resources that engenders so much aggression, violence, and warfare in other societies?

Anthropologist Jerome Lewis lived with a Bayaka clan and explained how a unique system of sharing all the resources had evolved among the Pygmies in their rainforest fastness. "Komba, the creator and guardian of the world, made creation for all creatures to share," he wrote. "This is set out in *ekila* rules that organize sharing and are said to originate from this time. No individual has any greater right than any other to the forest and its resources."

Men and women are equal but generally have different tasks as I witnessed at Wasse's encampment. Komba, or probably trial and error over countless centuries, evolved strict commandments. According to Lewis, "The hunter's meat is the heart, the men get the liver and kidneys; a dog that participated would get the lungs and so on. The remaining meat must be shared fairly among all present or the hunter's luck will be ruined." If the rules are broken then the camp will be endangered. The rules "instill an ideology of proper sharing that is the key to the safe enjoyment of forest resources and the guarantee of their continued abundance."

As I walk back to the bungalow, the hotel's night guard, an elderly Bantu, prowls the compound gripping a crossbow. A quiver of arrows is slung over his back. "Bon soir," I murmur. "Bon soir," he replies. I wonder whether the arrows are poisoned like those of the Pygmies, but the guard does not speak English.

William had gone home for the night to Bayanga where Jacob also stays, and I am the hotel's only guest. Mosquitoes throng the balcony, and even though the lotion protects me from their malarial attacks, their furious buzzing annoys. I retreat to the room where the one feeble light bulb prevents me from reading. I rub soothing ointment into the many insect bites that spot my arms, legs, and face and climb into bed beneath the mosquito net.

These are some of the worst moments of a life on the road. Alone at night in a strange place and homesick with no diversions to nudge the mind away from long contemplation of the misery of it all.

Even so, my loneliness must pale in comparison with that of Ota Benga, the young Congolese Pygmy brought to the United States by Samuel Phillips Verner in 1904 to be displayed in what in effect was a human zoo. Ota was twenty-three years of age, 4-foot-11. After being exhibited to the public at the World Fair in St Louis, Missouri, causing great excitement, Verner took Ota to New York to be displayed at the Bronx Zoo in a cage in the Monkey House. As with every other animal cage in the zoo, the cage had a label on it: "African Pygmy."

William Temple Hornaday, the zoo's director, a devotee of the pseudo-science, eugenics, had sought Ota because he believed Pygmies to be half human, half ape, the elusive "missing link." This was the Western version of the Bantu *bambinga*, the ape-man. Hornaday even had Ota share the cage with an orangutan. Tens of thousands of New Yorkers rushed to the zoo to see him.

Ota had his teeth filed to sharp points in a ritual of puberty, just like Jandu, and Hornaday ordered him to give the crowd a scary thrill by repeatedly rushing at the cage's bars and baring his "animal" teeth at them. A newspaper reported that one visitor peered at Ota in amazement and asked, "Is that a man?"

There was influential opposition to this degrading of a fellow human. The *New York Times* thundered: "We send our missionaries to Africa to Christianize the people and we bring one here to brutalize him."

Ota spent just twenty days in the Monkey House and then Hornaday released him from the cage and allowed him to wander around the zoo, usually followed by a crowd jeering and laughing at him. Up to 40,000 visitors a day crowded into the zoo to see him. Frustrated, Ota threatened a keeper with his knife and shot arrows at people mocking him.

Paula Newkirk wrote a book entitled *The Astonishing Life of Ota Benga* (2015). The breaking point at the zoo, Newkirk says, "was both his own apparent resistance to captivity, along with the mounting protests by individuals who courageously defied the racial conventions of the time to highlight his humanity." There was not the same protest at the World's Fair where "he, like many others, was part of a human exhibition. In the Bronx, he was exhibited with apes."

After Ota left the zoo, he took on several jobs, including one at a tobacco factory in Lynchburg, Virginia. But he never settled into the life of an American. Pygmy life was its exact opposite—communal. The rituals of the rainforest spirits, Ejengi and the *boyobi*, the sharing among all the clan of all the food, the unique singing and dancing formed a powerful social glue that bound the clan together in harmony, peace, and joy. No concrete jungle could ever be a substitute for his beloved rainforest. He plunged into deep despair and on March 20 1916 shot himself with a bullet in the heart. Ota lies to this day in an unmarked grave half a world away from his clan and his beloved rainforest.

It had been a long and tiring day, brimming with enthralling experiences, and I swiftly fall asleep once again to the baritone lullaby of the hippos in the river outside my bungalow.

CHAPTER 4

At breakfast I discover another guest at the hotel. An American academic in her thirties, Carolyn Bocian arrived late the previous night to buy supplies at Bayanga. We share a table at the outdoor riverside restaurant and order omelets, freshly baked bread, jam, and coffee. She is a gorilla researcher with New York University and spends weeks at a time in the jungle about thirty miles downriver in the neighboring Republic of the Congo, observing the lifestyle of the shy, elusive lowland gorillas. They are far harder to track than the famed mountain gorillas in Rwanda, she says, because they live in the dense rainforest and rarely encounter humans.

"Pygmies are the most skilled trackers, and so I use them all the time. Their senses are much more acute than ours; they see, hear, and smell things that go unnoticed by me, and even the Bantu. They seem to have 3-D Vision. It would take me ten times longer to find the gorillas without the Pygmies, and this shows their mastery of the jungle."

"Do you know Wasse of Mossapola?"

"Of course. He was one of my best trackers, but he returned home because he missed his wife and family."

"He took me to a family of gorillas somewhere in the jungle near here."

"You're lucky. I'm sure it was a memorable experience."

William arrives soon after in a dugout canoe. It is so narrow that I have to force my backside into the seat, the roughly hewn wooden sides pressing against my thighs. He stands at the stern and thrusts a pole into the water, sending the canoe gliding across the water. "When I was a child, our family had a pirogue and I often took it onto the river," he says, smiling at the memory.

Brightly colored kingfishers flash by as we slice through the shallows by the riverbank. About fifteen minutes later, William steers us into a creek branching off the river. It is carpeted with blue lotus flowers, but the sharp-prowed pirogue cuts a clean path through them. Above us soars an avenue of tall palm trees.

A pirogue is already tied to a palm tree by the water's edge, and its owner has shinnied up it and cut the trunk with a machete. He thrusts a peg into the cut and hangs a small bucket from it to gather the sap. "He'll collect it tomorrow," says William. "It sells for about 1,000 francs a liter in the market at Bayanga where it's fermented into wine. It's very popular, but I prefer beer."

He had baited me the previous day and now the question at the tip of my tongue is whether he prefers it to altar wine. But that would be unfair and also disruptive because William, having begun the day with a smile, is far friendlier than yesterday.

He is bathed in sweat and when we return I offer him a shower in my bungalow. At mid-morning in Mossapola we go to meet Ieki, the clan's *motuwanganga*, the medicine woman. She is in her thirties and her slim body is clad in a floral wraparound of considerably better quality than the other women's rags. The practice of medicine must be lucrative in the Congo even among the Bayaka. "My mother was a famous *motuwanganga* and since childhood I've studied how to cure illness with forest plants and roots," she says.

What does she think of the Bantu medicine man at Bayanga?

"I think he's a sorcerer. He can cure sickness that I can't. How does he do it? I think he casts spells to make people well."

Several days earlier Mimba, Jandu's sister, had gone to Ieki pleading for help. Bayaka cherish their children—I never once saw a child punished. But Mimba had been in a trial marriage, Bayaka style. Her partner's father had refused to pay the bride price and she had just been forced to return to her own family. She is two months pregnant, and it is a disgrace for an unmarried Bayaka woman to give birth. "That's why we've asked Ieki to help," Jandu explains. "Her medicine always works with this problem."

Ieki knows the jungle as well as Wasse and we trek for more than two miles into the leafy gloom, her alert eyes scanning the rainforest floor for plants. Suddenly she kneels and uses a machete to dig up a knee-high speckled green plant.

"We call it *sambolo*," she explains, "and it will abort a woman without fail, up to five full moons after she becomes pregnant. When we get back I'll cut its roots into five pieces and boil them in a pot. They turn the water very bitter, but if Mimba drinks it this afternoon, the baby will be aborted during the night."

The medicine woman claims the side effects last for just a day or two. Ieki places the plant and its straggly roots in a bamboo basket, and then discovers another prized plant nearby. "This is called *motunga*," she says while digging it up. "It will stop Mimba's stomach from hurting."

At Mossapola, Jandu's baby is looking much healthier. He breathes easier and his nose is cleared of most of the snot. "Did you ask Ieki for medicine for your baby?" I ask her.

The Bayaka's way of life has changed little over thousands of years, and for almost all that time they only had the *motuwanganga's* cures. "Ieki's plants can't cure many of the illnesses that kill many of our babies," she says. "So it's best we use Bayaka medicine when it works, because it doesn't cost us money, and then try to find money for the Bantu medicine when it doesn't. Usually we have no money and the baby dies."

"That doesn't mean the Pygmies regard life as cheap," William says. "Two years ago Jandu lost a baby who died from influenza a few weeks after birth. She, Wasse, and the clan grieved openly at Mossapola for many days. The high death rate among babies is why Pygmies don't give a name to a baby until it is about a year old."

Wasse is sitting cross-legged by his small hut, stringing a crossbow. "I'm going hunting monkey," he calls out. "Want to come?"

He has a bamboo quiver with about twenty dart-like arrows, each about twelve inches long. A small triangular leaf is notched at the blunt end while the pointed end is stained green with Bayaka poison. "We call it *ndambele* and we make it from special vine, bark, and roots ground into a paste," he explains. The poison kills a human, or a gorilla, in about two hours by attacking the nervous system.

As Jacob drives us deep into the jungle, Wasse tells me that he once fired three arrows into a gorilla he tracked through the rainforest. She fled up a tree, but soon crashed to the ground, killed by the poison on the arrowheads. The Bayaka were on a nomadic journey through the jungle and they carried the gorilla back to their makeshift encampment for a feast.

As a reward for finding and killing the gorilla, the Bayaka hailed Wasse as a great hunter and he was idolized for a long time after by the village girls. He took full advantage of his fame. Bayaka youth enjoy free love without any stigma, unless a pregnancy results, but must end their dallying when they marry. Pygmies are monogamous and infidelity is then strictly taboo, though divorce is permitted.

This is common among the many remote tribes I have been with. Teenagers can sleep with as many partners they can attract because there are few consequences except for ensuring that the girl does not become pregnant. But once a couple marry, adultery is taboo, forbidden, Wasse would tell me later, because a man wants to be assured that any child his wife gives birth to is his child and not another man's. And divorce seems a safety valve to diminish conflict within the clan. The families in a clan live close to one another and constant open disputes between unhappy couples would be disruptive.

Jandu comes from another village and Wasse met her at a traditional dance where young Bayaka go to find a mate. His playboy days ended when they married soon after.

"She loves me because I'm a good hunter who can feed my family, and I love her because she has already given me two children and that's how we Bayaka count our riches," he says. "When I die, people will still know my name because of my children."

"Here," Wasse says, asking Jacob to stop the car about an hour after we had left Mossapola. We pad quietly through the jungle, Wasse stopping often to cock his head this way and that. I don't know how he can hear anything through the cicadas' screech and the birds' chatter, but he seems to have detected prey. "Monkey, near here," he murmurs.

About five minutes later a monkey high in the trees emits a *woo, woo, woo* cry. "Too high to see," Wasse murmurs. He snaps a branch thick with leaves and shakes it, producing a loud *sssshhhhhhhh* noise. Then he whacks the branch against a tree. "The monkey will come down to see what is making the noise," he whispers.

Wasse withdraws a poisoned arrow from the quiver and grips it between his teeth. I suspect this is to prevent it breaking his skin should he slip. We wait a few moments, as still and quiet as trees, and then he nudges me and points towards the sky. A rust-brown monkey with a white face peers at us through the leaves. Wasse slots the arrow into the crossbow and fires. The arrow hits the monkey in the arm. It screams in terror and flees into the canopy.

About ten minutes later the monkey crashes to the ground. The poison has worked. Wasse fashions a rope from vines and ties it to the monkey, slinging it over his shoulder. "This will make Jandu's milk good," he says. "I want the baby to grow as strong as our other boy."

He and Jandu have a boy aged seven, but because it is primary school holidays the child is on a two-week trek into the jungle with Wasse's brother and his family. Wasse takes him on journeys into the jungle as often as possible because he wants to prepare the boy, knowing that one day he will face a dilemma that Wasse senses but barely understands. "I'm raising my children in both worlds, showing them how to live in the jungle, and how to live in town," he tells me as we head back to Mossapola.

It sounds an ideal compromise between the demands of a modern world and Wasse's desire that his family keep a grip on traditional customs. However, the risk is that Bayaka children who succeed at school will spurn the precarious life of a hunter and gatherer in the often-dangerous jungle, choosing the comforts of town life.

I am privileged to be with Wasse on a hunt, despite hating to see animals killed, because for thousands of years Pygmies have been masters of the rainforests that swathe Africa's equatorial belt. Millions of nomadic Pygmies shared the jungles with elephants, gorillas, leopards, and numerous other creatures.

But from about 2,000 years ago, Pygmy numbers began plummeting as their homelands were invaded by the taller Bantu, farmers and cattle herders who destroyed much of the forests. They transformed it into savannah for their villages, grazing land for their herds, and fields for their crops. With the Pygmy numbers decimated, modern education now threatens a catastrophic dilution of a culture that has evolved over the millennia in a symbiotic relationship with the rainforest.

The path that must be taken by Wasse's children will not be easy. At Bayanga, William introduces me to a friend, Mekite Sylvanus, a tall, kindly schoolmaster who is frustrated by the demands of teaching Bayaka children. "They like to eat the chalk I give them to use on their slates," he says. "Also, the Bantu children bully them and call them bad names, and so they often refuse to come to school. They are just as smart as our children, but have many more barriers to their learning."

During the school term more than sixty Bayaka children, including Wasse's eldest son, attend a straw-hut school at Yandoumbe, five miles along the road from Bayanga. The Pygmy children must walk to school and back each day. There they must leap across the enormous chasm separating the Stone Age from the Book Age, and many drop into the gap, neither here nor there. In the current year only a third of the Bayaka children were promoted to the next class. "They sometimes take three to four years to complete a single year of normal schooling," says teacher Sylvanus. Despite the barriers, the CAR government claims to be determined that the Bayaka children will be fully educated in the pursuit of what the politicians claim is national unity. That echoes a slogan more similar to overblown Western political rhetoric than African culture. William is skeptical. "It's only words, they don't mean it. I like Wasse and his clan but we are very different. They're thousands of years behind us in human progress and we can't expect them to catch up to us in a few years."

Several years ago the government banned the Bayaka from ever again going into the jungle to live or hunt. It was a ham-fisted attempt to modernize their lifestyle at the stroke of a legislator's pen, in reality to homogenize their lifestyle so they follow the Bantu way.

Yet, Pygmies in an important way are more far more modern than the Bantu who are destroying vast areas of rainforest each year to house their burgeoning population. Many African towns and villages resemble garbage dumps with the detritus of our modern society–plastic bags and bottles, empty cardboard boxes, discarded burned-out electrical appliances, cast-off ragged clothing, and even piles of soiled babies' paper nappies dumped by the roadside. Rivers close to settlements are fouled with filth.

In contrast, the Pygmies at Mossapola keep their village perfectly clean.

In the bungalow next to Blom's, William introduces me to Ngatoua Urbain, a tall Bantu administrator whose fashionable suit and supercilious expression mirror his name. "The Pygmies have to understand that they must live and work in the same way as all the other people in our country. That's why we spend good money to build schools here, to educate them, and that's why we will build clinics to make them healthy."

"If you care about them, why did you stop all the Bayaka from becoming citizens of the CAR for so long? They've been here much longer than your people."

Urbain glares at me. "When the Pygmies become educated, that's when they qualify to become citizens."

If this was a white man talking about Pygmies under his rule, he and his government would rightly be pilloried around the world. The UN would denounce them as racists. So, too, would progressive politicians, Hollywood movie stars, and concerned white citizens writing to newspapers and on social media. His government might be punished with tough economic sanctions and exclusions. But, if you are black, it seems by definition that you cannot be a racist, even though the CAR government's Bayaka policies are among the world's most repugnantly racist.

"You mean the Bayaka have no choice?" I ask Monsieur Urbain. "They must give up their traditional ways?"

"Correct. They can live next to the jungle and visit it from time to time, but the government forbids them to live inside the jungle for months at a time. It is an unpleasant, unhygienic, and primitive way of living, and it must end."

How can a government ban birds from flying into the sky? The Bayaka have blithely ignored the government order to abandon their jungle life, but in doing so they have pitched their children into facing the same difficult choice confronting many nomadic tribes I have been with around the world.

The biggest threat the Bayaka children face is ill health. Ann Kretsinger, working with limited funds, has tried to stem their shocking mortality rate. Her jungle camp is thirty miles along a track that cuts through the rainforest by the Sangha River. Jacob halts the vehicle at a footbridge that spans a stream linking the track to a slope. It leads to a spartan lodge on a hill overlooking the river.

Ann is nursing her two-year-old daughter when I arrive. "This is a lodge for hunters, mostly from France and the US, who come to shoot big game," she says. "The lodge is empty because it's not the hunting season, and I work as the caretaker until it reopens in three months. For the rest of the year I work in a health clinic I've established for the Bayaka. When I came here years ago, I was appalled by the state of their health, especially the children. Throughout the country, one infant in ten dies, and that's already too high, but among the Bayaka it's one baby in five."

"I've seen that at Mossapola. Jandu's baby could barely breathe and needed medicine urgently. Without it, the baby might have died. But Jandu told me they have no money to buy the medicine," I told her.

"That's true. I got so frustrated when I saw babies dying needlessly that, with the WWF's financial help, I set up a mobile clinic for the Bayaka. A doctor from Bayanga visits the villages around here each week, covering about 1,000 Bayaka. But our funds are limited and many Bayaka go untreated. The children die from a variety of illnesses, mostly malaria, pneumonia, and the flu, but also from bad water. So another of my projects is to put water pumps in the Bayaka villages."

She can only protect the Bayaka from harm while they are close to Bayanga, but many still prefer to live in the jungle for much of the time. "They stay in the jungle for up to seven months at a time, and there's not much I can do to help them then."

"What about government help? Urbain says the government runs clinics for the Bayaka."

She shrugs. "If they were effective, we wouldn't need to set up our clinics. The CAR is a poor country and much of what wealth there is never gets beyond Bangui. The Bayaka are at the bottom of the pile."

Back at Mossapola, timber trucks trundle by as Wassse looks on forlornly. "When the trees are gone, so is our life," he tells me.

It is a sobering thought. An apocalypse faces Pygmies across Equatorial Africa as timber companies snap up logging concessions, often doled out by corrupt politicians. Daily, lumber trucks speed past Wasse's village bearing away enormous hardwood logs from trees more than a century old.

The logging company has the concession to log a huge swath of the Dzanga-Sangha Reserve, threatening to devastate wildlife and open the rainforest to poachers by gouging a network of tracks through the jungle. To prevent this tragedy from continuing, the WWF, supported by the German government, has tried to buy out the concession and then let it lapse.

"The company is basically bankrupt and I've spoken to the country's president about buying out the company," Blom had told me. The logging concessions can be purchased at 10 percent of the logging company's debt level. "That's no more than two million dollars and then we can guarantee the Bayaka the chance to live a traditional lifestyle for as long as they want."

Despite this ambition, Blom knows that the Pygmy lifestyle is undergoing immense changes across Central Africa. "Many Pygmy children have only a rudimentary knowledge of the rainforest because their way of life has altered dramatically over the past decade," he explained. "The Pygmies are moving rapidly from being hunters and gatherers to becoming agriculturalists like the Bantu."

So, Wasse and Jandu and Wunga could be the last of countless generations of Bayaka who are truly people of the rainforest, although Wasse has signaled that he will try to pass on his great love and knowledge of jungle life to his children.

At the village an old man pulls Wasse aside. "You're very lucky," Wasse tells me when they finish speaking. "Our god Ejengi, who rules the forest, has heard you've come from far away to be with the Bayaka. He wants to meet you. Ejengi will come from the forest and greet you here tomorrow night. He only comes to us at night."

The hotel is once again empty except for me. I read a book as I eat dinner at the open-air restaurant by the river, a habit that I have developed over the decades of lonely nights on the road. It is so ingrained in me that when I return home I have to push myself hard to put away reading material when I share meals with my wife and daughter. Sometimes it is a struggle even though their conversation is always interesting and entertaining. What good is a habit that helps keep me sane on the road morphs into a very bad habit at home if I succumb?

The next morning a loud knock rattles the bungalow's wooden door. I had set the alarm clock for 7 a.m., but the sun has yet to rise and the room is in darkness. I check my watch and see that it is 5:34 a.m.

"Who is it?"

"Would you like to come to Mass with me?"

I pull on a sarong and open the door. "Of course. In Bayanga?"

"No, they're pagans," William smiles. "There's a Catholic mission for Pygmies fifty kilometers north of here. Jacob has the car ready."

As we pass Mossapola on the way to the mission, many of the Bayaka are already awake. A chilly mist drifts across the slope and the Pygmies huddle around cooking fires. The Land Rover dips and weaves along dirt roads cut through the jungle, crosses rickety log bridges fording murky creeks, and slips and slides through the many mud patches.

About two hours into the journey, we turn off the road and drive through a settlement with well-kept green fields, a neat school, and an infirmary. "It's called Monasao and about 1,000 Pygmies live here," William says.

As we arrive a church bell clangs, announcing Sunday. Near the church, at a bungalow shaded by a huge leafy tree, a young Polish missionary priest, Father Waclaw Krzempek, looks surprised when he answers a knock on his door and finds me. "We don't get many western visitors, but you are most welcome," he says in Slavic-accented English. He looks pleased when I reveal I'm a Catholic and have come to attend Mass and to meet the Bayaka at the mission.

With his keen, intelligent, youthful face, Father Waclaw looks like a Warsaw university student. In his mid-twenties, he is clad in frayed blue jeans, gray T-shirt, sneakers, and has fair hair curls over his slim neck. "Father Rene, a missionary from France, founded Monasao in 1974," he says as we stroll across a compound that has a workshop for the mission vehicles, a simple log cabin church where a Bayaka boy is enthusiastically ringing the bell, and a small trade store. It sells everyday goods at prices much cheaper than the Bantu shop down the road.

"All that you see in Monasao is Father Rene's work. He was devoted to the Bayaka and he's our inspiration."

The dangers of life in an African country tormented for many decades by violence almost ended Father Waclaw's missionary life before it got into gear. He flew from Warsaw to Bangui with three other young Polish missionary priests to spend a year in the capital learning the language and culture before being assigned to missions around the country.

One night, just weeks after the priests arrived, a thief broke into their bedroom. "He stabbed my friend to death in front of my eyes," the priest says. "He was so devoted to his future as a missionary in Africa and it ended in such a horrible way. I was downhearted, and considered going home, but my faith helped me overcome my grief and after finishing my training in Bangui I was sent to Monasao."

We jump into the Land Rover and Jacob drives us around the fields, cleared by hand from jungle by the Bayaka. The manioc, green vegetables, and potatoes are planted in tidy lines. "When he first came here, Father Rene was appalled at how the Bantu made the Bayaka their serfs by trading their manioc for poorly paid labor. So he taught them how to grow crops to break the Bantu's economic stranglehold on them," he explains.

When we return to the bungalow, a little girl runs up to the priest and shows him her catch, a basin writhing with scores of green striped caterpillars. "It's a Bayaka delicacy and she asked me if I'd like some for my breakfast," he says with a boyish grin. "They eat them raw. I've not been here long enough yet to stomach that, but I hope to remain for many more years, serving the Bayaka, and someday I might enjoy eating caterpillars."

Father Waclaw is one of two Polish missionary priests living at Monasao and he not only has to say Mass, hear confessions, and preach the gospel, but also be an expert agriculturalist, a mechanic for the mission's trucks, a medic, an accountant, and his own cook, all in the service of the Bayaka. "The most important achievement of Father Rene was to give the Bayaka dignity and belief in themselves as humans," he says.

The tradeoff has been the presence, if not the total acceptance, of Christianity, because only a quarter of Monasao's Bayaka have abandoned their jungle spirits and become Catholics. "We don't discriminate between the Bayaka who are Catholics and those who still follow the traditional religion," Father Waclaw explains. "We encourage all of them to send their children to our school, use our subsidized shop, and till the fields."

Another loss that springs from a settled life at Monasao bas been the Bayaka's link with the rainforest. A church elder, Midinato, taking coffee with us in the missionaries' lounge room, tells me that the Bayaka at Monasao do go to the jungle from time to time to hunt with crossbows, but rarely stay longer than a week or two. "Our children must go to school, and we must look after the crops," he explains.

"Do you miss living in the jungle?"

"A part of me does; we Bayaka have been jungle people since the Creation. But it's a tough, dangerous life, and holds no future for our children. We're so proud when we see them going to school every day. One day we'll even have Bayaka doctors. I couldn't imagine that when I was young. The Bantu always told us we were stupid people, no smarter than the animals. Father Rene helped us to prove them wrong."

At mid-morning we join about two hundred Bayaka who are filing in to hear Mass in the simple log cabin church with its dirt floor and pews hewn out of jungle wood. Father Waclaw throws a long green vestment over his jeans and T-shirt, so that only the sneakers show. Trailed by a pair of altar boys in white surplices, he enters the church to the accompaniment of a hymn sung in the distinctive yodeling Bayaka style.

A Bayaka priest in his mid-twenties is already there and joins the Polish priest to say Mass. Father Waclaw is about the same height as me, and the Bayaka priest barely reaches his shoulder. I notice him smiling at William as we kneel in the front row. It is a musical Mass with the Bayaka yodeling hymns for most of the service to the heart-prodding rhythm of their hand clapping and a pair of drums pounded by teenage boys.

At the end of Mass, Father Waclaw invites me to speak as an Australian Catholic to the churchgoers. I tell them how deeply moved I have been by attending Mass here, far more than in many of the great cathedrals where I have prayed. "More than at any time in my life, I feel here at Monasao the universal goodness and moral power of the Christian religion. Two thousand years ago, Jesus of Nazareth died on the Cross, leaving us all a message for eternal salvation. And that message was so powerful, and so imbued with goodness, that it carried across the seas and across 2,000 years."

As Father Waclaw translates, the Bayaka stare up at me with dark solemn eyes. "Today, Sunday—this holiest of the days—in my own country, Australia, in far-off France, in Bangui, in a very big village called New York, in thousands of places across the world, and here in beautiful Monasao, among people who are black, white, golden, we Catholics are gathering in our churches to honor Jesus. We chant the same prayers, hear the same gospel message from our priests, pray to the same God. I feel humbled that you have invited me to share that message of hope and salvation and I will carry back to my own country word of the Bayaka kindness and goodness."

Outside the church the Bayaka women, men, and even children line up to solemnly shake my hand. William calls me over to where he stands with an arm around the Bayaka priest's shoulder. "This is my good friend Andre. We were at the seminary together."

"Ah, but William was always a handful for our teachers," Father Andre says with a smile. "A very holy boy, but also a very mischievous boy. I always thought he'd make a better politician than a priest."

"Why is that?"

Father Andre looks at William with a grin. "Money and girls. He liked them too much."

"Is it easy for a Bayaka to become a Catholic?" I ask.

"We believe there is a supreme being, and so that helps. Christ's sacrifice on the Cross also means a lot to our people because sacrifice is a vital part of our traditional religion."

"But is there something of what the Chinese call 'rice Christians' in the attraction, the fact that Bayaka who live and worship at Monasao have a higher standard of living than any other Bayaka I've seen?"

"Perhaps among some of our people. But we don't discriminate between Catholics and non-Catholics. All Bayaka are welcome to settle here. We just hope that Christ's message that he loves us all moves our people to seek baptism. It's not easy with the older ones, but many younger Bayaka are attracted to Christianity because of the dignity it gives them."

"Were your parents happy that you became a priest?"

"They're Catholics and my mother was very happy. But my father was angry when I told him I wanted to be a priest. He knew I could never marry or give him grandchildren. I have a brother and sister, but I'm the eldest and my father wanted me to marry a Bayaka girl. So he wanted me to give up my ambition."

"Would you have liked to marry?"

"I'm a man, my feelings are much the same as yours and William's, and so, yes, I would like to marry and have children. But mine is the sacrifice a priest makes willingly and I'm happy with my choice."

"Are you happy that you and the Bayaka here have given up the jungle? It must be hard to be a Bayaka without the jungle."

Father Andre shrugs. "It must have been hard for your people to give up their fields and cattle two hundred years ago and go to live in crowded cities. Yes, it is hard for us. But we've been slowly coming out of the jungle for centuries. Here at Monasao, we are no longer under the Bantu thumb, our children go to school, we enjoy good health, have a better diet than if we lived with the Bantu, and of course we receive the word of Jesus."

"But do you ever go to the jungle, or even want to go to the jungle?"

"Of course, as a Bayaka the jungle is my blood; even now I look across the fields to the jungle with longing. But I'm a priest and my place is here at my church. Sometimes I go into the jungle for a week or two, with my brother, sister and uncles, but I must always come back to Monasao."

"What happens on Sunday when you're in the jungle? Do you say Mass?"

"Yes, because Jesus is everywhere, especially in the jungle among the trees and the many creatures God created. I take the Host to give

Holy Communion, and I say Mass by the biggest tree wherever we've made camp. I think Jesus would like that."

On the drive back, I wonder about the Bayaka's future. They face the same soul-shaking challenges as other nomadic tribes I have been with in jungles. So much of their culture flows from their ancestral home, the rainforest, and yet modern life is luring them away, sometimes gradually and sometimes with a destructive rush. Is Monasao the future for the Bayaka, where they have abandoned most of their traditional ways in sight of the tribe's jungle wellspring? Or is Wasse's groping for the middle path for his children to follow, mingling the rainforest and the settled village, the way for the Bayaka?

These are questions I can't answer. What I do know is that at Mossapola, Wasse and the villagers refuse to abandon their ancient religion, forged across the millennia by the stresses and delights and challenges of rainforest life. And, this night I am to see it manifested when the supreme jungle spirit Ejengi meets me.

I spend the afternoon writing my notes, transcribing the interviews at Monasao. The three weeks I have spent with the Bayaka have gone far too fast. With the sky darkening, William arrives to take me to Mossapola. "I don't have much to give, but please take this as a memory of our time together," he says. It is a blackwood Madonna and child, carved with African features.

I give him one of my two tape recorders. "It'll help me practice my English," he says and wraps me in a hug.

"The doctor at Bayanga says three months of treatment are needed to cure Jandu's goiter. How much do you think that would cost?"

"For the visits every week, no more than ten American dollars altogether. The medicine will be expensive, he'll have to get it sent from Bangui. All together, I'd say about a hundred dollars."

I give him a one hundred-dollar note. "Please ask the doctor to start the treatment tomorrow."

We drive to Mossapola for the last time. Wasse is waiting for me seated cross-legged by his hut. Jandu suckles the smiling baby. "Jandu and I have decided to call him after you, Powl, for saving his life. We're poor people, we don't have many possessions, but Jandu and I want to give you this so that we will always remember the time we hunted together."

Wasse hands me an arrow, its tip stained green. "It's still got poison on it."

"Of course," I say. "It would not be a Bayaka arrow without the *ndambele.*"

I hand it to Jacob. "Be careful with it because if the tip breaks your skin it could kill you. Put it in the back of the Land Rover so we don't sit on it."

I grip Wasse by the shoulder in thanks. "Before I left my home to come to Mossapola, my daughter asked me to bring back a Bayaka arrow. You must have known."

Wasse smiles and points up at the purple sky. "Now, it's time for you to meet Ejengi."

The Bayaka worship a supreme being, but as I had seen in the jungle encampment they also revere *mokoondi*, rainforest spirits, good and evil, who visit them from time to time. "Ejengi is the most powerful *mokoondi*," Wasse explains as we cross the dirt road to a meadow nestled against the treeline at the jungle's edge.

The meadow is home to thousands of fireflies that flit among the grass, their dot-sized lights twinkling like a city at night seen from a plane. A hundred Bayaka have gathered to greet Ejengi. Like Jandu, many of the women have tiny babies cocooned in cotton carry bags slung around their necks and resting on their bosoms. The men beat drums as the women chant songs in their strange but seductive style in honor of the rainforest god.

Suddenly, the drums stop, the singing ceases, and there is an eerie hush as all eyes turn to the jungle. Emerging from the shadows are six Bayaka men accompanying a creature swathed from top to bottom with hundreds of long strips of raffia. The creature has no head, no legs, no arms.

"It's Ejengi," says Wasse, his voice trembling with awe, fear, anticipation.

"Ejengi!" the Bayaka murmur.

At first I'm sure it is a Bayaka camouflaged in strips of foliage. But in the dark, as Ejengi glides across the meadow, as the drums begin beating louder and faster, as the Bayaka chanting grows more frenzied the closer the spirit gets to us, I begin to doubt my own mind and bend to the magic of the moment.

A little taller than Wasse, the jungle spirit starts to dance, his raffia cloak rippling like water over rocks. Suddenly, Ejengi charges at the Bayaka who scatter screaming in terror. "Be careful, if any of Ejengi's strips touch you, it will tear away your skin," shouts Wasse.

He sways to the drums, eyes glued to the *mokoondi*. Ieki, the medicine woman, has spun into a trance. Her head jerks from side to side, her eyes turn inwards, and her hips thrust forwards and backwards as she spins in a tight circle screaming, "E-e-e-e."

The Bayaka edge towards the jungle spirit, terrified and yet awed by his presence. Ejengi charges them once more, whipping them into feverish chanting. Spying the stranger, he glides towards me accompanied by his guardians. The rainforest spirit cannot speak and his wishes are always voiced by his companions. They surround me, grim-faced. "Ejengi wants to know why you've come here," shouts a squat man who tilts his head at a strange angle as he questions me.

"I've come to honor Ejengi, the great *mokoondi*," I reply.

Ejengi rustles his strips of straw. The Pygmy bends his ear close to the creature. "Ejengi welcomes you," he yells. The Bayaka scream their delight.

Ejengi begins to dance once more, charging the Bayaka, flopping to the ground in a pile of straw, then leaping up to dance and charge again. The music thuds against my heart as the chanting grips my mind, drawing me deep into the ritual. I spin like a top to the wild singing, captured by the ritual, unaware of time's passing.

At my side Wasse nudges me to safety each time Ejengi races at us. I twist an ankle trying to get out of his way as the *mokoondi* lunges, but the flare of pain melts into the thudding of the drums. The hours pass as so many minutes.

Jacob has gone back to the car, but William stays by my side. He too is dancing, his eyes are on fire, and each time Ejengi races at us he jumps nimbly out of the way. "Do you believe Ejengi is a spirit?" I ask "Or do you think it's one of the Bayaka?"

"Of course Ejengi is a spirit from the jungle," he shouts, pitching his voice over the drums and singing. "I believe he is with all my soul."

"But you're a Catholic."

"I'm an African too, and there's no conflict."

Ejengi retreats often into the jungle and stays hidden for several minutes only to surge out again into the ritual with his worshippers.

Just after 2 a.m., short of breath and now feeling pain stir in my ankle, I decide to leave. Wasse grips my arm in farewell, our eyes lock on each other, a silent affirmation of brotherhood. But then he turns back into the grip of Ejengi. As the Land Rover pulls away from the clearing, the chanting drifts back into the trees until it melts into the night sounds of the jungle.

Returning to my river bungalow, my eyes glisten with tears. I am moved by Wasse's immense dignity and courage under great duress, his irrepressible humor and deep love of the rainforest. Questions pound my mind, keeping me from sleep. I sit on the balcony overlooking the river, insect repellent slathered on my face, arms, and ankles to ward off the rapacious mosquitoes. For how much longer can Ejengi and the Bayaka roam the rainforest, I wonder, living in vibrant harmony with nature? For how much longer can Wasse and his people resist the modern world's destructive effects?

As population explosions and greed threaten their ancient rainforest homelands, the future of the Bayaka across Central Africa looks bleak. Yet they have warded off challenges before and held fast to their traditions for thousands of years. In the darkness, with the shadowy jungle looming overhead, I pray to Ejengi that the Bayaka will find their own unique way to survive.

CHAPTER 5

Pygmy populations across the Congo Basin suffer "appalling socio-economic conditions and the lack of civil and land rights," according to a study conducted for the London-based Rainforest Foundation. They have been pushed from their rainforests and forced into settlements on Bantu lands, the study says, by eviction from newly established national parks and other protected areas, extensive logging in Cameroon and elsewhere in the Congo Basin, and continued warfare between government and rebels.

The belief that Pygmies are less than human is common across Equatorial Africa. "They are marginalized by the Bantu," says David Greer, the American primatologist who was with Wasse and the Mossapola Pygmies for nearly a decade. "All the senior village or city leaders are Bantu, and they usually side with other Bantu in any dispute involving Pygmies."

A Bantu tribe in Rwanda, the Hutu, even tried to wipe out the nation's Batwa Pygmies during the infamous genocide in 1994 when *Interahamwe* militants slaughtered 10,000 of Rwanda's 30,000 Batwa. Another 10,000 Pygmies fled across the border into Uganda, a stronghold of the Batwa.

The Rwenzori Mountains, also known as the Mountains of the Moon, straddle the Equator to form part of the border between Uganda and the Democratic Republic of Congo. The rainforests here have long been home to the Batwa, with 80,000 people, the largest Pygmy tribe. I have come to see what changes have occurred in their traditional lifestyle.

On the Uganda side of the border, my LandCruiser trundles over a dirt road high along the flanks of the steep foothills. The hills have long been stripped of trees, but their slopes plunge to verdant valleys— a vast rainforest set aside as a national park. My guide, John Nantume, keeps one hand on the steering wheel as he points at the rainforest that runs parallel with us on the right hand side of the road. "A few thousand Pygmies used to live there, their homeland for thousands of years, but our glorious President, Museveni, may he burn in hell, forced all of them out at gunpoint a few years ago. They refused to leave but soldiers were trucked into the rainforest to herd them away. Pygmies are passive people and did not resist."

"Why were they forced to leave? That's callous. Surely they were not threatening any creature with extinction."

"Museveni gets about 80 percent of his government's budget from Western countries, especially Europe, and he's always sucking up to them. Western conservation organizations like WWF pressured him, using support for their aims from their governments, to clear out all humans from rainforests like this one and declare them national parks so the animals and birds there can flourish.

"But the rainforest creatures flourished alongside the Pygmies for thousands of years. The Pygmies always took only what they needed."

"Pygmies are human. To the Western conservationists, humans are bad and that also meant the Pygmies. So Museveni pushed them out and made it a serious crime for anyone to live or hunt in the new national parks like the one over there."

"What happened to the displaced Pygmies?"

"You'll meet some today. Museveni gave them small plots by the roadside, close to Bantu settlements, and told them to get on with their lives."

Western conservation organizations are among the most pious, holier than thou, of our civil society groups, and they exist largely on donations from the public. They mail out slickly produced brochures showing their good deeds in far-off places such as Africa. Many focus on preserving animal and bird life in national parks, especially creatures under threat of extinction. In doing so they prompt a money flow to pay their overheads, such as employing staff at home and experts in the field. Their aims are usually worthy, and this is the first time I have heard that some have prodded Museveni to expel Pygmies from their traditional homelands in the rainforests.

Several hours from Fort Portal, the nearest large population center, we stop at a Bantu town swarming with people. It is market day and scores of vendors have spread out their wares—goat carcasses, sarongs, soap, mirrors, scissors. Nantume points to a huddle of mud huts about fifty yards away, nudging the road, and identifies it as the local Pygmy village.

I am surprised that the Pygmies are living so close to their traditional enemies. Mubiru Vincent, of Rural Welfare Improvement for Development, a body that promotes Batwa welfare, later explained in Kampala, Uganda's capital, that his organization tries to resettle the displaced Batwa clans on land they can farm.

About thirty Batwa sit dull-eyed outside their huts, which resemble those of the Bantu. The smallest adult Pygmy I have ever seen strides toward me, introduces himself as Nzito, and says that he is "king of the Pygmies here." This, too, surprises me; traditionally, Pygmy households are autonomous, though I had seen how they cooperate on communal endeavors such as hunts.

Nzito says, "President Museveni forced us from our forests and never gave us compensation or new land. He made us live next to the Bantu on borrowed land."

His clan looks well-fed, and Nzito tells me they regularly eat pork, fish, and beef purchased from the nearby market. When I ask how they earn money, he leads me to a large field behind the huts. It is packed with hundreds of marijuana plants. "We use it ourselves and sell it to the Bantu," Nzito says.

The sale and use of marijuana in Uganda is punishable with stiff prison terms, and yet "the police never bother us," Nzito says. "We do what we want without their interference. I think they're afraid we'll cast magic spells on them. They fear we'd make their penises fall off."

The fate of Nzito's clan is similar in the Congo Basin. Congolese conservationist Dominique Bikaba told anthropologist Jerome Lewis that Pygmies in the Democratic Republic of Congo were evicted from their tropical rainforest after it was proclaimed a national park. "They were forbidden to use the economic resources of the forest (i.e., wild game, wood, etc.) and forced to live on the margins of the park. This helped destroy their culture, because their traditional ceremonies and lifestyle were linked to the forest and were now severely restricted."

In Uganda, government officials rarely bring charges against the Batwa generally "because they say they're not like other people and so they're not subject to the law," says Penninah Zaninka of the United Organization for Batwa Development in Uganda, another group, when I meet her in Kampala a few weeks later. However, Mubiru Vincent says his group is working to prevent marijuana cultivation.

Because national parks were established in the rainforests where Nzito and his people used to reside, they can never again live there. "We're training the Batwa how to involve themselves in the nation's political and socioeconomic affairs," Zaninka says, "and basic matters such as hygiene, nutrition, how to get ID cards, grow crops, vote, cook Bantu food, save money, and send their children to school."

"In other words, to become little Bantu," I suggest.

Zaninka nods. "Yes, it's terrible, but it's the only way they can survive."

The Pygmies also face diseases ranging from malaria and cholera to Ebola, the often fatal virus that causes uncontrollable bleeding from every orifice. While I am with the Batwa, an outbreak of the disease in nearby villages kills more than three dozen people. When I ask Nzito if he knows that people nearby are dying of Ebola, he shakes his head. "What's Ebola?" he asks.

Cameroon is home to about 40,000 Pygmies of the Baka clan. I board a jet at Nairobi in late afternoon and shoot across the continent, flying high above the Congo Basin. I am doing it the easy way; European explorers took months to battle through jungles like those far below. I could never have survived such journeys, if only because of my serious allergy to sand fly bites. In Sydney, after returning from my journey to Wasse and his people, I told my doctor that I gave up counting after finding one hundred red swollen lumps all over my arms, legs, and feet. These were the sand fly bites I got while we were at the jungle encampment. He warned that if I suffered too many sand fly bites at the same time, and a hundred were usually too many, then I could die on the spot from a life-threatening anaphylactic shock. It can happen swiftly from a surging overload of histamine from the bites.

The symptoms would begin with my heart beating faster, then vomiting and abdominal cramps, then my throat becoming swollen, making it hard to breath. I would then have a seizure, quickly losing consciousness and the ability to breathe. Death would follow quickly.

I asked the doctor how I could prevent such a fate. "By rushing to the nearest hospital for an injection of adrenaline to counteract the massive amount of histamine in your body. You might even need a second injection."

"But I'm often in places like the Congo, where there are no clinics let alone a hospital. What do I do then?"

"Pray."

On the flight, in reading a book about Cameroon's history, I discover that its name is derived from *camarão*, the Portuguese word for prawn. Portuguese medieval mariners discovered that its coastal waters teemed with prawns and they gave the land the world's most curious name for a country. "Prawn Land."

Four hours later we land at Yaounde, the Cameroonian capital. The road into the city resembles a roller coaster, as Yaounde spreads across waves of hills. The street life is familiar, with shantytowns mottling the lush green landscape. Cameroon is resources rich with offshore oil fields, logging, and ocean fisheries including the ubiquitous prawns, but the BBC says it is one of the most corrupt nations on the planet.

President Paul Biya is one of Africa's so-called Big Men and has been in power for three decades. Dissent is choked by his brutal secret police. In *Tyrants: The World's 20 Worst Living Dictators*, David Wallechinsky lists Biya alongside the genocidal Robert Mugabe of Zimbabwe and the murderous Teodoro Obiang Nguema Mbasogo, President For Life of neighboring Equatorial Guinea.

At mid-evening the shantytowns along the road to the city roll on, fronted by rickety wooden roadside shops. Outdoor butchers offer meat hacked from fat-streaked sides of beef hung on hooks and goat heads staring dumbly into space from blood-splattered benches. They are pushed against mom-and-dad stalls offering not much more than packets of biscuits, tinned meat, toothpaste, washing powder, and cans of Coke.

The most colorful are the numerous barbers with just one or two dilapidated chairs and cracked mirrors in their small stalls. At their entrance they boast florid paintings of the oiled and greased high-top styles you can have fashioned inside.

My hotel is in the middle of downtown Yaounde, and well into the early hours very loud music booms from several shabby bars, keeping me awake. But it does not trouble me. West African music is one of the world's glories, bouncy and zesty, spurred along by an irresistible beat with the singers' voices melting into smooth harmonies.

The following night I visit the city's top nightclub to see how the moneyed class celebrate. It is owned by a former world soccer superstar, Samuel Eto'o, who played for FC Barcelona. He has clearly tipped some of his millions into the nightclub because it is as good as any I have been to in New York, Paris, or London.

On the dance floor, under flashing multicolored lights, a swirl of sharply dressed young women and men gyrate as music pounds from giant speakers. Expensively clad middle-aged men and women are seated in plush armchairs on a raised platform at the far end. This is Cameroon's elite. A steady stream of beautiful young women bear $200 bottles of Johnny Walker whiskey up to the privileged on the platform. Many Cameroonian families earn not much more than a dollar a day and the contrast is sickening. Soon enough I will be with Pygmies in the rainforest, and they must earn even less.

Despite my many journeys to Africa, I never get used to this very obvious contrast between the wealthy and those on middle class incomes and the poor. As the decades have rolled on from my first-ever trip to Africa, there never has seemed any solution to the gross inequality. The moneyed class is never going to give up the many privileges they have grabbed for themselves, and those on middle and low incomes have little chance of dismantling this hoarding of much of the national income by the rich.

One of the most pernicious privileges is higher education. Free education through primary school is common and secondary education is often also free. But the chance for advancement largely stops at the gates of the universities through a cruel system. The cost of tuition in the many private universities throughout Africa is usually about the same as in my country, but the average annual income of even the middle class is up to fifty times lower. That shuts the gate on most middle class students, and the poor have no chance. It deliberately limits upward income mobility, reserving professional qualifications largely for the children of the rich. That, in turn, allows them to then become the elite of the next generation.

On the following morning I take a taxi to the office of Samuel Nnah, who directs Pygmy aid programs for the Centre for Environment and Development (CED). Nnah is a ruggedly handsome bearded man who resembles Joe Frazier, the world champion American boxer, when he was in his prime. Nnah tells me he struggles against a federal government that allows timber companies to log Cameroon's rainforests, which effectively drives the Pygmies out of their homelands. "The Pygmies have to beg land from the Bantu owners, who then claim they own those Baka," Nnah says.

The next day on the road from Yaoundé to Djoum, a ramshackle town near Cameroon's southern border, I pass more than one hundred large timber trucks, each bearing four or five huge tree trunks to the port of Douala. Cameroon's 1,000-franc note, worth about two dollars, bears an engraving of a forklift carrying a huge tree trunk toward a truck. In effect, the government glorifies the destruction of its precious rainforests.

My companion is Manfred Mesumbe, a Cameroonian anthropologist and expert on Pygmy culture. "The Bantu governments have forced them to stop living in the rainforests, their culture's bedrock," he tells me. "Sadly, within a generation many of their unique traditional ways will be gone forever."

At Djoum the CED provincial coordinator, Joseph Mougou, tells me he is battling for the human rights of 3,000 Baka who live in sixty-four villages. "Starting in 1994, the government has forced the Baka from their homes in the primary rainforest, but the Baka are allowed to hunt in the secondary forest where they hunt mostly rat moles, bush pigs, and duiker," Mougou says. "But that's where the government also allows the timber companies free rein to log, and that's destroying the rainforests."

Sixty miles beyond Djoum, along a dirt track, and after passing scores of timber trucks fully loaded with giant logs, we reach Nkondu, a Pygmy village consisting of fifteen mud huts. As in Uganda, the huts are built in the head-high rectangular Bantu style.

Awi, the chief, welcomes us and says the villagers, each carrying empty cane backpacks, are about to leave to forage in the rainforest. He says that the older children attend a government primary boarding school, but the infants go to the village preschool. "They'll join us later today," Mesumbe says.

"*Goni! Goni! Goni bule*," Awi shouts to his people. "Let's go to the forest!"

The clan leads Mesumbe and me single file through a steaming rainforest. Scrambling across tree trunks straddling fast-flowing streams, we hack through heavy undergrowth with machetes and cut away vine-like lianas hanging like shredded curtains in our path. The sweltering heat swaddles us like a sauna.

After two hours, we reach a small clearing beneath a hardwood tree canopy that almost blots out the sky. The women begin constructing the traditional igloo-shaped huts in the clearing where we will spend the next few days. They chop saplings from among the trees and thrust the ends into the ground, bending them to form the domed frame of each hut. Then they weave bundles of green leaves into latticework to create a rainproof skin. As with the Bayaka and Batwa, none of the men stands higher than my shoulder and the women are smaller.

At midafternoon, about twenty children between the ages of three and five stream unaccompanied into the clearing where their parents have fashioned the huts. "Pygmies know the forest from a young age," Mesumbe says, adding that these children followed jungle paths from the roadside village to the clearing.

As the Baka bring firewood to the camp, Mesumbe and I put up our small tent.

Suddenly the Pygmies stir. Three scowling Bantu brandishing

machetes stride into the clearing. I fear they are bandits, common in this lawless place. I am carrying a substantial amount of money in a bag strung around my neck, and news of strangers travels fast among the Bantu here. Mesumbe points to one of them, a stocky man with an angry look, and in a low voice tells me he is Joseph Bikono, chief of the Bantu village near where the government has forced the Pygmies to live by the roadside.

Bikono glares at me and then at the Pygmies. "Who gave you permission to leave your village?" he demands in French, which Mesumbe translates. "You Pygmies belong to me, you know that, and you must always do what I say, not what you want. I own you. Don't ever forget it."

Most of the Pygmies bow their heads, but one young man steps forward. It's Jeantie Mutulu, one of the few Baka Pygmies who have gone to high school. Mutulu tells Bikono that the Baka have always obeyed him and have always left the forest for the village when he told them to do so. "But not now," Mutulu announces. "Not ever again. From now on we'll do what we want."

About half the Pygmies begin shouting at Bikono, but the other half remain silent. Bikono glowers at me. "You, *le blanc*," he yells at me. "Get out of the forest now."

When the villagers continue to defy Bikono, the Bantu chief demands 100,000 francs (two hundred dollars) from me as a bribe to remain with the Pygmies. At first I ask him for a receipt, which he provides, and then, with one eye on his machete, I refuse to give him the money. I tell him that he's committed a crime and I threaten to return to Djoum and report him to the police chief, with the receipt as evidence. Bikono's face falls, and the three Bantu shuffle away.

The Pygmies greet their departure with singing and dancing, and they continue until midnight. "The Pygmies are the world's most enthusiastic partygoers," David Greer would tell me later. "I've seen them sing and dance for days on end, stopping only for food and sleep."

This was yet another of those incidents where, on returning home and even as I write this, I shake my head in wonder. No sane person would ever do such a thing, especially in a far-off rainforest many miles from the nearest police station. The risk of Bikono and his men attacking me in bloody retaliation was immense. He could claim later that I attacked him first and the Pygmies' denials would count for very little in a police investigation, Mesumbe had told me. Bikono was a wealthy man from the smuggling of elephant tusks and would have no qualms in bribing the judge if there was a trial.

But yet again I gained from the insanity because I was able to remain in the rainforest with Awi and his people and meet Ejengi once more. When Awi pauses from the dancing, he grips my arm. "You are a very brave man," he says with a smile. I accept his admiration in silence, not wishing to disappoint him by replying that bravery is not one of my traits.

You are only brave when you become afraid, when you are confronted with danger and then confront and surmount it. In those moments of madness, such as the Bikono confrontation, I never feel afraid. A kind of bold foolishness takes hold of me, allowing me to do the most daring actions without any sense of risk. It is only later, sometimes much later, that I realize how close I had come to death or serious injury.

Over the next three days, Mesumbe and I accompany Awi and his clan deeper into the rainforest to hunt, fish in the streams, and gather edible plants. In terms of their culture, the Baka here seem to fit somewhere between the Bayaka in the Central African Republic and the Batwa I had just visited in Uganda. They have abandoned net hunting and put out snares like the Bantu to trap small prey.

Sometimes, Awi says, Bikono will give them a gun and order them to shoot an elephant. Mesumbe tells me that hunting elephants is illegal in Cameroon and that guns are very rare. "But highly placed policemen and politicians work through village chiefs like Bikono, giving rifles to the Pygmies to kill forest elephants," he says. "They get high prices for the tusks, which are smuggled out through the port at Douala to Japan and China." The Pygmies, Awi tells me, get a portion of the meat and a little cash.

The Baka here have clearly begun accepting Bantu ways, such as anointing Awi as the clan's chief. But they cling to the tradition of revering Ejengi. On my final night with them, as light leaches from the sky, all the women in the clearing chant a welcome to the great rainforest spirit. The men dance wildly with flailing arms to the thud of drums. When I join them they smile.

"*Kwa Kwa.*" The high-pitched scream and thumping on trees reverberates through the gloom. "Ejengi is near," Awi says, his voice trembling.

As among the Bayaka, no sooner has the sky darkened than Ejengi emerges from the gloom, accompanied by four clansmen. The rainforest spirit's raffia strips are ghostly white and, as in Mossapola, he has no head, no limbs, no features, giving him a spooky look. He dances with the men for about an hour, the raffia strips swirling about him, and then four little boys are brought before him by their parents. Shoulder to shoulder, they sway to the drums' thump as Ejengi dances solemnly along the line, letting his rippling raffia strips brush their bodies. "Ejengi's touch fills them with power to brave the forest's many dangers," Awi tells me.

"Does he come often?"

"Rarely. This is the first time in many months. He's come to meet you."

Through the night Ejengi dances with the men and the boys as the women chant ancient rainforest hymns. Unlike Mossapola, where Ejengi gave the ritual the exuberance of a nonstop dance party, this rite is more somber, more sacred, with the tree canopy soaring overhead like the arch of a rainforest cathedral.

Nearing dawn, as the darkness drains from the sky, the women's chanting becomes more frenzied. "Ejengi will leave us soon," Awi murmurs, an ache in his voice.

Five teenage boys step forward and stand shoulder to shoulder. The drums beat louder and the women's piercing singing shakes the leaves on the trees as Ejengi pushes against each of the boys in turn, trying to knock them off their feet. They brace their shoulders and stand firm. Again and again in a powerful metaphor of the Pygmies' life, Ejengi moves along the line, shoving each boy, attempting to tumble them to the ground. Steeling every muscle in their bodies, they refuse to budge.

"Ejengi is testing their power to withstand adversity," Awi tells me as my throat chokes, aware of the charged emotion among a people being buffeted daily by the Bantu. "We Baka face hard times and the youngsters need all that power to survive as Pygmies."

And then Ejengi is gone, uttering his birdlike calls and thumping trees as his presence fades into the fastness of the rainforest. Quietly, the Pygmies gather their belongings and lead Mesumbe and me through the jungle back to their roadside village to say good-bye.

Later in the day, at Djoum, I meet the province administrator, a Bantu named Frédéric Makene Tchalle. "The Pygmies are impossible to understand," he says, more smug than puzzled. "How can they leave their village and tramp into the forest, leaving all their possessions for anyone to steal? They're not like you and me. They're not like any other people."

SECTION TWO:

WITH NEW GUINEA'S TREE-DWELLING CANNIBALS

CHAPTER 6

The New Guinea Korowai cannibals beckon.

The Bayaka Pygmies and the Korowai have evolved beliefs, customs, and behavior in their rainforests for millennia and I am intrigued to know how they differ and why. Very little is known about the tree-dwelling cannibals because they are among the most remote people on earth. They live in an isolated jungle in the Indonesian province of Papua. It was formerly known as Irian Jaya and for half a century rebel Papuans have been battling a brutal neocolonial federal government in seeking independence.

The journey begins as always with Cecilia, Cathy, and Freia—wife, daughter, and dog—standing on the porch, their smiles tight and eyes concerned as we await the taxi taking me to the airport. "I'll be very careful, I won't do anything silly," I promise, a ritual that began three decades earlier when my wife and I were courting.

She, and now my daughter, and probably the dog, know otherwise. After travelling the world's roads, airways, rivers, and oceans for three decades, journeying to tribal people living at the edges of the world is still a passion. I am still as excited as a birthday child when setting off on a new trip.

The promise means very little to Cathy. It is for her a formality. For many years she has avoided reading my magazine features based on adventure with meaning. She does not want to know about my Mad Dog incidents and even shies away when I describe my journeys to my wife when I return home. Hear no danger. See no danger. Speak no danger. I accept it, knowing that Cathy's aversion stems from a deep love and not disinterest.

Cecilia and Cathy are used to this eccentric zest for adventure with meaning whatever the risk. My Chinese wife has little urge to wander; her life is rooted to our patch of earth in Sydney. Time after time she waves me off to some remote place, but never lets me know of those many moments when she must fear for my life. Like many Cantonese, her gentle smile masks an iron resolve that gets her through the weeks and months until I come home again.

Cathy carries the blood of the Sicilian mariner who jumped ship in Melbourne a century and a half ago to join the great Australian gold rush, and who gave us our surname. However, she is never entirely happy about me travelling to some of the most isolated and perilous places on earth.

This time my family has much more to fear than usual, which is why I keep the details of this trip brief. I am at the first step of a journey to the land of the fierce Korowai, the last cannibal tribe on earth, deep in the remote rainforests of Indonesian New Guinea. Until recently, much of New Guinea, the world's second largest island, was unexplored. For centuries its very name stirred the hearts and travel lust of adventurers from Asia, Australia, Europe, and the United States.

It summoned images of a forbidding interior roamed by naked headhunters, bloodthirsty cannibals, and bizarre and beautiful creatures–kangaroos living in trees, rats as big as sheep, and the fabled birds of paradise with their beautiful plumes, hanging upside down on trees as if they were bats.

The eastern side, the independent nation of Papua New Guinea, has been largely pacified for decades, the warring tribes brought under the central government's control–though clan fighting still occurs, especially in the highlands. Four decades earlier I had spent two years among Stone Age people in the highlands, there as a trainee patrol officer. But to the west in Indonesian territory, where the tribes speak over two hundred fifty separate languages, there are still tens of thousands of square miles marked on the map as places unknown. There, the swamp-lands, highlands, and rainforests bristle with deadly animals, deadly microbes, and deadly warriors. The most feared are the Korowai.

Cecilia and Cathy help load my luggage and camera gear into the taxi, masking their concern with nervous laughter, but Freia hangs back with dark accusing eyes. She must hate the black suitcase and camera bag because each time she sees me haul them out she knows I will be leaving home. In her dog's way she must wonder if I will ever return.

My wife told me that Freia sits on the balcony of our home every day that I am gone. She faces the front gate, and though she sleeps for much of the day, each time the gate creaks open her head snaps up instantly as she hopes to see me arriving home. When I do, she barks loudly with what I expect is a happy greeting and jumps up to place her paws affectionately on my chest. Freia weighs about sixty pounds, most of it muscle and bone, and it is like being charged by a professional wrestler. I would not have it any other way, even though sometimes she tumbles me over in her eagerness to lick my face.

Her devotion often reminds me of Hachiko, a faithful dog at Shibuya, a suburb in Tokyo. I learned about the extraordinary devotion to her master, a professor at the University of Tokyo, when I was based in the Japanese capital for three years. Each workday Hachiko would accompany her beloved owner to Shibuya station to farewell him as he took the subway to work. And each afternoon Hachiko returned at the correct time to the station. The professor always found Hachiko wait-ing faithfully for him on the pavement by the exit.

I expect Hachiko could tell the time by the darkening of the sky. When I am home, each afternoon at about 4:30 p.m., Freia pads into my study and begins pawing gently at my leg. It's time for our walk in the park near our home, she is signaling. When I am busy and neglect to take her she grows anguished, crying and whimpering, until I relent and put on her leash. Then we walk to the park, where she can romp about and play with her many dog friends.

Hachiko always greeted the professor at the subway exit. But one day he collapsed at work with a cerebral hemorrhage and died. Each afternoon at the same time from then on for nine years Hachiko padded to the station hoping to greet her owner. Of course, he never returned. Hachiko did this until the day she too died.

No wonder we love our dogs so much. Moved by this devotion, the Japanese built a statue of Hachiko waiting faithfully for her master and placed it at the very spot at the subway exit.

But human devotion to our dogs, and they to us, might not necessarily go back to the Neolithic era when wild dogs began to join us in our villages. At the Bayaka encampment I never saw a single moment of affection by the Pygmies towards their dogs.

Wasse could not understand why I displayed affection towards his basenjis. He valued them because they played a vital role in the net hunting, no more, no less, and were not regarded as friends. The Korowai, another Neolithic people, probably have hunting dogs and, if so, I am eager to see whether their bonding includes affection on both sides.

"Look after yourself, and come back safely," says Cathy as Freia barks what is either a farewell or her upset at me leaving yet again. Completing the farewell ritual, my wife kisses me and my daughter turns me around in a complete circle three times for good luck. This time I may need it.

"I'll see you in a few weeks," I call out through the open window as the taxi roars off. Through the rear window they drift back into the muddle of suburbia.

It takes six hours to fly from Sydney to Bali and, fearful of being arrested on arrival, my stomach is in a knot for most of the way. I wave away meals, concerned that I might throw up after eating. Years before, the Indonesian government banned an edition of *Reader's Digest* featuring my story exposing the brave struggle of the East Timorese against the occupation of their country by the brutal Indonesian military.

I had gone into East Timor clandestinely, and knew that the government was angered and embarrassed internationally by my story, a profile of Bishop Carlos Belo, who was leading the fight for independence. The bishop stated publicly that my profile of him, read by up to a hundred million people worldwide in the *Digest*, helped him win the Nobel Peace Prize, a major factor in the Indonesians having to retreat from their colony. Soon after, East Timor gained independence. Now, I wonder if Indonesia has blacklisted me from entering the country.

But the lure of travelling in a time warp, journeying back to the Stone Age to be with the Korowai, is too strong to resist, and I have gambled on knowing that the Indonesians are the Mexicans of Asia. Mañana, or never do today what you can do tomorrow or the year after next, translates loosely to *tidak apa* in Indonesian, an everyday expression meaning, "Don't worry, don't hurry, it'll be okay." So I trust that the tardy Indonesians won't have placed me on the banned list. But if they catch me at the airport, then it will mean days or even months in the filthy, disease-clogged prison at Bali, my cell mates murderers, rapists, and foreigners from a dozen countries caught with illegal drugs.

The twist in my stomach tightens as the 747 skids to a halt on Bali's rain-splattered tarmac a few minutes after another jumbo landed from Tokyo. The arrival hall is thronged with holidaymakers. G'days and *ohaiyos* mingle as Japanese honeymooners in look-alike tropical shirts share the immigration queues with Aussie surfers sporting bleached dreadlocks and surfboard shorts. One of the immigration lines moves twice as fast as the others. Slipping into it, I step up to the counter and hand over my passport.

"*Selamat siang*," I say. It means g'day in Indonesian.

The immigration officer grunts a reply. By his elbow is a computer that must contain the names of blacklisted foreigners. A click or two of it and he could have me. This very day, I could be sharing dinner and a cell with cockroaches and rapacious stomach bugs. At the booths on either side, the officers click the computers, carefully checking each passport name, but in front of me the man with the bored eyes can't be bothered. Taking my passport, he bangs an entry visa into it.

"*Terima kasih*," I say with a smile, thank you. "Stay calm, keep smiling," I say under my breath while walking towards the baggage claim area.

Papua is officially one of thirty-four provinces of this enormous country, but in reality it is an old-style grab-what-you-can-from-the-natives colony. The Javanese rule by the power of the gun and the threat of long terms in brutal prison. The troops with their assault rifles hold the people in bondage all across the vast archipelago while, unchallenged, politicians and generals funnel immense amounts of money into their bank accounts from Papua's treasure trove of rainforest hardwood, and gold, silver, and copper mined from rich rocky veins in the Papuan mountains.

The flight from Bali to Jayapura, capital of Papua, is a milk run, the jet taking most of the day to fly east in a zigzag. Most of the passengers are sleek, golden-hued Javanese and Balinese, new settlers or colonial officials, and they struggle onto the jet loaded with carry-on luggage.

I have learned over decades of travel in the Third World that if you truly need to fly to a destination, then never fret about the condition of the plane, no matter how dilapidated it looks. Just say a prayer and trust in whatever god you worship. If you do worry, then cancel your ticket and stay home, or take a train, car, or ship, because too often the planes look as though they have not been serviced in months. Today, the seatbelt buckle is broken. If the jet has to brake suddenly on takeoff or landing, I may be flung into the back of the seat in front of me.

The flight attendant shrugs when I show her. "*Tidak apa!*" she says. "Don't worry, we'll fix it tomorrow."

"Tomorrow never comes," I murmur.

The man sitting next to me smiles. "So, you know Indonesia well," he says in the soft, sensuous manner of a true Javanese, that race of mystic poet-warriors who rule Indonesia. He is slim, warm-eyed, in his thirties, clad in khaki slacks, a green polo shirt, and a black *peci*, the peaked cap worn by Muslim men in Indonesia. His chubby wife is swathed in a brown batik robe that covers her from neck to ankle, but does not disguise her rotund shape. This is a mark of beauty in Java, as is her plump face, like a golden apple with dimples, framed by a black cotton scarf that covers her hair and is pulled about her throat.

This is called a *tudung* in Indonesia and a hijab almost everywhere else in the Muslim world. It is the clearest sign of the way hundreds of millions of Muslim men oppress their women. A female must display her modesty and piety as a Muslim, even in the hottest countries such as Indonesia, but the men, by theological definition, do not have to show modesty and do not have to wear similar head coverings.

I have been journeying through Muslim countries in the Middle East and Asia for four decades and have seen the regretful rise of the hijab to become almost obligatory wear. In Southeast Asia, even until twenty years ago, the hijab was not seen often, but now in Muslim-dominated countries such as Malaysia and Indonesia almost every Muslim female, even small girls, wears the hijab. They must swelter under its confining wrap about their heads.

In Jakarta on an earlier journey, I asked the daughter of a Muslim friend why she wore the hijab, even though she was a fan of Western pop culture and studied at university. "I don't want to," she said quietly, out of hearing of her father and mother, "but our religious teachers and our parents make us wear it. I think my parents are afraid of being criticized by the mullahs and even by our neighbors if we don't wear it."

She and most girls you see in the streets signal their rebellion by using makeup on their faces, the lipstick drawing attention to their lips, and wearing tight jeans that defiantly display the curves of their bottoms and tight T-shirts that outline the seductive shapes of their breasts.

All power to them. Nonetheless, Indonesian Muslims are relatively tolerant when compared with their religious cousins in many Middle Eastern countries along with Afghanistan and Pakistan, where I have been many times. There, a girl risks having her father and brothers slit her throat in what is known as an honor killing if she flaunts herself in the street, elopes, or refuses to marry the man chosen for her by her parents. Such behavior is regarded as a stain on the family's reputation, and even though the girl's father and brothers know they will go to jail or hang for the heinous crime, they still carry it out.

"My name is Ahmed," the man in the seat next to me says. His handshake is soft as putty, like that of most Asian men I have met (with the exception of South Koreans). They don't feel the need to forewarn and impress a stranger of their strength with a finger-crushing handshake like that of many Western men. "I'm an army captain, we're returning to Jayapura after a wedding at home," he confides.

So, here is the brave Indonesian military. My time in East Timor reporting the army's barbarity there still shakes my soul. I try to imagine Ahmed taking part in the pack-rape of a teenage prisoner in her cell, or torturing a schoolteacher to death, or shooting an old man for the fun of it—crimes that were common among the occupation forces in East Timor—but cannot.

He seems too refined, too gentle-mannered, but then, from captured pictures I have seen, many of the torturers and rapists and killers look just as gentle as he does. After more than thirty years of international reporting I am still amazed at how ordinary many of the truly evil people in the world look.

The Indonesian army has been just as brutal in Papua, using terror tactics to instill fear in a people who have never accepted their rule. For all I know, Ahmed might never have harmed a mosquito, he might have a job as innocuous as he looks, but I'm wary of talking to him about the army's role in pacifying Papua. I keep our conversation to mainstays of meaningless babble with strangers on the road–family, food, and the curious animals of Australia, the bouncing kangaroo, the cuddly koala, and the mysterious platypus.

The day drones on, echoed in the jet engines as we swoop over the jagged green cordillera, the chain of mountain ranges that bisects the 1,600-mile length of New Guinea. Archeologists believe humans arrived here more than 40,000 years ago, probably from Southeast Asia when the much lower sea levels made travel much easier.

One of the enjoyments of travelling to far-off places is to study the history of the countries on the journey. Before departure I often spend many days at the excellent state library in Sydney reading dozens of books to gain a sense of where I am going, those countries' past and present, their geography, economics, politics, and social systems.

The first Europeans to reach Papua were mariner explorers, the Portuguese and Spanish, in the sixteenth and seventeenth centuries. The Spaniard Yñigo Ortiz de Retez landed on the great island's southern coast in 1545 and in an act of supreme arrogance took possession of it for his king. He came up with the island's name, its dark-skinned inhabitants reminding him of those in Guinea on Africa's west coast.

In 1660 the Dutch also claimed sovereignty over the island "in an effort to keep other countries from encroaching on its profitable Dutch East Indies (now Indonesia)," according to the *Encyclopedia Britannica*. Over the next several centuries Britain, the Netherlands, Australia, and Germany established colonial claims. "Colonial disruptions continued throughout the twentieth century and into the twenty-first."

But the cannibal Korowai, secure in their remote rainforests, were unaware of these outsiders with skin the color of ghosts for another three centuries.

Soon after midday, following lunch of a curried egg sandwich, a bottle of water, and a biscuit, the pilot announces that we are approaching Biak. New Guinea is shaped like a hovering bird, and little Biak is flying loose just behind its head.

As the jet passes over a turquoise coastline fringed with multicolor coral gardens, Ahmed asks why I am travelling to Papua. "We don't see many tourists," he says.

"When I was eighteen, I lived in the highlands across the border and longed to visit Jayapura. It was called Hollandia then. But the Dutch discouraged us from going there."

"The Dutch are long gone, we liberated the people in 1962 and returned them to the motherland," he smiles, a conqueror's gleam in his eyes. "Now, you are welcome. Where are you going to visit?"

Ahmed could be an army accountant engaging in polite chitchat to pass the time on a plane, but he could also be an intelligence officer checking me out. I have to be cautious. The cannibals live in a jungle that is closed to regular travel, and there is no point forewarning him.

"Jayapura, of course, and Wamena in the highlands."

"Ah, Wamena, land of the giant cocks!" he grins.

I glance at his wife in the window seat to see if she is shocked, but she continues reading a glossy women's magazine in Indonesian. She must not understand English. As a Muslim, Ahmed would never talk openly with another man about sex in front of her.

"Cocks? You mean roosters?" I ask, feigning innocence.

He digs me in the ribs with a sly smile. "I mean men's cocks. I've been there several times. The tribal men walk around naked, even in town, except for a long tube they wear over their, what do you call it, pennies."

"You mean penis."

"Yes, their pennies, their cocks. They tie the tube so that it sticks up like your cock when making love. Even though we have friends in the army there, I won't let my wife go to Wamena because she would see the men's pennies."

"Do any Indonesian women live in Wamena?"

"Yes, it's a trouble spot, we have a base, so some army wives live there. Their husbands tell them not to mind when they see the men in the market or on the street, because the tribal people are like animals. It's the same as seeing a pig with no clothes on."

Ah, the racism of neocolonialism rears its ugly head, the Indonesian version of the Bantu word, *bambinga*. Conquering and then exploiting a people is much easier on the conscience when you believe, or are told, that they are not fully humans. Ahmed's comment sets my teeth on edge but then I grew up in the 1960s in Australia when even a woman's breasts were banned from the screen and in print.

A white woman's breasts, that is. *National Geographic* got around the ban by featuring naked tribal women, mostly Africans, though I didn't think them sub-human. Far from it. Many were so beautiful that the sight of their nipples and buttocks in sharp-focus Kodachrome stirred many sinful thoughts.

"They might look harmless, naked, but once you leave Jayapura, be on your guard at all times," Ahmed warns. "Village people are primitive, many still live up in the trees and eat each other. They can't be trusted and they'll attack you if they get the chance. We're here to civilize them, but from what I've seen it will take centuries."

So have spoken conquerors from Caesar, my own white tribe in Australia, down to the Indonesian army whose method of civilizing backward tribes is often a sustained burst from a line of assault rifles, or a long spell in a very nasty prison.

We make five stops and, as the sun slides into the ocean, the jet descends over a wide lake dotted with straw-hut fishing villages and lands at Sentani airport in the shadow of an emerald mountain. The jet drops onto a concrete strip that General Douglas MacArthur laid down in 1944 as a vital stepping-stone in his push to dislodge the Japanese from the occupied islands to the north.

A cocky young man strides up as I wait for my suitcase. "Hi, my name is Sam," he says, extending a hand. My well-developed antennae quiver. At many a Third World airport, a newly arriving foreigner is a prime target for the local Sams, sharp as stilettos, eager to sign you up for a tour, help you ease sensitive luggage through customs, or introduce you to their sister. All for a price and they are keen estimators depending on your nationality.

I usually shrug them off, but now I need all the help I can get. Below his almond eyes, Sam has an American college boy look with white teeth, shiny black hair curling over his collar, muscled biceps, a Chicago Bulls sweat-shirt, faded jeans, and road-stained white Nikes. The uniform of globalised youth. I hire Sam to drive me into town in his Nissan Patrol.

"I take tourists to the villages around Jayapura," he says. "Want to go on a tour?"

"I'm leaving the day after tomorrow."

"Where for?"

Sam could be in the pocket of the army intelligence, paid to report on suspicious-looking tourists, but my instincts sense his question is well meaning. "Wamena, first, and then down south on a trek to the Korowai, the tree people."

Sam whistles through his teeth. "The Korowai! The army won't let you go down there," he says, taking a hand off the steering wheel and waving it dismissively in the direction of the Korowai jungle, more than five hundred miles to the south over the central cordillera. My spirits sink. The Sams of the world are know-it-alls, their financial health depends on it, and they never say a trip is impossible unless it is so true that they can't squeeze a single dollar out of it.

"Why won't the army let me go?"

Sam shrugs. "Haven't you seen the newspaper reports? Rebels captured some university students a few weeks ago and are holding them for ransom not far from where you want to go. At the best of times you need a military permit to go there because the Korowai are very dangerous, they're cannibals, but the government has banned all travel there until the military rescues the students."

"Thanks for the advice, but I've got this far, mate, and I'm not going to give up now."

The pot-holed road to Jayapura winds by green mountains with plunging slopes, and coastal inlets where children splash in the ocean, diving from straw huts perched on long poles over the water. At the halfway point Sam gestures towards a track that veers off the road down to a huddle of wooden huts overlooking the sea. "That's Girls' Town," he says. "Best girls in the country. You want to go there tonight? I can get you a good price."

I'm glad at least that his sister doesn't work there. "No thanks. I'm married and perfectly happy."

Sam sniggers. "Says you. You're probably too tired from jet lag. Maybe tomorrow."

Fixers such as Sam are usually subservient, rarely disagreeing, setting the visitor up for a plea at the end for a hefty tip. Sam seems different and I like him for that.

"Thanks but no."

Sam looks peeved, perhaps because he won't get a kickback from the mamasans at Girls' Town, and remains silent as he drives to a seaside hotel, the steamy seaside town's finest at forty dollars a night. I politely refuse his offer to be my chauffeur while I am in Jayapura, driving me to where I want to go in the province's capital for fifty dollars a day. I intend making a risky visit that night to some young rebels and Sam is the last person in Jayapura that I want to hire to drive me there.

After checking in, I sit by the ocean eating fiery fish curry washed down with a bottle of the local beer that tastes like it has been brewed from spiders' eggs. Then I take a taxi to downtown Jayapura.

A shadowy friend in Sydney—I'll call him Bill—has arranged for me to meet some of Papua's freedom fighters.

Five decades ago, in a cynical Cold War romance, John F. Kennedy wooed the flamboyant Indonesian President, Sukarno, away from the arms of the Soviet Union and into the embrace of the US by promising the then colony of Dutch New Guinea as a love gift. Kennedy pressured the United Nations to transfer control from the Dutch to Indonesia. With a stab of the pen the mighty UN betrayed the one and a half million tribespeople from Biak in the far west to Merauke in the far south who wanted independence or amalgamation with their Melanesian cousins across the border in Papua New Guinea.

The army terrorized the new province into a reluctant acceptance of their new overlords. Jakarta then accelerated plans to tame, exploit, and populate its timber and mineral-rich Wild West frontier. Fortune seekers are pouring into the province from hopelessly overcrowded Java and other islands and over 300,000 transmigrants have already settled in Papua.

The first step was to transform Jayapura into a Javanese metropolis. In the main street, Jalan Ahmad Yani, the conquerors—Javanese soldiers in wraparound sunglasses and tight khaki uniforms that hug their slim, taut bodies—strut along the crumbling pavements. Javanese shops and food stalls line the potholed streets, and Javanese bureaucrats occupy the desks in the government offices.

The food stalls on the main street are thronged with newcomers from all over the archipelago—Javanese, Sumatrans, Buginese, Balinese, Makassarese, and many more ethnic groups—and they squat on the pavement or sit on plastic stools at street stalls as they slurp up bowls of pungent chili noodles. They threaten to overwhelm the locals, dark-skinned Melanesians with coiled hair, who share little in common with the outsiders.

Papua is the Malay word for frizzy hair. The Papuans are Melanesians, an ethnic group who spread across the West Pacific from Fiji to the Arafura Sea, which laps the southern shoreline of the Indonesian province. The word comes from the Greek *melas* meaning black and *nesoi* meaning island.

Many Melanesians have one thing in common above all else. "The cultural orientations of many Melanesian peoples were shaped by a warrior ethic—an ethos of bravery, violence, vengeance and honor—and by religious imperatives that prompted aggression," according to the *Encyclopedia Britannica*. "Evidence from the New Guinea Highlands and other parts of the island suggest that warfare or in some areas clandestine raiding had a high cost in human life."

Even so, for Melanesian men to make war is glorious. In *Melanesian Religions,* Professor Garry Trompf wrote of the ever-present warfare prompted by the abduction of women and the stealing of pigs and land. "The muscular vigor, the armed skill, the brilliant flashes of energy as the spear-shafts are hurled quivering in the air against the enemy, the exhilaration of victory itself, as well as the precarious exploit to retrieve one's dying clansman from the field in the moment of defeat, are all close to this primal anthem of life."

The contrast between the pacifist Congo Pygmies and the many

New Guinea warrior clans could not be starker, and I expect that includes the Korowai cannibals. Another significant contrast is payback, or violent circular retaliation, unknown to the Pygmies, but I know from living in Papua New Guinea for two years that along with pitched battles it is the core cultural imperative of most New Guinea tribes.

You kill one of ours, prompting us to kill one of yours in vengeance, and then you must kill one of ours in return. The lust for reprisal is akin to the Sicilian practice of vendetta and can last for generations. Not even children are safe from a payback killing in New Guinea. As I would discover, payback in an eerie, unique form is the most powerful prompter of Korowai cannibalism.

When the Indonesian President Sukarno sent his troops to occupy Papua, although brave in defense of their homeland, the Papuans were no match for the Indonesians. They targeted Papua's multi-billion-dollar natural resources, most destructively its lucrative stands of rainforest timber, among the world's largest. Of its one hundred three million acres of virgin forest, sixty-nine million acres have been licensed for logging. Vast forests have already been hacked down and bulldozers have begun carving with great difficulty a cross-country highway through virgin jungle.

Even remote tribes like the Korowai, cut off from the rest of the world for thousands of years, are under threat from the relentless destruction of their land. "Their isolation has long protected them, but within a decade or two, if the Indonesians start logging the Korowai forests, their traditional way of life will be destroyed forever," Gerrit Van Enk, an expert on the Korowai, had told me by phone from his home near Amsterdam.

The Papuans in the highlands and on the coast are fighting back, mostly with bows and arrows against the army's assault rifles, in a brave but so far hopeless struggle to regain their land. Leading the fight since the 1960s has been the OPM, the Organisesi Papua Merdeka (Free Papua Movement), a loose federation of freedom fighters that numbers more than a thousand guerrillas, many of them Stone Age tribesmen. But the Korowai jungles are so remote that the fighting is still very far away.

The OPM has bases in highland hideaways, in the jungles on the border with Papua New Guinea, and secret cells formed among the students at Jayapura's university. I have been given a contact with the resistance by Bill, who has been to Jayapura several times on what he denied with a wry smile were missions of espionage for a certain foreign government in the Pacific whose first three letters are Aus.

Crossing Jalan Ahmad Yani, I enter a coffee shop and sip a cappuccino while reading a two-day-old copy of the English-language *Jakarta Post*. International direct dialing and emails are the bane of modern-day spy catchers; it is very hard to monitor a thousand or more phone lines, emails are even more difficult, and Bill had emailed ahead to Jayapura, arranging for me to meet some of his friends in the resistance. I am not here to explore Papua's politics, but to journey to the cannibal Korowai in their rainforest. Nevertheless, I want to know more about the resistance to Indonesian rule, so that I can better understand the province's present and its past.

It is just after 6 p.m. and my eyes wander around the half-empty shop, trying to pick up any contact. A wiry girl in jeans and Bon Jovi T-shirt catches my glance as she sits at another table drinking a Coke. She is a tall, slim, coastal girl with Afro-style frizzy hair, coffee skin, and a lean, angular, intelligent face. I wink, hoping to God she is not a hooker. Just behind the coffee shop is the notorious Tropicana bar, and Bill had warned me that the girls sometimes use the coffee shop as a pick-up spot when business is slow in the bar.

The girl saunters over to my table. "Paul?" she asks. I nod. "I'm Kori. Let's go."

Taking my hand, she leads me into the street as if she has just scored a customer for the night. As we stroll down Jalan Ahmad Yani, heading for the waterfront, Kori's eyes move from side to side. Now and then we stop and chat by a street corner while Kori discreetly looks around to see if we are being followed. It's a cat and mouse game I've also played in Beijing, Hanoi, Baghdad, and Pyongyang, but I never get used to it, wary that a posse of secret policemen will suddenly collar us.

Although she is just twenty-two, Kori must have played the game hundreds of times because she looks ice cool. "We have to make sure that Intel agents are not following us," she explains. Intel is the military's murderous secret police. In my banned *Digest* article I slammed their reign of terror in East Timor where they raped, tortured, and killed thousands of victims.

"I know Intel from East Timor, so I understand."

"Yes, I read your article. Bill emailed it to us. I know you're going to the Korowai this time, but I hope that you'll return and write about our struggle."

The waterfront curves like a horseshoe around a bay. A blue Toyota is parked outside a Catholic church near the sea. Kori opens the rear door. "Once we've travelled a little way it's best that you crouch down in the back."

I hunch over so no one can see me, but can't see where we are going. The car climbs a hill, but then most of Jayapura's suburbs slope up from the shoreline. The journey takes about twenty minutes, and it is dark when we reach a bungalow on a dirt road without streetlights. The other houses are like giant lumps of coal in the gloom. Kori looks about to see if anyone is watching. "Let's go inside," she says.

The front door of the safe house opens onto a narrow hallway that leads to a lounge room dominated by an independence flag with a blue eagle bearing on its outstretched wings the slogan, "One People, One Soul," on the wall.

Like many political slogans, it is a half-truth. Papua is fractured like a smashed full-length mirror into more than two hundred tribes ranging from sophisticated city dwellers to naked Stone Age warriors with a wealth of customs and traditions. Many of the tribes fear, hate, and constantly fight each other, though usually with bows and arrows and stone axes.

The concept of nationhood is alien, and even unknown, to many of Papua's people. Even its name is alien and has no meaning.

Yet, there is some truth in the slogan, because the only way the Papuans can expel the Indonesians is if they unite as one people. My sense is that, tragically, Indonesia will rule as Papua's colonial master, the exploiter of its vast natural resources' wealth, for many decades to come.

Two men in their early twenties sit beside a girl about the same age on a frayed gray sofa. When I enter they rise and solemnly shake my hand. The only weapons I see are the knives and forks laid out on the dining table.

"*Selamat malam*," they say in unison. "Good evening." Although most educated Papuans are devoutly anti-Indonesian, they speak Bahasa Indonesia, the conquerors' language, to each other. "Our country is like the Tower of Babel, we have hundreds of different languages, and it's easier this way," Kori explains.

They all attend Jayapura's University of Cenderawasih, Indonesian for "bird of paradise." Johannes, one of the two young men, studies agriculture and wants to help villagers grow more effective crops. At university vacation time he joins the OPM guerrillas in the jungle. He pulls up his white cotton shirt. The flesh to the left of his belly button has been torn apart, leaving a patch of mottled purple scar tissue that shimmers in the lamplight.

"I was in the jungle with our troops last summer when we ambushed a patrol," he says. "We killed three soldiers, but I was hit by a bullet. My companions plugged the hole with cloth. Luckily, we were near Papua New Guinea and they carried me on a stretcher across the border to a medical clinic."

Hannah, the young woman, gazes at me with unflinching eyes. "I'm a student teacher at the university, and an OPM member," she says. "I was taken to Intel headquarters last year for questioning about a demonstration I organized on the campus against Indonesian rule. We raised the OPM flag. Two Intel men held me down on the floor while their Javanese boss raped me. He told me to tell the other girls in the movement that he'll get them too. They tried to break my spirit, but they only made me stronger, more determined to resist."

Dirk, the other young man, is also studying to be a teacher. His eyes are heavy with sadness. "The troops came to our highland village in two choppers just before dawn. They herded us into the open and burned down our huts. Then they shot most of the men, including my father. We still don't know why we angered them. That day I joined the OPM."

My eyes glisten in admiration for the iron spirit that carries these young people through suffering that would shatter most people. "I heard many similar stories in East Timor," I tell them, "and the Intel agents here must use the same manual of terror."

Kori's dark eyes catch fire and her lips tighten with the fervor of a freedom fighter. "We'll never give up the struggle against the Indonesians until we win freedom just like the East Timorese. The outside world can help us win justice, or it can ignore us, but we'll never give up the fight."

Usually my discussions with rebels are wide-ranging and without restriction. But on this night I hold back from commenting on their wish because they have been hurt enough already. The cases of East Timor and Papua are entirely different, according to the consensus in the byzantine corridors of the United Nations in New York.

East Timor was a Portuguese colony and so, according to the UN, the Indonesians had no right to take it over when the Portuguese departed in 1975, but to this day the other half of the island, known as West Timor, which was formerly a colony of the Dutch in their East Indies colonies, has been an integral part of Indonesia. The UN consequently stays clear of any demand from West Timorese for freedom and right to independence.

Papua was also part of the Dutch East Indies, ruled from their capital at Batavia, now Jakarta, and when the Dutch departed, the newly independent nation of Indonesia claimed all the former territory of the Dutch. In UN-speak, that meant Indonesia had the legal right to incorporate into its territory Papua, the western half of the island of New Guinea, and no other nation should object.

Realpolitik, whatever its aims, is usually a very ugly business and can cause significant suffering for the millions of people caught in its ruthless maw.

We talk about war and the rebels' resistance for another hour and then Kori, a law student, drives me back to the seaside Catholic Church, from where it is an easy walk to my hotel. As we say good-bye with a hug, I wonder what will become of her. Perhaps one day she will die in a jail cell, her youthful body broken by torture; or perhaps one day she will stand before the United Nations in New York and hail the independence of her country. That last possibility is a dream and not a realistic assessment, unfortunately.

"Tell the Korowai that we're fighting for them too," she says. "If the Indonesians remain, their traditional life will disappear in a few years, but we'll save them by banning logging in their jungles when we come to power."

Kori grips my hand. "Take care, Paul, because the Korowai are still cannibals. Even the soldiers don't go there."

It has been a long day and, troubled by the OPM tales, I sit by the sea at my hotel and down several bottles of spider-egg beer. I fall asleep the moment my head touches the pillow. Just before dawn, I race through a jungle pursued by wild-eyed cannibals with blood foaming from their mouths. Again and again I escape, only to find them waiting around the bend in ambush, shooting at me with their arrows until I look like a pincushion.

The alarm clock ringing ends the nightmare.

At mid-morning John Wolff arrives at the hotel. Tall, lean, and silver-haired, Wolff was posted to Papua more than two decades ago as an army officer. I got his name and phone number from Bill, who nimbly moves across both sides of the political fence.

"John owns the best hotel in Wamena, but he once held high rank in the army of occupation," Bill told me. "He still has excellent contacts in the army, and if anyone can get you into the Korowai jungle it will be John."

Wolff sits on the sofa next to me. "What you need is a travel pass called a *surat jalan*, or 'document to walk,'" he says, his voice and manner silky smooth. But, unlike Ahmed, his fellow soldier, Wolff's friendly manner is betrayed by his battle-hardened eyes and he looks as though he would not hesitate to try to win the hearts and minds of backwoods tribesmen with a well-aimed burst of bullets or incendiary mortar bombs lobbed into their straw huts.

"The army has banned travel to Korowai territory, but for a price I can get the pass for you."

I hand over my passport, a couple of head-and-shoulder pictures, and an envelope containing $3,000 US dollars in one-hundred-dollar bills. Wolff counts the greenbacks. Expenses for the visit to the Korowai cost $1,500, with the remaining $1,500 going, he tells me with a sly wink, "to a good home." His army friends' retirement fund and his own, no doubt. I feel a stab of guilt, but there is no other way to reach the Korowai. Later that day, Wolff arrives back at the hotel with the precious piece of paper, my military permit to enter the land of the Korowai. It is in Indonesian, has my photo at the top, and the stamp shows it has been issued by Intel.

"What is Intel?" I feign innocence.

"The army's secret police, military intelligence," Wolff replies. "To tell you the truth, most of them wouldn't know if a guerrilla's head was up their butt."

The Jayapura branch of Intel must not have sighted my Bishop Belo article or known about it being banned in Indonesia. Despite Wolff's scorn, it is possible that the agent who approved the *surat jalan* might hear about it and make the connection. Then I will be in serious trouble. I have to get into Korowai territory, spend plenty of time with the cannibals, and then get out of Indonesia before that happens, or I might yet be signed in as a guest in an Indonesian prison. Or worse.

That is the kind of risk you have to take in my world. I have been called an adrenaline junky many times but that is a foolish remark prompted by a fallback on an overused cliché. I get an adrenaline rush when on a steeply inclined roller coaster or rushing to the tennis net to volley a shot. But I cannot recall a single time when I got an adrenaline rush when faced with danger. At such a time you must remain cool-headed, calm, and with an intense concentration on averting the risk you face. The last thing you need at that time is a rush of excited blood to your head.

That night for the umpteenth time I take dinner alone, far from my home, in a remote city at the edge of a journey into a remote and dangerous rainforest, this time in search of cannibals. Do cannibals really exist in the twenty-first century? After a meal of delicious ocean prawns and musty beer, I lay on my back in the sparse hotel room, with an overhead fan lazily slapping the torpid air, and trawl through the controversial question of so-called institutionalized cannibalism, whether it exists or whether it is an historical hoax.

The doubters' guru, anthropologist William Arens, stirred the pot in 1979 with his book *The Man-Eating Myth: Anthropology and Anthropophagy*. He challenged: "I am dubious about the actual existence of this act as an accepted practice for any time or place." He contended that such cannibalism was "unobserved and undocumented."

About the same time that Arens was casting doubt about the existence of tribal cannibalism, Dutch pastors from the Mission of the Reformed Churches in the Netherlands were risking their lives by journeying to the Korowai. For two decades they suffered much hardship, living in rough conditions, as they studied the Korowai language and documented their culture, which had as a core ingredient ritual cannibalism, the killing and eating of village men branded as *khakhua* or witch-men.

The Dutch pastors were no culture destroyers. One of the missionaries, Gerrit Van Enk, and linguist Lourens De Vries wrote the only book on the tribe, *The Korowai of Irian Jaya*, published in 1997 by the authoritative Oxford University Press. Van Enk told me, "We went to the Korowai to convert them to Christianity, but when we got there realized we'd destroy their unique culture if we did that. So, we gave up our plans to convert them and remained for many years as observers, documenting their culture, which was radically different to ours, and so ancient, while attempting to influence them as little as possible."

Unwilling or unable to tramp into the dangerous Korowai jungles to see for themselves, the doubters disputed this testimony with no evidence except their own prejudice. Arens wrote in 1998: "I continue to aver that the Caribs, Aztecs, Pacific Islanders, and various African, native American, and New Guinea tribes have been exoticized but also—and equally important—that Western culture has congratulated itself for putting a stop to the cultural excess through colonial pacification and introducing Christianity to once-benighted natives."

Arens's eagle eye roamed wide in geography and history in search of fake cannibals and he singled out New Guinea, an island infamous for centuries among Westerners for its cannibal tribes. (In 1998 the Duke of Edinburgh congratulated an Australian student for successfully traversing the swampy and mountainous Kokoda Trail in Papua New Guinea. "You managed not to get eaten then," he joked.)

Besides Van Enk and De Vries, Arens could have found numerous first-hand witness accounts of cannibal feasts there. My first-ever job was as a trainee colonial official in Papua New Guinea in 1961. I flew from my home in Sydney to the capital Port Moresby on my eighteenth birthday and among my colleagues there were *kiaps* or patrol officers.

These brave men risked their lives to take the rule of law and the liberating concept of modern Western-style justice to remote tribes who had been living under a simple and brutal code of kill-or-be-killed for millennia.

The patrol officers filed meticulous reports of their contacts with people still living in the Stone Age, and among these is considerable evidence of payback murder and ritual cannibalism among the tribes. In 1920, Ernest Chinnery, a patrol officer turned anthropologist, wrote of cannibal raids in the Gulf Province of Papua, not too far across the border from Korowai territory. He lectured about his finds to the Royal Geographical Society in London, and in 1920 won its Cuthbert Peek award for his anthropological work among the Papuans.

"The people had been classified as Papuan, and all those except those under control, practice headhunting and cannibalism," he noted in his report to the colonial authorities almost a century ago. "Before a house can be occupied or canoe launched it is the custom to sprinkle the building or boat with human blood . . . the heads of people are slain and collected . . . bodies are cut up, cooked in various ways and eaten."

In one village Chinnery visited he reported: "The people were living in one large house, which was entered by my party at dawn while the Moreri were eating the bodies of Irumuku natives they had killed."

Like Chinnery, other patrol officers mostly wrote their reports in a matter of fact style, even their accounts of cannibalism. In contrast to the slander of doubting anthropologists, they usually resisted the temptation to make judgments on the locals' sense of morality or the notion that the *kiap* with his Western culture was in any way superior to these people.

Just two years before I made my first trip to Papua New Guinea, seventeen warriors from the Mianmin tribe on the Sepik River, about three hundred miles northeast of Korowai territory, formed a raiding party and attacked a communal hut inhabited by the Sowana tribe. They killed six men and abducted their wives. John Mater, a patrol officer, investigated the attack at the remote location and wrote in his official report that the raiding party cut up the bodies with bamboo knives.

"The Mianmin left the heads and entrails and carried the rest of the bodies away to be eaten." The raiding party carved out the livers as snacks and after several days, when they returned home, "the remains of the bodies were cooked with taro and eaten."

At their trial a year later, at which the men admitted guilt, the judge noted: "Apparently they have to rely on raids of this kind to obtain wives for their young men, and that the killing, cutting up, and eating of the women's husbands appears to be accepted by the women as something inevitable and final."

The Amazon also experienced tribal cannibalism. Beth Conklin, an American anthropologist at Vanderbilt University, studied an Amazon tribe whose members were until recently cannibals. She wrote: "We assume that cannibalism is always an aggressive, barbaric and degrading act. But this is a serious oversimplification, one that has kept us from realizing that cannibalism can have positive meanings and motives that are not far from our own experience."

The cannibal doubters would probably wrinkle their noses and snort disbelief. But, as with the Dutch missionaries and the Korowai, Conklin did the hard yards in the Amazon, journeying to the Wari jungles and shrugging off the tribulations to live with them for nineteen months, between 1985 and 1987. The Wari were cannibals until missionaries and government pacification teams in the 1960s stopped them from eating human flesh.

Older tribespeople confirmed to her their cannibalism, and missionaries and government officials described to her how they had witnessed cannibalism among the Wari in the 1950s and 1960s. Conklin returned to the Wari three more times, the latest visit in 2000 to reconfirm her findings.

The Wari described to Conklin how their cannibalism came in two forms. "Eating enemies was an intentional expression of anger and disdain for the enemies," she said. "But at funerals when they consumed members of their own group who died naturally, it was done out of affection and respect for the dead person and as a way to help survivors cope with their grief.

"This 'mortuary cannibalism' helped mourners emotionally detach from memories of the dead," Conklin wrote. That helped them "deal with the loss of a loved one. For the dying, being incorporated into fellow tribesmembers' bodies was far more appealing than being left alone to rot in the dirty, wet, cold and polluted ground."

She said that the Wari "may have understood ways that made the destruction of the body through cannibalism seem to be the best, most respectful, most loving way to deal with the death of someone you care about."

The work of Jens Bjerre, a distinguished senior fellow of the Royal Geographical Society of London, took place closer to my own early wanderings. His book *The Last Cannibals,* published in 1956, tells of encountering cannibalism among the fierce Kukukuku who live in the rugged southern foothills of Papua New Guinea. I was based not far away in 1962 and at that time they were regarded as the most warlike of any tribe in the Australian colony, the eastern half of the great island. Short, stocky, and bellicose, the bare-chested men wore bark skirts tied at the waist and carried their bows and arrows with them wherever they went, even to their outside hole-in-the-ground toilets.

I only ever saw the Pygmy-sized Kukukuku once when a band of warriors was brought to Mount Hagen, the Western Highlands' provincial capital where I lived, for the annual "sing-sing" of the tribes. The field set aside for the sing-sing was thronged with several thousand Stone Age highland warriors, tall, strong men who made the hills shake with their warlike chanting during spear dances. Their vividly painted faces gave them the appearance of multicolor demons. To these warriors, making constant war on each other was a core element in their reason for living.

But there was a sudden hush when the highlanders saw the Kukukuku warriors, and they warily shuffled back en masse to allow the outsiders, clad in straw matting clasped about their waists and carrying bows and arrows, to pass through the throng without challenge. They well knew the Kukukuku's fearful reputation, gained by centuries of merciless bloody raiding and cannibalism, and I saw fear in the highlanders' eyes as the little men strode defiantly past them.

Bjerre bravely trekked among the Kukukuku hills with an Australian government patrol while I was still in primary school. He observed that when a party of Kukukuku warriors capture an enemy prisoner, either in combat or by kidnapping, they tie the captive to a solid tree trunk and carry him back to the village. "So that the prisoner shall not escape, they then break his legs with the blow of the club, bind him to a tree, and adorn him with shells and feathers in preparation for the forthcoming orgy."

Fresh vegetables are brought in from the fields and a big hole is dug in the ground for an oven. As a rule, the children are allowed to "play" with the prisoner; that is to say, to use him as a target, and finally stone him to death. This process is designed to harden the children and teach them to kill with rapture.

When the prisoner has been killed, his arms and legs are cut off with a bamboo knife. The meat is then cut into small pieces, wrapped in bark, and cooked together with the vegetables in the oven in the ground. Men, women, and children take part in the ensuing orgy, usually to the accompaniment of dances and jubilant songs. "Only enemies are eaten. If the victim is a young, strong warrior, the muscular parts of his body are given to the village boys so that they can absorb the dead man's power and valor."

Bjerre wrote that an Australian patrol officer named Jack told him, "six months ago, two men had been eaten in a village, Jagentsaga, not far away; and that a month ago he had, by chance, found the hand of a man who had been eaten shortly beforehand. The rest of him had been hidden in the jungle." The patrol officer said, "They know that we will punish them for cannibalism, so they do everything to conceal it now. But it still occurs and probably will do so for a long time."

Arens and his supporters seem to have shrugged off the wealth of such easily available evidence of tribal cannibalism. Enough of this musing, I think to myself, or I might suffer nightmares. I need to be up early for our departure. Within days in a remote jungle far to the south I will come face to face with men whom John Wolff says truly are tribal cannibals faithfully practising an age-old ritual.

The next morning Sam arrives at the hotel to drive me to the airport. "You missed a great time at Girls' Town last night," he says with a sympathetic look as I load my bag into the boot. "I took a German there and he had two girls in the same bed." He laughs at the memory. "The hut shook so much it nearly fell down."

"Thanks, mate, but I'd rather reserve my energy for finding the Korowai."

"Well, if you get lucky and do return from the cannibals, the girls will be waiting for you. If they know you've been with the Korowai, they'll probably give it to you for free."

"There's your plane," Sam says as we arrive at Sentani airport. He points to an unmarked Boeing 737 parked by the waiting room, sharing the tarmac with a Merpati Airlines jet. As part of the deal, Wolff had arranged a flight to Wamena from where I will take a single-engine Cessna to an isolated landing strip in the jungle to the south. But he had not given me a ticket. "The airline you're going on doesn't have tickets," he said.

"Where do I check in?" I ask Sam.

"You don't check in on this airline."

"But what about my luggage?"

"You carry it on board."

"Does the airline have a name?"

"Not really, but we call it Pirate Airlines."

"What does that mean?"

"You'll see."

Sam shows me to a seat in the crowded waiting room. An hour passes, then two as I watch passengers clutching boarding passes called on board over the PA stream onto their planes. The air conditioners in the waiting room have gone on the blink, and sweat pours from me, but I read a local newspaper and drink several bottles of orange juice, accepting the delay without boiling over.

A survival trick when travelling in remote places is not to get fussed over delays, especially if beyond your control. Otherwise, you only hurt yourself. Many Third World countries have expressions that condone their less than fervent devotion to the passing of time on a clock. It's usually called Fiji Time, or Samoa Time, or Malay Time, something like that. In Indonesia, they call it Rubber Time.

The hours stretch on. Finally, near midday, Sam walks towards me, smiling. "Time for you to board," he says.

"Do you work for Pirate Airlines?"

"Nah, but the pilot is a friend and I help him when I can."

I look around for fellow passengers. The waiting room is almost empty, so I trudge across the tarmac alone and struggle with the suitcase up the steps to the jet. The interior is piled high with cargo, draped with tarpaulin and tied down, the rope looped under floor rails on either side of the aircraft. A single three-row set of economy-class seats is bolted to the floor just behind the cockpit.

The pilot, stocky and round-faced, emerges from the cockpit. He is clad in a faded brown bomber jacket, jeans, scuffed cowboy boots, and a New York Yankees cap. A black pirate-style patch hides his left eye, or where it should be.

"Welcome aboard, I'm Tommy," he says in an American accent, holding out a hand to grip mine. "You're the only passenger, so you can sit with us up front if you like."

I ease into the jump seat at Tommy's shoulder. This time the seatbelt buckle does work. His co-pilot is bent over the controls, going through the pre-flight check. "That's Faisal, he doesn't say much, but he's a damn good flier," says Tommy. "You have to be to survive over here. The weather is clear today, but it can get real hairy when there's plenty of clouds and you have to fly among the mountains as you ascend and descend."

Tommy takes the controls as we taxi to the runway. He guns the engine and halfway along the runway we soar into the air, the steep takeoff thrusting me back into the seat. "I used to fly fighter jets in the Air Force, and did a few courses in the US of A," Tommy explains with a grin. "Never got to learn how to take off a plane politely so you don't frighten the customers, like the guys in the big airlines."

The jet soars over a lake by the airport, and climbs above desolate swampy marsh. Minutes later we swoop along a valley folded between two craggy mountains. It is the passageway through the mountains into the highlands, and Wamena. Beyond the coast, New Guinea is a land of massive, sheer-sloped mountains rammed together for hundreds of miles on end, so that flying is risky, especially as most days are cloudy. The mountains were formed when trillions of tons of sedimentary limestone, sandstone, and shale were thrust up through ruptures in the earth when the continental plates slammed into each other about five million years ago.

I can see the high cordillera, like the jagged spikes stretched along the back of a giant crocodile. Because the sky is empty of clouds today there is no risk that the plane will crash into a mountain, a common flying accident on both sides of the border in New Guinea. Without warning, what look like army barracks appear below, more than a hundred wooden huts dotted along the valley. They are so precisely aligned, with the same distance between each hut, that it looks as though a sergeant major is drilling them.

"What's an army camp doing in the middle of nowhere?"

"Army camp," Tommy snorts. "More likely, it needs the army to keep the poor bastards there, to stop them from fleeing home. You've heard of the *transmigrasi*?"

I had. It is a desperate effort by the Jakarta government to disperse the dramatic overflow of people to less populated territory in Indonesia, a vast country straddling the equator. With 260 million people spread across 733,584 square miles, it is the world's fourth most populated country. But of its 17,508 islands, only 2,342 are inhabited.

About half of Indonesia's people live on the relatively small and desperately overcrowded island of Java. To tempt millions of the poorest Javanese to go away, as far as possible forever, the government offers each immigrant family a free air ticket to a distant province, five acres of virgin land, and a year's supply of rice.

"A few weeks ago, I picked up some of those families below in Jakarta and flew them over here," says Tommy. "We loaded their rice and belongings down the middle of the plane and they sat along the sides in bucket seats. Most were terrified of flying, it was their first time, and they threw up all the way to Sentani. The smell was terrible, and so was the noise. The children screamed and the women sobbed. Once we were in the air I think it finally dawned on them that they were going to a place far away. Most are so poor that they'll never see Java and their relatives again. I felt so sorry for them. At the airport, soldiers guarded the trucks they were loaded onto to make sure none ran away to Jayapura."

The brave soldiers again. The only time the Indonesian military has been in a fight against regular soldiers was during the *Konfrontasi* (Confrontation) war over the formation of Malaysia between 1963-6, and they were trounced by British, Gurkha, and Australian troops. But they are world champions at fighting unarmed civilians.

"If the immigrants only get one season of rice seed, what happens if their crops fail?"

"They do it tough. In some islands *transmigrasi* people starved. But that won't happen here, the land is very fertile. Their biggest worry is the locals. The natives hate the newcomers and, given half a chance, they'll shoot them full of arrows. Maybe even eat them."

Tommy peers out the window, taking a final look at the barracks village as the jet leaves the valley and weaves between high-peaked mountains that flow to the horizon. "Poor bastards!"

Poor bastards indeed. While the politicians and generals loot the country of its riches, the millions of poor who live at the fringes of national largesse are forced to abandon their ancestral villages and fields and seek a new life in lands conquered by their military. And what awaits them here? Tribes whose cultures have been honed over thousands of years by unrelenting warfare, and the custom of "payback" or uncompromising revenge. Kill or be killed.

The tribes in Indonesia's remote provinces have fought back many times when the pressure of living side by side with the newcomers became too great. In 2000, frustrated at the thousands of immigrants streaming into their lands, the headhunter Dyak of Indonesian Borneo exploded in a killing frenzy, their target the *transmigrasi*.

The warriors hacked to death hundreds of women, children, and men in the streets, in their beds, in their shops and offices. Dyak warriors lined up their severed heads on the roads as warnings for their kin to flee the horror and return to their own lands. To escape the carnage, more than 10,000 immigrants fled Borneo on an emergency armada, leaving behind most of their possessions. They will never return.

"Some day the same thing will happen here, because the *transmigrasi* have been dumped in the middle of some of the most warlike people on earth, the highland clans especially," says Tommy. "You've heard of the Dani?" I nod. "Well, Wamena is the stronghold of the Dani."

He turns back to the controls and fixes his one eye ahead as the plane begins its entry into the valley of the Dani. Around us rise mountains, up to 12,000 feet high. Their sheer slopes and razor peaks are like the walls and turrets of a giant's castle that blocked this land from outsiders for thousands of years. Through the mountain mist I see glimpses of a green fertile land, the Grand Valley of Baliem, home of the Dani. They are a Neolithic people whose culture demands perpetual warfare, but who are just as skilled as farmers, among the ancient world's most successful.

Journeying into Dani territory while on the way to the Korowai allows one of those enjoyable surprises you encounter when you travel to the most remote places. I had long wanted to visit the Dani, but never until now had the chance. In the early 1970s, a favorite book of mine was *Gardens of War*, a stirring account of a pioneer expedition by Harvard University anthropologists into the Grand Valley of Baliem in 1961.

As a teenager, I had spent the same year living among Stone Age warriors in the highlands of Papua New Guinea, across the border, and the people there shared a similar culture to the Dani. I kindled my taste for adventure when I lived among the highland tribes. Shining with pig's fat, sporting headdresses of golden birds of paradise plumes, flaunting crescent breastplates carved from mother-of-pearl, and with their faces and bodies swathed in crimson and yellow ochre, the highland warriors were the grandees of Papua New Guinea. As they strode the mountain passes and villages, they carried themselves as proudly as any Spanish count.

Any slight on their manhood, or any dispute involving women or pigs, quickly brought out the dueling weapons: bows and arrows, spears, or stone clubs. Then, hundreds of warriors would face off against each other. Australian patrol officers walked for weeks at a time among the remote valleys, demanding an end to warfare and punishing it with fines and jail sentences, but the clan battles flourished because ritual fighting defined the meaning of life for the highland men.

What largely wiped out that ancient culture was the invasion of Western culture starting in the mid-1970s. In the town of Mount Hagen, where I lived, the clans still adorn themselves with feathers and ochre for the "sing-sings," which are important tribal gatherings. But most of the time the men slouch around in grubby jeans and pullovers, wolf-whistling girls in tatty cotton dresses, eating fried chicken, and watching violent and pornographic movies.

To pay for such delights they must work in shops or on coffee plantations, and that leaves little time and energy for plotting war and revenge killing. But, in Wamena, it seems the Indonesians and Western culture have failed to tame the naked Dani. Famed anthropologist Margaret Mead called the Dani way of living "the long, relentless cycle of killing and being killed."

For the highlanders I lived among, much of the fighting was bluster and display, a way to work off frustrations while demonstrating solidarity with friends and kin. It was as much warfare as the chanting, jeering, and flurries of scuffles that used to break out among rival fans in the soccer crowds on chilly English Saturday afternoons.

Although I witnessed highlanders shouting bloodthirsty threats at their enemies across the battlefield, ax and arrow wounds were common, death was rare and usually prompted the war chiefs to call a halt to fighting for the day. But it also meant that the clan whose son had perished vowed to extract payback for the mortal insult, and the warriors would plot revenge until they had killed a warrior from the enemy clan.

Ritual warfare is also at the heart of the culture of their cousins, the Dani. Peter Matthiessen was on that pioneer expedition to the Dani and in his book *Under the Mountain Wall* wrote of one battle he witnessed: "Several men from each side would dance out and feign attacks, whirling and prancing to display their splendour. They were jeered and admired by both sides and were not shot at, for display and panoply were part of war, which was less war than ceremonial sport, a wild, fierce, festival."

But blood is spilled when the Dani rouse themselves for battle. "They are tough, unmerciful fighters," Tommy says. "Most weeks somewhere in the valley a Dani is murdered because of payback."

Forty minutes after leaving Sentani airport, the jet descends into the Grand Valley, a forty-mile stretch of fertile land that nestles like the floor of a giant amphitheater surrounded by 12,000-foot-high walls of towering limestone. A coffee-hued river, the Baliem, winds in tight loops along the valley floor. Dotted across the valley, clusters of straw huts with conical tops, like Chinese coolie hats, sit strategically on rises in the land and by the foothills to blunt surprise attacks. Smoke spirals into the air from cooking fires within the huts, mingling with clouds that drift by at treetop level.

Surrounding each village are quilt-works of land hemmed in by reed fences. Most are fields of sweet potato, the staple food of New Guinea highlanders. These warrior farmers cultivate their vegetable gardens as neatly and obsessively as any rose gardener in Sussex.

Coming in low over the villages, Tommy aims the jet at the airstrip and lands at a far steeper angle than the Qantas jet three days earlier at Bali. At the last moment, he levels the plane over the tarmac and then drops it onto the concrete with a thump that rattles my teeth.

"Sorry about that, but it's the safest way to land," he says with a grin as he steers the jet towards the terminal, a wooden bungalow at the edge of a small town that seems to float among the low-lying clouds. "The reason the airline boys put you down light as a feather is that passengers think a soft landing is the safest landing. It's not. It's much safer to drop the plane onto the tarmac once you level out a few feet over it."

Wamena is 5,349 feet above sea level. The mountain air chill hits me like a blast of cold air from a refrigerator as I leave the plane and struggle down the stairs with suitcase and camera bag.

"Mister Paul! Over here!"

CHAPTER 7

The caller is a slim Javanese in his twenties standing by the terminal fence. He strides onto the tarmac to help with my luggage. "My name is Agung Djarmono," he says with a wry, gentle smile. "Welcome to Wamena. John Wolff asked me to take you to the Korowai."

Agung gestures to a man standing by his side. "This is our cook, Dawut."

Our cook? Dawut is stark naked, except for a Rasta-like net covering his coiled hair and a cream-colored gourd fitted over his penis, leaving only his dark testicles visible. So, this is one of Ahmed's giant cocks. Proudly erect, the gourd rises from Dawut's groin to his nipple. His testicles settle like a roasted walnut shell at the base of the gourd.

Dawut is about six feet tall and bristles with muscle. With his distinctly Semitic features—broad hooked nose, high cheekbones, sharp eyes, and square ebony beard—he resembles many of the warriors I knew in the highlands on the other side of the border. He sees me glancing at his rampant gourd and smiles.

"We must hurry because we're leaving tomorrow, and we've got to buy food at the market for the trip," says Agung.

"Shouldn't Dawut put on some clothes if we're going to the market?" I ask.

"Why? That *is* the Dani's clothes. You'd better get used to it. The Korowai wear even less."

A Toyota LandCruiser owned by John Wolff waits for us at Wamena airport. Agung drives with Dawut next to him, and me in the back seat. "You looked surprised to see Dawut's penis gourd," Agung says over his shoulder as he turns the car into a dirt road that runs by the airport.

"I've never seen anything like it. It's spectacular."

"It's called a *koteka* and it's a Dani man's proudest possession."

"I'd be very proud if I had something as impressive as that."

Dawut smiles at the joke when Agung translates this for him. He turns back to me. "I'll give you a *koteka* if you wear it today," he says, grinning. "Our women would laugh for a long time if they saw an *orang putih*, a white man, wearing one."

I have been willing to mumble an off-key version of "Candle in the Wind" or "Waltzing Matilda" to humor a remote tribe if it made them happy and the journey easier. But parading through Wamena in a *koteka* is far beyond the call of duty, even though the Dani would probably tell tales about it around the village fires for generations.

"No thanks," I laugh. "I'd get sunburned in some sensitive places."

As we drive along a dirt road lined with provision shops in the center of the small town, I see what Ahmed, the soldier on the plane, meant. Most of the pedestrians strolling by the roadside are Dani men, bare-bum naked, and flaunting their giant "cocks." The penile gourds, standing stiffly to attention, jiggle as they walk, making the Dani seem to be in a perpetual state of sexual excitement.

The few Dani women I see on the way to the market are more modest, bare-breasted but clad in grass skirts called *youngal*, slung low on their hips. In other tribal societies where the men wear little or no clothing, I have noticed that usually the women keep their buttocks and genitals covered at all times, even when they bathe. I only know of the Australian Aborigines, and some remote African clans and Amazon tribes where women traditionally went about as fully naked as the men.

There is no single answer as to why humans took to wearing clothing however skimpy or bulky. It seems obvious why humans living in cold climes did. Somewhere along the human timeline they discovered that the fur of large animals such as bears provided body-covering protection against the cold. The answer is not so clear among humans living in the rainforests.

David Reed, a mammologist at the University of Florida, used the evolution of a species of lice unique to humans to hypothesize that the first humans to wear clothes began 173,000 years ago. His reasoning was clever rather than authoritative. Using lice gene sequencing, he calculated this time span by determining when a new species of lice on humans began evolving that was specific to the body and not the hair on our heads.

It does not explain why many societies, despite living for thousands of years in almost identical conditions such as the rainforests, went about clothed, partly clothed, or entirely naked. The Congo Pygmies traditionally wear grass skirts while others such as the Korowai and certain Amazon Indians, especially the males, have never worn clothes.

The reason why the Dani never developed clothing, apart from the females' brief straw skirts, is clear. The largest furry creature in their territory is a possum and they use its skimpy golden fur to decorate their spears.

One reason why many societies developed clothing, perhaps thousands of years ago, could be because of male sexual jealousy, the size of a man's penis. That could explain the evolution of the Dani penis gourd, where all the men are roughly the same size down there. Perhaps, long ago, a warrior chieftain was less endowed than the other men and, mortified, invented the penis gourd to make all men seem equal. After all, the solution was daily in front of his eyes in his vegetable garden patch.

Shaka, the great warrior king who led the Zulu nation into dominating all the other tribes in South Africa's Eastern Cape in the nineteenth century, had an undersized penis when he was a young boy. His diminutive genitals were clearly visible for all the tribe to see. The other young boys, who also went about naked, mocked him and for years he seethed in humiliation.

His tribe's adult males wore the traditional *inJobo*, a knee-length kilt made from animal skins. By the time Shaka entered manhood his penis had grown to an impressive size and he enjoyed flaunting it in public. Soon after he was made king he had his royal executioners club to death the boys who had mocked him.

Sexuality also plays a role in why the Dani women must cover their genitals. "Why do Dani women wear skirts when you men wear nothing but your *koteka*?" I ask Dawut.

"We Dani are proud of our manhood, we want everyone to see it, but a woman must keep what is hers only for her husband to see," he says in a voice that rumbles from his broad hairy chest. "If a man looked at my wife naked, I'd attack him."

"But the women don't see what you've got because it's covered by the *koteka*." I'm struggling for polite words and hope Agung selects the Dani equivalent.

Dawut touches his *koteka* fondly. "They do, soon enough."

"Isn't a Dani girl disappointed when you first sleep with her? Isn't she expecting something the size of a snake?"

Dawut laughs when Agung translates. Modern man, Stone Age man, we can still connect through sexual humor that must have made men laugh through the millennia. "From what I've seen of Indonesian men, ours are snakes when you compare them to the worms they have between their legs."

He says this in Bahasa Indonesia, but Agung must voice it in English and he blushes as the words tumble out. This assures me that he will provide faithful translations, much like William with the Bayaka, when we journey to the Korowai, rather than tell me what he thinks I want to know. In most Asian countries face is all-important and a translator will sometimes alter blunt and critical comments to avoid causing offense.

Another bonus is that Agung speaks excellent English. Capturing the nuances of our talk about the Dani's unique sexual advertising requires a skilled translator, also needed when I ask the Korowai about their fondness for eating human flesh.

The two, though firm friends, are evidently quite different. Dawut, raised in a warrior tribe, is like a Spartan, bold, steely-eyed, and swathed in muscle. Agung is quiet-spoken, somewhat shy in this early stage of our relationship, and is probably happier wielding a pen and writing poetry than wielding a spear or a bow and arrows in a battle.

Though the hub of a province with more than 100,000 highlanders, Wamena itself is a settlement of only 10,000 people. The neocolonialists' bungalows surround the town, where a few dirt roads link offices, shops, a bank, and the Pasar Nayak market where we go to buy supplies. The market covers a city block and you can smell it from a hundred paces. Indonesian butchers sell goat meat and fish in covered stalls, but most traders stand or squat by their wares displayed in the open on long concrete tables topped by tin roofs, or on the ground between the tables.

Dani men wearing *koteka* and woven fiber hair covers, and Dani women clad in grass skirts, offer piles of sweet potatoes, yams, and the gruesome smoked corpses of tree kangaroos. Others sell bows and arrows, spears, axes, *koteka*, and belts of cowrie shells, traditional money still used to purchase brides.

The Dani believe the cowries are powerful magic, a superstition stemming from the time when they knew nothing about the distant sea, and it took years for the shells to be traded from tribe to tribe up from the coast. The cowrie shells are also embedded in clay in the chieftains' breastplates. The price range of the six types is astonishing.

American John Cutts, whose parents were Christian missionaries, grew up among the highlanders. He wrote that the cost varies from fifty cents for the more common type to twenty-five hundred dollars for the most expensive shell called *indo*.

"Shells of the top three grades are all given names and a detailed history of every transaction," he wrote. These give the shells their value. Most Dani are lucky to earn a hundred dollars each year. Only the most powerful chieftains with the most garden land can own *indo* shells.

Dawut and Agung are after more prosaic goods at the back of the market, where more than a dozen smoky stalls run by Indonesians sell everyday supplies: rice, tinned fish, clove cigarettes. They buy two sacks of rice and bargain for a carton of sardines. Whatever other pleasures adventurers get from journeying to remote places, they rarely do it for the food.

I point to a Dani man with a farmer's dirt-ingrained fingers squatting before a pile of sweet potatoes. "What about vegetables?"

"Too bulky to carry, so we'll get them as we travel, trading some of our rice with the tribal people," Agung says.

Moving among the stalls are Indonesian women, distinctive in ankle-length batik dresses and scarves. As they hand over bundles of grubby rupiah notes in exchange for vegetables wrapped in large green leaves, they cast their eyes modestly away from the male Dani traders' exposed flesh.

To protect their womenfolk from such a shocking sight, in the 1970s the Indonesian government tried to force the Dani to cast aside their *koteka* and dress in pants and shirt. "It was called Operasi *Koteka*," says Agung as we wait for Dawut to finish shopping. "But the Dani threatened to go to war with us to keep their traditional clothing and, after trying for a year or two with little success, the government gave up."

Stark evidence of that failure can be seen all over Wamena. Outside the market, pairs of Dani men hold hands as they stroll along the crumbling pavements, careful I imagine not to get their *koteka* entangled. A bizarre thought pops into my mind. If two Dani men get into a fist fight, down below do their *koteka* duel like fencing epees?

I know from my time among the highland clans across the border that hand-holding does not necessarily mean that the pair are lovers. It is the way men show friendship. But there is a hard core of male homosexuality in highland culture and this is often a feature of warrior societies. I came across it among the Dani's cousins in Mount Hagen, with manhood initiation ceremonies involving group masturbation and semen sharing among the young men and their uncle-sponsors at sacred sites beyond the village.

Also in the highland way, men and boys leaving the Wamena market walk at the front empty-handed while the family's women and girls follow at their heels, bent over almost double bearing heavy loads of sweet potatoes and other vegetables in *noken*. These are large scallop-shaped bags woven from bark fiber, carried on the back and tied to a band strung around the forehead. This distinct separation of male and female roles is seen most clearly in warrior tribes, where a family on the march needs the men unencumbered so they can immediately fight back against an enemy ambush.

So far I have seen no contact between the Dani and their neocolonial overlords. Indonesian public servants or low-level soldiers, and their wives and children, hurry by the market on foot or on pushbikes, eyes averted from the Dani, while the upper ranks zoom past in LandCruisers, hidden from sight by black-tinted windows.

"Agung, I've only been here a short time, but it seems obvious that the Dani and your people don't mix at all."

He shrugs as eloquently as a Sicilian, all shoulders, hands, and dark molten eyes. "How can they? Most Javanese here think the Dani are little better than apes. I thought so too when I first arrived three years ago. I was disgusted by the *koteka*, shocked by their unclothed bodies, and I thought only the most primitive people behaved like that. I'd read a book in English called *The Naked Ape* and thought it a good name for the Dani. But I now have Dani friends like Dawut, and when I got to know them they seemed much the same as us."

That kind of discrimination spreads across the globe, similar to the way many of the first settlers in Australia, and many afterwards, regarded the Aborigines. Now there is this Indonesian knee-jerk racism. But Agung is different and I immediately warm to him. He is a young man, from an upper middle-class Javanese family I suspect, thrown into the most alien culture imaginable to him and having the intelligence and sensitivity to try to make sense of it. He will be a good companion on the journey.

After loading the rice into the LandCruiser, we drive out of the town, over a bridge spanning the swiftly flowing Baliem River, and head towards Dawut's village for him to bid farewell to his family. It will also give me a chance to see the Dani in their tribal fiefdoms. "Dawut's village is about twenty kilometers from here," Agung says.

Minibuses scoot by on the paved road, going to and from Wamena, stacked with naked Dani who pay about fifty cents for the ride. Just a few decades from a full Stone Age existence, the clans in the Grand Valley are now captives of the cash economy and seek money by selling their vegetables and fruit so that they can ride to town in the buses, instead of walking. There, they meet friends from other clans, go to the movies, or purchase luxuries such as rice and sardines.

Surely it is the only cinema in the world where you can walk in naked and not prompt the ticket seller to summon the police. Ironically, all movies shown in Indonesia are heavily censored with no nudity allowed, not even female nipples.

The road keeps to the valley floor, passing villages nestled among the foothills. Above them soar the sheer slopes of the mountain walls, marbled by drifting clouds. The fertility of the land is amazing, the patchwork fields and forests fed by a rainfall of two hundred inches a year, and nourished by the hard work of the green-thumbed Dani.

Agung turns off the road and parks the LandCruiser by a reed fence, the boundary of Dawut's clan territory. A woman in a grass skirt and carrying a sharpened gardening stick hails him. "It's my father's cousin," Dawut says.

We stride along a path towards a village perched on a rise in the land. The path meanders between a mosaic of fields, clumps of banana trees, and rows of sweet potatoes, enclosed by a network of reed fences. The Dani are proud of their skill in growing the starchy food staple. "We have many kinds," says Dawut.

The village seems peaceful but close by is a reminder that for thousands of years, until recently, war chants and battle cries echoed daily across this valley. Looming over the fields is a watchtower made from tall poles lashed together with vine. Crowning the tower is a platform with just enough room for a lookout. "A warrior kept watch there from morning until night every day to raise the alarm if the enemy approached on a raid," Dawut explains.

I had seen these watchtowers in the book *Gardens of War*. Vital to the clans' security, they were dug in at distances of about four hundred yards throughout the valley. Between the fields of each village was a no-man's land where rival clans stole through the tall grass to launch surprise attacks. The sentries in the towers were also alert for enemies sneaking up to abduct and rape women working in the fields.

"We have no use for the towers because we rarely have big fights any more. The Indonesians have banned them."

"But do you still have payback?"

Dawut clenches his fists as if eager to fight the clan across no-man's land.

"Yes. My clan is involved in a payback with another that goes back generations. They kill one of us, we kill one of them as payback, and then they kill one of us to get revenge. Payback will never end."

A log stockade guards the entrance to the village. Crossing the knee-high step is like stepping back ten thousand years. Wispy clouds float by, a few yards above several mushroom-shaped straw huts clustered around one big hut in the middle of a cleared space. Dawut's mother, Sagat, is waiting by one of the smaller huts. She is smeared in white clay and clad in a grass skirt with an empty *noken* bag slung over her back. She has several joints missing on each finger.

"My mother is proud to tell how she lost her fingers," Dawut assures me. Her sacrifice played a vital role in the religious life of her clan because the Dani's world is full of vengeful ghosts who must be appeased with bloody rituals for the clan to remain prosperous and powerful.

"Whenever a relative died fighting, a girl had to give part of her finger to his spirit," Sagat says, holding up her hands to show me the many truncated fingers. She points to the middle finger on her left hand. All that remains is the stubby lower joint. "My uncle was shot with arrows in an ambush and died. He was burned that afternoon."

On the morning after the death, the holy man came to Sagat in her hut. He tied her finger tight, then hit her on the elbow, which made her arm go cold to numb the pain. "He used an ax to chop off most of my finger," she says. "Then he put it into the embers of the fire that had burned the dead man to make peaceful his spirit."

Dawut's mother wiggles her mutilated fingers. "Like the other girls in my clan, the holy man came for me more than once."

By the time they reached middle age, the hands of many women were little more than stumps. Agung notices me looking sympathetically at Sagat. "Only the older women are like this. Younger women refuse to do it. And our government bans it."

It seems a bizarre way to appease the spirits, the sacrifice of one of the most useful parts of the body. Women are the workhorses of Dani society. They do most of the heavy carrying and, while the men dig the irrigation ditches and turn over the new fields with hoes and adzes, it is the women who go there every day to toil from early morning to evening, planting, weeding, digging up the sweet potatoes, and planting new crops. They also need their hands to cook food and tend growing children, so why cripple themselves by chopping off several of their fingers?

Dawut shrugs. "It was the Dani way to make the ghosts happy, but I feel sorry for my mother. I'm glad the custom changed. My wife and daughter have and will always have all their fingers."

The biggest hut, twice as large as the others, is forbidden to women. It is where the Dani men sleep, eat, and plot war. Once a boy reaches puberty he is taken from his mother to live with the men. Although men and women marry, they rarely stay together. Sex is a hurried affair in the bushes or thickets beyond the fields, almost always with the woman bent over in front of the man.

"Do Dani men fear sexual intercourse and the supernatural power that women possess?" I ask Dawut. "Is that why you keep away from them as much as possible?"

He gazes at me with an uneasy expression. "How do you know this?"

I explain about my year in the New Guinea highlands. "The customs seem very similar. Even women chopping off part of a finger as a sacrifice when men are killed in battle."

But not all customs. Never over the border had I encountered what I come across next. Dawut's brother, Jonet, with a broader face and coiled, soot-stained hair soaked in pig's fat, leads us into the men's hut, which is dark and smoky. Bows, arrows, war axes, and spears are stacked against the walls. Dry grass is spread across the floor.

Most men are out inspecting their fields or their beloved pigs, often closer to their hearts than their wives, and the hut is almost empty. A flame flickers in a fireplace scooped out of the floor, but there is no chimney and the smoke is trapped inside. My eyes begin to sting and water, and it is hard to see through the shadowy gusts of smoke.

By the wall squats the oldest man I have ever seen, a living mummy, his skin shrunk to the bone, the flesh on his face barely clinging to the bones, his long bony arms clasped about his ankles.

Dawut beckons me to the old man. Close up, I see that he *is* a mummy, his skin smoked the color of ebony. A band of feathers perches on his skullcap.

"He is my ancestor and he is over four hundred years old. He was one of the greatest ever of our *kain*, a war chief, and led our clan to victory in many famous battles."

WHERE TIME STOOD STILL

THE CONGO
PYGMIES

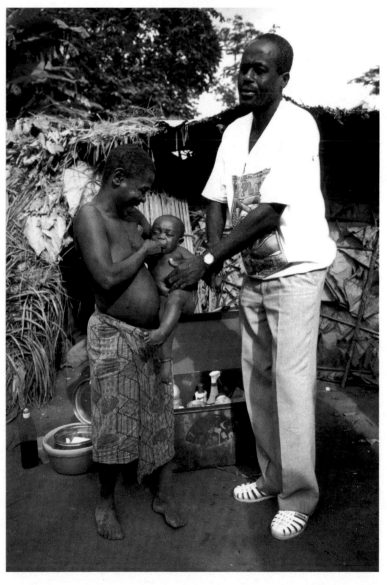

A woman and baby from the Bayaka Pygmy clan at Mossapola
in the Dzanga Sangha Reserve in the far southeast of the
Central African Republic. The Bantu doctor is about 5'8",
just a little taller than the author.

The main character, Wasse, hunting monkeys with his crossbow. He uses poison arrows that kill the monkeys in a few minutes.

Wasse with his hunting net. He is his clan's greatest hunter. The Pygmies only take from the rainforest what they need.

Wasse's wife, Jandu, with her very sick baby. I took them into the nearest town to see the Bantu doctor and he gave the baby medicine that saved its life. Wasse and Jandu in thanks named him Paul, after me.

The Pygmy women at puberty have their teeth shaped like shark fins, using a machete. They believe it makes them look more beautiful.

The Pygmies are the world's most enthusiastic party goers. They sing and dance for many hours each day. Here they are dancing to welcome their most important rainforest spirit, Ejengi.

Ejengi came in from the rainforest soon after to greet me.

The Central African Republic government has allowed overseas loggers
to go into the Pygmies' rainforests and start stripping them of giant trees.
Here, a Pygmy woman stands beside a giant log that is being hauled over a
bridge on its long journey to the port in neighboring Cameroon.

Most Pygmies in the CAR have been enslaved by the taller Bantu, but not
those at Mossapola. Here, Pygmy boys by the roadside wear tattered clothing
given to them by the Bantu. They retain the quiet dignity you find among
all of the Pygmies.

NEW GUINEA
Korowai

Closeup of the warrior Kili Kili with the skull of Bunop, the witch-man.
Kili Kili smashed open his skull to get at the brains, his favorite part.

The Korowai warriors had never seen a white man before and they barred our way, very suspicious of our intentions. To them I was a *laleo*, a ghost demon. My guide placated them.

The Korowai have no chiefs, but each clan has what they call 'the fierce man,' who leads them into battle. Here, the fierce man gives me a ceremonial welcome. He told me that he expected to see a ghost when he heard I was coming, and was very relieved that I was like him, a *yanop*, a human being.

The Korowai clans are always fighting and, for protection, live in tree houses built on the trunks of trees stripped of branches and leaves. When an enemy clan attacks, the women, children, and old men flee up into the tree house. It also helps them escape the mosquitoes, which are lower down. Here, the men are returning from a successful hunting trip.

Me with the warrior Kil Kili and his brother, Bailom. Both took part in killing and eating Bunop, the witch-man.

Agoos, the main character, with his bow and arrow.

Two friends, one with a stone ax and the other with a bow and arrows.

Korowai women. Unlike the men, who go naked, the women wear short skirts made from palm fronds. They have just brought me a breakfast of insects and a frog, which they caught in the forest.

(Above) The boys learn to be warriors from an early age. This little boy is using a toy bow and arrow, which helps him develop the skills he will need when he grows up.

On the way to the Korowai, I visited the Stone Age Dani, a warlike tribe in the highlands. Here, two warriors pose with the mummified body of their greatest war chief. They keep him in the men's house, where all males live together from puberty. The Dani men wear spectacular penis sheaths.

THE AMAZON
KORUBU

As we arrive at the maloca, the communal hut of the Korubo, they watch us carefully.

Ta'van, the Korubo war chief, leads two other warriors on a war patrol, checking their territory. Not long before, these three smashed to pulp the heads of three white men they found in their rainforest. They are the only Amazon Indians to use fighting poles. The day I arrived I did the haka, the Maori war dance, to soften their aggression towards me.

On the second day they wore their finery to thank me for performing the haka.

The war chief, Ta'Van, and me on the second day. With a smiling face, he is almost unrecognizable from the previous day. He is wearing his ceremonial finery to thank me for the haka.

Sydney Possuelo, head the Brazilian government's Department of Remote Indians and one of the world's greatest explorers. He made first contact with the Korubo and set a record of first contact with seven previously uncontacted Stone Age tribes. Here he is showing the warriors his gun.
They are so dangerous that he dared not stay overnight with them and would not let any anthropologists visit them for fear of them being attacked.

(Above) Jumi, our Indian guard, speaks with members of the tribe, asking them to allow us to stay.

The clan chieftain is a woman, Maya, seen here with her daughter and other Korubo. Life here is reasonably pleasant; they work about five hours a day in the gardens or going hunting, then spend the rest of the day chatting.

A group of Korubu women outside the maloca. They shield their babies with palm fronds.

Jumi, our guard. He is from the Matis tribe, which has a dialect similar to that of the Korubo. He wears the shells of giant river snails in his ears.

I tell Dawut that I had known a legendary war chief in Mount Hagen, Ninji, by then frail and elderly, but still feared by the clans for his courage and skill at planning battles. Ninji had that rarest of gifts, true charisma, not the media-manufactured Hollywood type, and I spent many weekends at the men's hut in his village on a hilltop strategically overlooking the valley, enthralled as he retold his most famous battles.

We became so friendly that he smiled on an affair with his seventeen-year-old unmarried granddaughter, Nengka, a high-spirited and sometimes haughty girl who wore a switch of tan possum fur between her breasts. When she went to a sing-sing with pig's fat shining over her entire body, with a mother-of-pearl shell nestled against her bare breasts, with circles painted on her face in red and yellow ochre, and with a golden plume of birds of paradise feathers as a crown, fluttering in the highland breeze, she was truly a mountain princess.

I was not her first lover but she was mine and so she was my teacher. I could not take her back to my bungalow because the three dozen white people who lived in Hagen frowned on any affair with a local girl, and if it became known, the District Commissioner, nicknamed "God," because of his unchallenged authoritarian power, would have sent me back to Port Moresby in disgrace on the next plane.

Ninji's people lived in communal huts and so we did what they did and strolled out into the bush, knowing that though we would have been noticed, it was bad manners to follow a pair of lovers to spy on them. Our favorite spot was in the thick bush that ran along a bank of a stream.

Unlike the other women, even those the same age, Nengka bristled at the warriors' domination over the clan's females. She told me she wanted to test her oratory powers, and she certainly had some of Ninji's charisma, but women were forbidden to speak at clan gatherings.

Nengka had learned English at a Catholic missionary primary school in the valley on the outskirts of Hagen, run by Father Ross, a kindly, diminutive American priest with a long white beard. He was not much taller than Wasse, my Pygmy friend. Father Ross selflessly devoted most of his priestly life to the Hagen people, far from the raucous stands of Yankee Stadium where he went as a teenager to cheer on his home team. Giving up that pleasure was true sacrifice.

He must have been one of the few priests outside remote jungles in Africa to look out on his congregation at Sunday Mass and see the pews packed with almost naked women. Nengka, like the other women, wore just a band of bark around her waist that held in place a length of woven fiber covering the dip between her thighs.

After mass one morning I asked Father Ross how he reacted to all that naked female flesh. I have never forgotten his reply. He smiled at my teenager impertinence. "Eve was also unclothed. I don't look upon their nakedness the same way as you. To you it may be the delight of a young man's eyes but to me it is sacred, how God made them in the image of Eve."

Nengka was not popular among the young men and Ninji suggested we marry, hoping to shield her from a possible attack by males angry at her rebellious nature. But I was too young to marry, at age eighteen, and was itching to go out and see the big world. Nengka told me she would never be happy in the white man's world, cocooned in a dress, underwear, and shoes, far from the mountains and her clan's customs. When I returned to Hagen on an assignment three decades later, I was told she had married a man from a highland clan far away over the mountains and was never seen again.

"She did the right thing by not marrying you," Dawut says when I tell him. "She would have been like a pig tethered day and night to a tree. The white man has many useful things, but, like the Indonesians, you breathe air that Agung tells me stinks, and wear clothes that scratch and itch. We Dani want the mountain air, every day, in our lungs, on our body."

"Come outside!" a man cries out.

A dozen men, newly arrived, squat in the open space. By the fence Sagat and several women, also clad in grass skirts, *noken* bags, and a covering of white clay, huddle around a fire to ward off the chilly mountain air, their long skinny arms clasped about their backs.

"It's my family here for a farewell feast," Dawut explains. He points to a plump young woman with a sad face. "That's my wife, she's unhappy that I'm going with you."

"And your daughter?"

"She's with my wife's mother."

Suddenly, somewhere out in the fields, a creature begins screaming, a terrifyingly human sound, as if a child is having its throat cut. I look at Dawut in alarm, but he doesn't react. Moments later a warrior bounds into the compound clutching a struggling, bellowing piglet.

Dawut's father, Jaja, fetches a bow and an arrow from the men's hut and lines up the victim as his two sons spread-eagle it in the air. Shot from close range, the arrow pierces the piglet's heart. It dies quickly. Jaja is the village chief, his badge of office a breastplate embedded with hundreds of tiny cowrie shells and with pigs' tusks flaring from each side of his nose. He also flaunts his status as a "Big Man" with three wives.

His skin is wrinkled, his hair is specked with gray, the muscles on his arms and haunches are withered, but his *koteka* still stands sprightly. The chief dismembers the piglet with a stone ax as Dawut makes the fire, furiously rubbing two sticks together, the friction producing sparks that fall into a bundle of dried grass and set it alight.

Jaja hands the body parts to the women, who steam the piglet, with dozens of sweet potatoes, in a primitive oven, a hole dug in the ground and covered with burning hot river rocks and banana tree branches thick with leaves.

"This is how the Korowai cook the flesh of the men they kill after they chop apart the bodies," Agung says. "Steaming makes the flesh soft and juicy."

Because I am a guest of the clan, Jaja gives me a chunk of piglet, and it is indeed sweet and moist. As we eat, he tells of a raid he went on at the time of the Dutch.

"We ate sweet potato in the morning and rubbed pig's fat into our bodies, put on our headdresses and pushed pigs' tusks through our noses," he says. At mid-morning, carrying spears and bows and arrows, Jaja and his clansmen went to the battleground beyond the watchtower near the fields. When the enemy arrived, they ran straight at each other and fought until noon. Men on both sides were wounded. Then they fell back, rested, and attacked again. This happened many times during the day. "I hit an enemy's leg with an arrow," says Jaja. "As the sun went down, we yelled curses across the battlefield, and then went home."

Jaja's eyes gleam with passion as he talks about the battle. "I enjoyed war. It is what men do. But now that the Indonesians have banned fighting, we men are frustrated. What else is our reason for living?"

"To make babies," Dawut grins.

The old man smiles indulgently at his son. "Yes, that too, although it's not as much fun as fighting. But don't go with your wife into the bushes too often or the ghosts will punish you."

Agung anticipates my next question. "The Dani don't eat any enemy they defeat. They are not cannibals like the Korowai. The enemy carry away from the battlefield their wounded and dead."

When we finish the food, the women begin wailing and slap their oily hair, thighs, and breasts. Tears stream down the men's faces. Dawut's father grips him by both arms and pleads with him. "He begs his son not to go to the Korowai," says Agung. "His family has heard of them from Dawut; they know they're cannibals and his father fears he'll be killed and eaten."

It is a poignant and worrying moment. For many years I have known of the Dani as born warriors, immersed in a culture of constant warfare, afraid of no one. And yet the thought of a human killing and eating another shakes to the core the courage of these brave men.

"I am a Dani, and when the Korowai see me they will tremble in fear," Dawut reassures his mother, father, and wife. Then he beckons us to leave. On the drive back to Wamena, he stares sad-eyed at the Dani fields. I tap him on the shoulder. "I'm sorry your parents were upset about our trip. Are you afraid to come with us?"

"No, I'm looking forward to it. Dani now don't get many chances to prove our courage and when I return I'll tell how I braved the Korowai. I'm sad because I was thinking about how much I'll miss going to the bushes with my wife. I don't think the Korowai girls will be as pretty."

At dinner in the hotel I order a beer to wash down my stringy steak. Agung shakes his head. "All alcohol is banned in the highlands because the government fears that the tribesmen, when drunk, will go berserk and attack Wamena. The hotel is the only place allowed to sell it and only at meals."

To sustain our friendship, I don't remind him that a far more potent stimulus to the Dani's anger is their hatred for their neo colonial masters. Dani warriors once attacked Wamena and slaughtered more than forty Indonesians before the army put down the revolt with telling brutality, leaving the bodies of dead Dani scattered about the town.

Later that night Agung, Dawut, and I go to the movies, the cinema a tin shed near the market. By the ticket booth, a garishly colored poster shows that "Rambo III" is playing. Hollywood released it many years before but Agung tells me it continues to be a favorite with the Dani. Sylvester Stallone is a hero to Dani men who are connoisseurs of his male posturing as much as his fighting skills. Inside, perched awkwardly on seats, more than two hundred naked Dani men cheer and slap their thighs, their *koteka* jiggling in full erection, as Stallone vanquishes one villain after another.

The next morning at seven, Agung arrives at the hotel to fetch me. I found the Dani culture interesting because it was so close to that of the highlanders I lived amongst across the border, but I have come here to visit another unique rainforest tribe and I am eager to meet the Korowai. My nerves are jumpy. It's not every day you journey back to history's misty reaches to be with a tribe of cannibals in a remote jungle. On the road you often look for a laugh to quiet the nerves and today Dawut is my savior, prompting a wide smile the moment I see him. I hardly recognize the Dani warrior in well-worn camouflage combat pants, a faded Ice Cube T-shirt, and wraparound sunglasses. He looks like an LA rapper. From Stone Age to Dance Party Age overnight.

"Where's your *koteka*?" I ask, still smiling.

He pats his groin with a grin. "Tucked down here to surprise the Korowai girls."

Dawut's homeboy gear is not convincing—it seems more like fancy dress than street gang uniform. Then I notice that he is barefoot. A homeboy would never leave the house without his high-tech sneakers.

"Where did Dawut get the clothes?"

Agung looks at our cook and grins. "He bought them yesterday at a second-hand clothing shop with some of the money I paid him for the trip. The sunglasses are an old pair of mine."

"I'd swear he was from Los Angeles, except for the bare feet."

"He'd rather jump off a cliff than wear shoes. He tried on a pair of mine once and told me they felt like rocks tied to his feet."

Waiting for us at the airstrip is Bill Wilson, a lanky American pilot working for the American-run Mission Aviation Fellowship. The MAF is the aerial workhorse of New Guinea on both sides of the border. The Christian missionary pilots ferry in hundreds of mostly American missionaries and supplies to their remote posts, while earning operating funds for the missions from journeyers like myself willing to buy a seat or charter a plane.

Bill pilots a six-seater single-engine Cessna that looks like a toy plane beside the jet revving its engines for the flight to Jayapura. I sit by him up front, with Agung and Dawut behind us and several hempen sacks, our supplies, stacked in the back. Leaving my suitcase at the hotel, I'm carrying a camera bag, sleeping bag, and an overnighter with a single change of clothing. As the Cessna buzzes into the sky and heads south over the valley, Bill asks, "Where are you going to end up?" the words stretching southern-style like chewing gum.

"The Korowai."

He whistles in surprise. "Be careful, because it can be dangerous as hell down there."

I point to Dawut. "I'll be okay, I've got my own Dani bodyguard."

"From what I've heard, one Korowai could take on several Dani."

The sky is clear of clouds and the morning mist has gone. Flying down the Grand Valley is like flying down the middle of a giant sports stadium with the sheer walls of the high mountains on either side angled in at the green fields. The highlands is the most densely populated part of rural New Guinea and clusters of Dani huts are dotted all over the valley and in the foothills that nudge the mountain slopes. Slicing through this primitive metropolis is the Baliem River, picking up speed as it rushes southwards to surge through a gap in the mountain chain, the Baliem Gorge.

It is one of the most spectacular views I have ever seen. The giant mountains magically part, allowing the river to tumble down to the jungle for more than 1,500 yards in rainbow-misted cataracts. At sea level we make for the Siretsj River, a wide tidal waterway that meanders in tight loops through the dense jungle to the distant Arafura Sea.

The Cessna drones on. Bill flies low to dodge thick cloud cover, skimming about six hundred yards above a never-ending tangle of rainforest, cut by the Siretsj and other coffee-colored rivers that snake through the jungle. He points to our location on a navigation map spread across my lap. Surrounding the spidery lines that mark the low-land rivers are thousands of square miles blanked out and shaded green. Unexplored territory. Forbidding, untamed. The Dutch missionary Gerd Van Enk called it, "The hell in the south."

This hell on earth was like a magnet to Christian missionaries, mostly from Holland and then from the United States, intent on bat-tling Satan in such a devilish place and determined to convert such demonic peoples, headhunters and cannibals. The missionaries spread out along the relatively accessible New Guinea coastlines beginning in the mid-1800s, eventually constrained by a curious pact enforced by the Dutch colonial officials called the Boundary Line of 1912. It mirrored the geographic separation of religion in their homeland, with Protestants keeping religiously to the north and Catholics confining their missions to the south.

In 1938, a year after European explorers first entered the Baliem Valley, the first missionaries, American evangelists, reached the high-lands following a hazardous eighteen-day trek through the jungles and across the mountains. Once again the sects divvied up the heathens.

"The missionaries agreed that the Catholics would spread the word of God among the highland tribes around Lake Tigi, while the Protestants confined themselves to the highland clans settled along Lake Paniai," Bill explains. "One of the first things they did was build airstrips so pilots could fly in the missionaries' families and supplies."

The coastal tribes welcomed conversion and the trade goods offered as sweeteners, while the proud highland clans largely resisted the mis-sionaries' pleas to abandon their ancient beliefs and commit totally to Jesus. "It's tough, but you never give up," says Bill.

About one hundred fifty miles in from the southern coastline, Bill lands the Cessna at a tiny dirt strip hacked out of the jungle at the edge of the muddy Ndeiram Kabur River. "Good luck, you'll need it," he says, shaking my hand. "I'll remember you in my prayers."

Agung has been here once before on a journey to the Korowai, intrigued by the chance to meet cannibals and hopeful that some day someone like me would give him a reason to return. As he hires porters to carry our supplies to the river, I feel a twinge of abandonment watching the Cessna take off and disappear in the clouds.

Hemmed in by the jungle nudging the airstrip are the sub-district police station and a few bungalows housing a doctor and several Indonesian bureaucrats and their families.

A radio mast rises by the police station, a single-story wooden building. A police private shows Agung, Dawut, and me to chairs on the porch. The sun has yet to gather its sting and a cool breeze flutters across the porch. "The lieutenant is eating breakfast," the private says.

An hour later we are summoned into the lieutenant's presence. He sits ramrod straight behind his desk, his khaki uniform crisply ironed. Like most Javanese men, he is slim and cat-like, and it might have been his posting that has given him that smug look you gain from believing yourself to be far superior to the people you live among. The lieutenant's good looks are marred by a scowl that seems etched into his features. Could it be from the sense that his fate is drifting away from the brilliant future he must have imagined for himself? This posting is about as far as you can be sent from Jakarta, and probably means he is still way down the totem pole and has little hope of reaching the heights.

He looks at my *surat jalan*, the Intel permit, and then at me, with loathing. "What are you doing here?" he asks in English.

"You can see by my *surat jalan* that I'm going to visit the Korowai."

"And what do you hope to gain from that?"

I pause, unsure what to say, not expecting the question. I can't tell him my real purpose because I have entered the country on a tourist visa. "For the fun of it," I blurt out.

"For the fun of it," he sneers. "And once you've had your fun, and got into serious trouble with the cannibals, I suppose you'll expect me to come and rescue you."

I could have humored him with a sycophantic reply, but I have a low tolerance of tin-pot petty dictators, whatever their rank, and it has led me into trouble too many times. "No, because if I get into trouble, you'll probably never know about it. I imagine they'll eat me."

The lieutenant glares at me and then hands back the *surat jalan*, dismissing me from his presence with a wave of his hand. As we walk towards the river, a frowning Agung lectures me on the protocol when dealing with an irascible police chief.

"That was foolish of you. He could easily have stopped us going to the Korowai. All he had to say was that he was checking with police headquarters in Jayapura and then tell us every day that he had no answer. We'd have tired of it before he did."

"I'll remember that when we reach the next police post."

"There will be no next time. That's the last police we'll see until we leave the Korowai."

At the river a dugout canoe, a long hollowed-out log powered by a 40 HP outboard, sits low in the water, tied to a stake driven into the muddy bank. Agung negotiates with the owner to take us downriver to a settlement at the edge of the Korowai jungle. As I sit cross-legged with a sack of rice at my back for support, the dugout scoots along a winding watery path slicing through the overhanging forest.

"From here on, the *orang pohon*, the tree people, make the laws," says Agung. "They punish wrongdoers by eating them."

A jet-black hornbill with a giant ivory beak keeps pace with us, flapping along the riverbank, a high green curtain of hardwood trees woven with tangled streamers of vine. The sun swiftly gathers strength. Stunned by its intensity, and with my head ringing from the siren scream of countless cicadas all along the river, I hardly notice the hours drift by as the dugout heads south along the Ndeiram Kabur.

The sun slips out of sight below the jungle, and nighttime descends suddenly as it always does in the tropics. About midevening, the boatman steers the dugout towards the riverbank. As he nudges against it, we scramble out and climb the muddy slope in the dark.

"Mbasman!" Agung says, pointing to a clearing where darkened wooden huts nestle in a tidy line against the towering rim of the shadowy rainforest. Agung knocks on the door of the biggest hut. A stocky man in his forties opens it and is surprised to find an *orang putih*, a white man, on his doorstep. After Agung shows him my *surat jalan*, he welcomes us inside.

"I'm Barnabas, Mbasman's village chief," he explains. "It will be safer for you to spend the night in my hut."

Barnabas sends porters to bring our stores from the river. At the back of the hut, Dawut places three river fish we had purchased at a village along the Ndeiram Kabur on a grill over a roaring fire. When the fish are cooked, Dawut coats them with sambal, ground chili mixed with tomato and oil, and serves it with bowls of boiled rice. It tastes delicious.

"Where did you learn to cook so well?" I ask.

"At John Wolff's hotel in Wamena. I was there for a few months until I got tired of working in the town. Going on trips is much more interesting, I have many tales to tell when I return home."

The headman explains that he belongs to a coastal tribe and works for the Jakarta government in this remote place as an administrator. "The government gives a hut and land at Mbasman free to any Korowai family willing to leave the rainforest," he says, pausing to let us reflect on the generosity of this offer. "We do it because we want to stop the tree people from killing and eating each other."

Confident that Barnabas cannot speak English, Agung sneers: "What Jakarta really wants is the rainforest hardwood, and that's why they want the Korowai out of their jungles. The licenses to log the land here are worth millions of American dollars and belong to a powerful general in the capital."

Barnabas explains that about three hundred Korowai have chosen to settle at Mbasman and two other government villages to the south. More than 3,500 Korowai have scorned the bribe, refusing to abandon their clusters scattered over 1,500 square miles of jungle.

"You've chosen a dangerous time to come," he warns as we drink river water boiled over the fire. "A man who lived in the jungle died recently. To the Korowai no one ever suffers a natural death, there's always witchcraft involved. You'll need Korowai from this village to guide you through the swamp to the tree people, and carry your supplies. But they're terrified to enter the jungle at the moment because they fear they'll be blamed for the death, then murdered and eaten in revenge."

In a small bare room by the porch, I settle uneasily into my sleeping bag, hoping to prove that mind can conquer matter by softening the hard wooden floor. Dawut sleeps the moment he closes his eyes, but Agung is restless, tossing this way and that on his sleeping mat. "If you're frightened, Paul, then we can forget about the Korowai and take a boat downriver to Yaniruma village, about two days from here," he says softly. "I've arranged for the plane to fetch us there in a couple of weeks."

It's a tempting offer. Although I constantly encounter danger, I have managed to live this long by tempering my desire for it with a commonsense evaluation of each risk to my life. This time, caution threatens to overwhelm courage. Witchcraft, revenge killings, cannibalism. It's the stuff of horror movies. And yet, surely, I reason, the rare chance to enter the jungles of the last human flesh eaters on earth is worth the risk.

Angry voices awaken me soon after sunrise. Agung squats on the porch of Barnabas's hut surrounded by a dozen sullen-faced men clad only in ragged shorts. They are slimmer and much shorter than the Dani. Are these the feared cannibal warriors?

Agung points to the men. "We need six or seven porters and guides to get us to a Korowai village I've been to before, but they refuse to go. They say the jungle Korowai will kill them with black magic and eat them if they enter the jungle."

I offer double the usual porter's fee, then triple and quadruple, but they will not budge. Fight fire with fire, I decide, and grip Agung by the shoulder. I have an idea as mad as any I've had in three decades on the road, but it might work. "Tell the Korowai that I'm a shaman from a far-off land and I'll use my spells to protect them in the jungle."

Agung's eyes widen in surprise but as he translates my mind races back to the days when I was a Catholic altar boy. "Please have the men, women, and children come here," I ask Barnabas.

More than one hundred Korowai drift from their huts to gather in front of us. Standing on the porch, I gaze down at them and spread my arms like a priest. I stay silent for a few moments to heighten the suspense, and then look up at the heavens with beseeching eyes as I begin chanting the opening prayer of the Mass in Latin. *"In nomine patris, et fili, et spiritus sanctus, Amen,"* I shout in a holy-roller voice. *"Introibo ad altare Dei."*

A murmur ripples through the Korowai.

I might as well be chanting in English for all it matters to the villagers, but the sonorous cadences of the Latin give me courage. If there is a God of travelers, then He might answer my prayers. But the novelty effect is short-lived and the Korowai begin muttering among themselves or walk away. I shout louder, rolling my r's, making signs of the Cross, holding my hands to Heaven, but see that I have lost them. After finishing the "Confiteor Dei," I give up.

Agung glances at me sympathetically. "It was a nice try, they believe you have magical power, but they say it's only strong in your own land. We're stranded and we'll have to start back to Wamena now."

CHAPTER 8

As the sun rises over the tree line, I pack my sleeping bag and camera equipment for the journey home. Until now, there has never been a time on the road when I have been unable to get where I wanted to go, however difficult, but this time I am up against primeval sorcery and cannot blame the Korowai for turning their backs on me. I have rarely felt so disheartened, to be at the edge of one of the most thrilling adventures on earth, only to be turned away.

But reality as blunt as this cannot be overcome merely by wishing it away. I tried my best and it seemed it was not good enough to convince the Korowai, still steeped in their primordial beliefs even though these Korowai seem to have largely abandoned their ancient lifestyle. But I know, even by the history of my own people, that belief in black magic, bewitchment, casting spells, devilry, and witches can persist for centuries after we turned our backs on wizards and tribal sorcerers. There always has to be a first tine, I think, justifying my decision to abandon my quest.

Sitting on the floor with my back resting against the camera bag, attempting, but failing, to adopt a comforting "Such is life" acceptance of my fate, I await the summons for our departure. An hour passes and then suddenly Agung calls me back onto the porch. "Let's go," he cries boyishly, pointing at four men and a woman heading in single file towards the jungle with our supplies. "Barnabas forced them to take us to the tree people."

"Are you certain we should go?" I ask Agung. "I don't want to put them in danger."

"Paul, what you will see later today are humans as our ancestors must have lived thousands of years ago. Few outsiders have ever seen them. I think I know why they fear going into the jungle. I know they will be safe."

"What do they fear?"

"You'll know soon enough."

From decades on the road I know that it is wise not to push my guide, Agung, to act against his will. He must have a reason for not telling me now.

The five Korowai turn back to glare at me, and then walk towards the rainforest. The men are clad in shorts and they balance our bags and supplies on their heads, but the middle-aged woman, our guide to the tree house dwellers, has cast aside her ragged dress and donned Korowai garb, a tiny grass skirt about twelve inches long. Her shriveled breasts flap against her wrinkled stomach.

"*Terima kasih* [thank you]," I tell her in Indonesian as we catch up.

She looks at me with dark eyes that throb with hatred, and spits in my face.

"She believes you're an evil spirit forcing her to go into the jungle where one of them will be killed and eaten," Agung says with a shrug. To the Korowai, all outsiders are what they call *laleo*, ghost-demons.

As I wipe away the spittle from my cheek with the edge of my collar, I wonder if the heat has turned me seriously mad, trekking into the rainforest with people who hate me and likely wish me dead. Agung, Dawut, and I are trusting them with our lives, because if they abandon us deep in the jungle then we have little chance of finding our way out alive. I should have marked our path every twenty yards with bent twigs, just as Wasse did when we tracked gorillas, but I did not think of it, my mind focused on the danger ahead.

Entering the Korowai rainforest is like stepping into a giant watery cave humming with malice. One moment the sun is bright overhead, we breathe easily, but as the porters chop through the undergrowth, towering trees jammed together abruptly close in over us, blocking the sky. The heat is stifling and the air drips with humidity; it clutches at my throat. Halting to catch my breath, I peer at the shadowy world ahead, plunged into a verdant gloom by the dense weave of the tree canopy. It's the haunt of giant spiders, killer snakes, murderous microbes, and warring cannibals.

I suddenly feel very frightened and even consider turning back. My wife, daughter, and dog back in Sydney wait for me to return home. Am I being selfish by pushing on when my life could be at risk? Possibly, but then my wife is proud of my journeys and my daughter knows that the primary aim is to bring knowledge of unknown or little known tribes and animals to millions of people across the globe.

"Keep walking or we'll never get there," Agung shouts, noticing me lost in thought and yanking me back into line. I press on even though the fear does not lessen. To witness people still living as our ancestors might have done 10,000 years ago makes the many risks bearable.

High in the canopy, sulphur-crested cockatoos screech a warning as we follow the porters along an invisible pathway that winds through rain-soaked trees and primeval palms. The shirt clings to my back, soaked by sweat. The annual rainfall in this flooded jungle is even higher than the Grand Valley's two hundred inches, making it one of the wettest places on earth, and the forest floor swims with murky swamp water and mud pools.

The Korowai have laid a line of logs along the surface of the otherwise impassable mud and the barefooted porters cross it with ease, even with their loads. Desperately trying to balance as I edge along each log, time and again I slip, stumble, and fall into the knee-deep mud, bruising and scratching my legs and arms as I claw back on my feet.

More worrying are the solitary logs, up to fifteen yards long, slung across the many deep dips in the land. More than once while inching across like a tightrope-walker, I peer down into the shadows and wonder how the porters would get me out of the rainforest were I to fall and break a leg.

Agung shrugs when I ask him. "Don't think about it." I want not to think about it but it is impossible not to.

I thought the Pygmy rainforest was tough but that was like a pleasant stroll along a Los Angeles beach when compared with this hell. Hour melts into hour as we push deeper into this nightmarish place, dive-bombed at each step by squadrons of black-striped mosquitoes threatening to inject malarial parasites into our veins. The mosquitoes also carry the microscopic worms that cause the terrible affliction of elephantiasis, which swells the legs and the testicles to giant size. Only repeated dousings of insect repellent keep the mosquitoes at bay.

I constantly reach for the water bottle to try and replace the sweat that pours from all over my body. Suddenly I feel a knife rip into my stomach. The pain is almost unbearable. That bloody chili fish. Mumbling apologies I rush behind a tree, strip down my jeans, and rid myself of much of the previous night's meal, now a khaki slosh. As I stand up, I vomit. My head starts pounding with pain as if someone is bashing me with a hammer.

A few minutes after resuming the march I have to seek cover again. Sweat flows down my face and I grow dizzy, the world about me tosses from side to side like a yacht battling high waves. I'm dehydrating badly. My body is losing the fluids and salts it needs to operate. I wonder if we have enough water left for the journey. Moments later the jungle falls apart as my eyes lose focus. I struggle to regain sight, but am consumed by a blur. My head whirls like a top out of control, dragging me downwards. Unable to stop myself, I plunge into darkness.

I regain consciousness on the ground, my head nestled in a bed of mulchy leaves. The blackness splinters into the jagged pieces of a jigsaw puzzle strewn across my sight, and they jiggle into place. Agung, Dawut, and the Korowai crouch around me.

"You've got to stand up," Agung whispers. "Now!"

"Water," I murmur weakly.

"There's none left, you've drunk more than we expected."

No water? I know from the Australian desert that the body can dehydrate to the point of death in just a few hours. Here, we are surrounded by water, but it is foul and evil-smelling. I must get to my feet, as Agung demands. I try to move my legs, then my arms, but nothing happens.

Hundreds of ants, big green brutes, march in single file towards me across the mulch. I try to move my hand to brush them away, but nothing happens. In desperation I struggle to move my little finger. It is paralyzed. If I can't get up on my feet now, I'm going to die of dehydration or from ant bites, I think. My mind is so blurry that I do not realize that Agung and Dawut would crush the ants with their feet before they reached me.

"Stand up, Paul," Dawut growls, using my name for the first time. "You must do it by yourself, now!"

It is a desperate struggle with my own body. One moment I'm powerless, and then adrenaline surges through me, like water suddenly released from a dam. Dawut hands me a stout branch. Gripping it, I totter to my feet, arms and legs trembling from the effort.

Moments later one of the Korowai runs into the clearing bearing a pot of water. "You were unconscious for half an hour," says Agung as he boils the water over a fire. "I knew what was wrong, so I sent the Korowai to get water from a running stream he knows nearby. I didn't help you get up; I made you do it yourself, so you'd know there's still strength left in your body."

Even just a mouthful of the precious liquid instantly clears the blur from my mind. More mouthfuls surge through my body like the most powerful drug imaginable. We begin the march again, me with iron again in my legs.

Four hours after leaving Mbasman we slump to the ground beneath a giant sago palm to eat rice and fish washed down with the boiled stream water. My muscles lock into place and they shiver with pain even when I move a little to shake off a cramp. After twenty minutes' rest, Agung looks at me with sympathy warming his brown eyes. "Time to go," he says.

We only trek another one hundred yards when the jungle begins to echo eerily with yodeling war cries. Agung grabs my arm. "Korowai!" he whispers. My heart pounds, but it is too late to turn back; as I am obviously now in my Mad Dog Raffaele persona I do not want to turn back.

Wary of attack we press on and for more than an hour the sounds shadow us through the jungle. Then, as we slash with machetes through a wall of bamboo and enter a small clearing, a hard-muscled man suddenly leaps from behind a tree, obstructing our path. Naked except for a leaf covering the knob of his penis, he brandishes a blackwood bow and several wicked-looking barbed arrows. A pair of bat bones flare from holes pierced into his ebony nose.

"Jesus Christ," I utter in astonishment. In three decades of wandering the world's most remote places I had never seen anything like him. No tribal warrior in a *Tarzan* movie looked a tenth as frightening.

As the warrior steps menacingly towards us, he shouts in a threatening voice. Our female guide holds out trembling arms to placate him. "He demands to know why we've come here," says Agung, using the woman as a translator. As Agung tells him he has been to the tree house clan before, the Korowai rattles his bow and barbed arrows in warning. He glares at us for a few moments, this fierce cannibal from the Stone Age, then turns and disappears into the jungle.

"He's gone to warn his people," says Agung, his face a few shades paler.

Even Dawut is impressed. "He's a true warrior, afraid of no one," he says.

At mid-afternoon the jungle gloom dissolves as shafts of silvery light stab through the trees ahead, signaling a clearing. The woman points ahead. "It's a Korowai village, so we must be careful," says Agung. "She warns that we must move slowly and stay in the open, or they might think we're going to attack, and then there'll be much trouble."

Through the thinning foliage I glimpse a straw hut perched high in the trees. In the clearing, which is about the size of two football fields and littered with fallen trees, I sink to my knees, exhausted, unable to take my eyes off the tree house. It is the strangest-looking dwelling I have ever seen, like the nest of a giant prehistoric bird.

About twelve yards long, seven wide, and soaring twenty yards into the trees, it is as high as a four-story building and nestles against a backdrop of rainforest giants. The floor is held up by a central pole, the decapitated trunk of a massive banyan tree that still has its roots anchored in the ground. Several smaller tree trunks and a dozen sturdy poles dug into the ground help prop up the floor. The thatched leaf roof rests on slatted walls lined with flattened bark. A notched climbing pole dangles from the verandah. The tree house looks deserted.

"Hello! Is Agoos here?" Agung shouts in Bahasa Indonesia, his words translated by the woman. Their voices echo unanswered through the forest.

Suddenly, a child's shriek shatters the silence. "*Laleo!*"

Agung looks worried. "Remember, all outsiders are *laleo*," he says warily. "To them we are ghost-demons."

Through binoculars I glimpse a small boy peering from a verandah jutting from the tree house. Clad only in a necklace of curved dogs' teeth, he shakes at us a tiny bow slotted with an arrow. An unseen Korowai yanks him inside.

Agung knows just one Korowai well here, Agoos the warrior, from a journey he made to this village a year ago. "Agoos will welcome us into the tree house," he says, "but most other Korowai hate outsiders, and they'll shoot us full of arrows if they get the chance."

The woman from Mbasman approaches Agung, they talk for a few minutes, and then he takes out a pile of rupiah notes from his satchel and hands them to her. Satisfied, the five Korowai head back into the jungle.

"What the heck is going on," I ask Agung. "Are they going back to Mbasman?"

"Yes, I paid them the equivalent of ten dollars each. They still fear being killed and demanded to go home."

"Then how do we get back to Mbasman? We don't know the way."

"We have to hope that Agoos will return soon. He may be away for days. At another village."

"Will we be safe?"

"I don't know. Agoos brought me here from Mbasman last time, stayed with me all the time, and took me back to Mbasman."

The minutes drag by as we wait, tense and nervous, in the clearing. I cannot blame the child for believing me a demon. Few outsiders have battled through the swamp to get to this tree house clan since the first foreigner, Johannes Veldhuizen, a Dutch Reformed Churches missionary, came here in 1978. "Because the Korowai were known to be cannibals, I wanted to bring them the word of Jesus," he had told me by phone from his home in Holland.

The tree house people were shaken to their very souls by his ghostly appearance and refused to believe he was a *yanop*, a human. It was only when they saw him bathing in a creek, observed that he came equipped with all the necessary human parts, and when they watched him eating and sleeping that the Korowai accepted him as a true man, though his curious skin color and very odd habits also marked him as a *laleo.*

It took Veldhuizen more than a decade to fully win the friendship of a few clans and even then he and a handful of fellow Dutch missionaries toiling among the tree people never converted a single Korowai to Christianity. As I knew from Van Enk, that was not their aim.

"A very powerful mountain god warned the Korowai that their world would be destroyed by an earthquake if outsiders came into their land to change their customs," Veldhuizen explained. "So we went as guests rather than as conquerors and never put any pressure on the Korowai to change their ways."

The Indonesian government, planning to empty the Korowai forests of the clans and turn it over to loggers, felt it better that there were no outside witnesses. So they forced Veldhuizen and Van Enk to abandon their study of the tree house people's customs and return home after Jakarta refused them an extension of their work visas.

A yodeled shout interrupts my musing. "Agoos is coming!" Agung cries joyfully, pointing to a small, compact, ebony-colored man in his mid-twenties loping into the clearing. He is clad only in rattan belly strips and a leaf covering the knob of his penis. The Korowai warrior clutches a bow and several arrows in one hand as he leaps nimbly over the rotting logs that litter the clearing.

Agoos has a square face, a curved nose, and slim, muscled limbs. He greets Agung, but does not take his sharp dark eyes from me. The proud expression he wears as a birthright is marred by a frown.

"It's good to see you again," he tells Agung. He can speak Bahasa Indonesia, learned from Korowai who have lived for a time at Mbasman, and Agung knows many words in his language. "I've just come from a beetle larvae ceremony at another Korowai village."

I know from Veldhuizen that this is a sacred ritual where hundreds of tree people from many of the fifty Korowai clans gather for several days to cement alliances, seek brides, and exchange gossip while they feast on consecrated grubs and chant fertility songs. Inevitably, when spirits are so high, fights break out and they can lead to murder.

"This morning I got into a fight with another man over a pig and he and his friends said they would come here today to kill everyone in my clan," says Agoos, his wary eyes still hooked to mine. "I've run through the jungle to warn my people."

As we talk, a young warrior climbs nimbly down the tree house pole. Clad like Agoos, he also grips a bow and arrows. "His name is Tinoos," says Agung. Agoos tells him of the threat. Korowai clan warfare is never-ending and, like the wars of Dawut's Dani, is almost always over pigs and women, often as a payback revenge for an earlier killing.

"That's why we build our huts among the trees," Agoos explains. "If our enemy attacks, the women, children, and old people can retreat up into the tree house while we warriors fight it out in the clearing."

"Have there been fights recently?"

He grins at my sudden look of concern. "Yes, *laleo*. Not long ago, warriors from a village near here came because they believed we'd stolen one of their pigs. We fought with bows and arrows. One of their men was killed, along with one of ours, and several were wounded."

Agoos and Tinoos exchange smiles, remembering the clash. "The enemy carried away their wounded and the dead man."

He yanks out one of the arrows from a bundle he carries. The Korowai along with the Amazon Indians never considered or felt the need for a quiver. "This is to kill men."

It is a yard of slender weathered bamboo lashed with vine to a hand's span of cassowary bone with six sharp barbs carved on each side. This ensures the arrowhead will cause terrible damage when removed from the victim's flesh.

"What should we do?" I ask Agung.

"We should stay and fight with the Korowai," says Dawut, who had asked Agung for a translation of my English. "I can use a bow and arrows."

Agoos is amused when Agung explains our conversation. "Korowai fight Korowai," he says to Dawut. "If the enemy come, you three must stay in our *khaim*, our tree home. You'll be safe there."

Up close it looks like an impossible task for a bulky *laleo* to climb up into the *khaim*. Slanted against the ground at an angle of about 45 degrees is a jungle ladder, a yard across, made from boughs, the side struts tied to a pair of the poles that support the tree house. About five yards long, the ladder slants back in midair to meet a long pole called a *yafin,* which joins the verandah where I saw the boy. The ladder looks strong enough to bear my weighty body, but the pole?

"Do people ever fall from the pole?" I ask.

Agoos wistfully touches a hand-sized patch of scalp where the skin and hair have been ripped off, leaving just shiny scar tissue. "I slipped and fell when I was a little boy," he says, pointing to his crooked right elbow that was also broken in the fall. "I came close to dying."

He explains that mothers carry their babies up the pole until they are about four years old, when the toddlers begin to scramble up without help. Falls are frequent for young and old, some fatal. A teenage boy died not long ago when the pole snapped as he was climbing up to the tree house. "He fell backwards onto the pole which ran through his throat," says Agoos.

The clans occasionally bury their dead in abandoned tree houses, sometimes in the jungle, but most often beneath the tree house they inhabit. Agoos points to a patch of earth near my feet. "That's where we put the boy."

I follow Agung and Dawut up the ladder. Sweat pours down my body as I nervously grip the pole with both hands. Although it is twice as thick as my fist, it feels as solid as a stick of candy. The pole has foot notches cut into it every thirty inches. When I place a foot on a notch and swing the full weight of my body onto it, the pole bends perilously as it takes the strain. The upper end rattles against the verandah, a primitive burglar alarm to warn of intruders.

For a few moments I freeze, remembering the doomed boy, and then with gritted teeth slowly ascend. At each notch my heart seems to shake like the pole until I haul myself onto the verandah. Inside, wreathed in a haze of smoke split by beams of golden light, are a man and the small boy with the toy bow crouched around a hearth. They stare at the flame, ignoring me, perhaps hoping I am an illusion, soon enough to drift away like the smoke that curls up from their fire. Three wild-eyed piglets, khaki-hued with yellow stripes, huddle against the wall they are tied to with rattan string.

"Where are the women?" I ask.

"In the sago fields, but they'll return soon because Tinoos has gone to tell them of the threat," Agoos answers.

Smoke from the cooking fires has coated the bark walls and sago-leaf ceiling, giving the hut a sooty odor. The floor is a densely woven latticework of bamboo strips and boughs, which bend and creak as I tread carefully across them. Every nook and cranny is crammed with the haunting bones from clan feasts—spiky fish skeletons, blockbuster pigs' jaws, the skulls of flying foxes and jungle rats. They even dangle from hooks strung along the ceiling, near bundles of many-colored parrot and cassowary feathers stuffed into the leafy rafters.

"Seeing the bones and feathers makes visitors feel they are welcome, that they've come to the tree house of a prosperous clan," Agoos tells me as he slips the bow and arrows into a bamboo holder strung to the wall, near several stone axes.

There are no human bones, no grisly reminders of feasts where human flesh was consumed. In the longhouses of Borneo's Dyaks I had seen hanging from the ceilings the gruesome skulls of victims murdered in headhunting raids. The skulls sanctify each longhouse, impart added muscle to its warriors, and magically fertilize the sago fields.

Agung says that because the Korowai know their victims, there are no such displays in the tree houses. "They use stone axes to cut notches in trees outside the clearing and jam the bones of the murdered in them to ward off evil spirits," the Dutch missionary Van Enk had told me. "On a visit to one clan I saw trees full of human bones of all types. The Korowai were able to point to each bone and tell me the name of the person who'd been eaten."

From the verandah I spy two other tree houses on the far side of the clearing, half the height of this *khaim*. Agoos tells me that about ten people live in each tree house, all members of the same clan. "The older people find it hard to climb the pole, so they live closer to the ground," he says. "Our war chief lives in *khaim* there."

"Has he killed and eaten humans?"

Agoos nods. "Of course, we all have."

"Will you tell me why?"

"It's better that the war chief tells you. Tomorrow, I'll take you to meet him."

The forest silence is suddenly shaken by loud yodeling that echoes around the clearing. "Is it the war party?"

Agoos grins at my dismay. "It's the women!"

Each clan has its own password calls and, as they near the clearing, the women are signaling so they are not mistaken for invaders. An enemy war party could imitate the clan password, but a code of combat must forbid such an unchivalrous act.

A dozen near-naked women troop into the clearing. Most are in their twenties, two are pre-teens, and their backs are bent under bulging loads of firewood and food carried in hand-woven vine bags strung around their foreheads, much like those of the Dani women. All are wiry with whipcord leg muscles that tense as they climb the pole to the tree house, still toting their loads. One girl also carries under her arm a lean fawn dog resembling a miniature greyhound and probably having the same speed and agility, most useful in a hunt.

This is the first sign that the Korowai have moved an evolutionary step closer than the Pygmies to the bond that we humans and our dogs share today. The dog is the only one in the treehouse, there must be more, and so it is probably kept by the girl as a pet.

"It's time to reveal your *koteka* to the girls," I say with a wink to Dawut.

He frowns at the thought. "I didn't tell you but I packed it into my bag last night at Mbasman and won't wear it until we're in the mountains again. Agoos would probably eat me if I dared take one of the Korowai girls to the forest."

"But Agoos is much smaller than you."

"It's not the size of his body, but the size of his heart that matters. He might smile at us and treat us as guests, but I can see in his eyes that, like a true man, he'll kill you if you anger him."

Agoos, the potential assassin, nods to his wife, Lali, a round-faced girl in her late teens clad like the other women in a tiny skirt made from strips of dried palm frond that perches on her hips, barely covering her upper thighs. Circles of scar tissue the size of large coins run the length of her arms, around her stomach, and across her pendulous breasts.

"They're beauty marks," Lali says shyly, avoiding the *laleo's* gaze.

Such marks are flaunted by men and women, she adds, to make them sexually attractive.

The seductive marks are formed by thrusting burning-hot pebbles onto the bare skin. I cannot see how bubbles of flesh covered by scar tissue can excite a man or a woman sexually but then lipstick and rouged cheeks leave me cold and new jeans deliberately torn in a kind of ugly poverty chic baffles me. Why is that fashionable? Apart from anything else I suppose it signals that the wearer, even a billionaire singer such as Beyonce who could afford a thousand pairs of unsullied jeans, is one of the modern post-millennial tribe and is therefore hip. Whoops, that is an expression from my youth. Now the word my daughter told me is "cool." Curiously, cool, like hip, comes from the slang first used by African American jazz musicians in the 1940s.

"Of course it hurts very much but to be beautiful is worth the pain," Lali explains.

I considered at first that the marks might relate to the women being proud members of a warrior tribe, with the wearer flaunting her willingness and ability to withstand pain. You might expect that from the warriors, but the women do not fight. Among my people the allure of tattoos is surging and devotees told me that the tattoo needle jabbing repeatedly into the flesh on an arm, a leg, or even the face hurts like hell.

Agoos's hunger has been spiked by his exhausting run through the jungle and Dawut, sitting by me, watches intently as he starts a fire in a way similar to the Dani and other Neolithic tribes that I have been with on three continents, a method humans must have relied on for tens of thousands of years. Planting his feet at either end of a stick resting on a pile of wood shavings, Agoos loops a length of rattan string around the stick and rapidly pulls it to and fro. The friction produces tiny sparks that set fire to a handful of shavings. Blowing hard to fuel the tiny flame, he places the glowing shavings beneath a pile of twigs on the hearth. Within minutes we squat around a blazing fire.

The hearth, one of two in the hut, is made from strips of clay-coated rattan suspended over a hole in the floor. "That's so it can be quickly cut loose, to fall to the ground, if a fire starts to burn out of control," Agoos explains.

The Korowai staple food is flour made from the pith of sago palm and it has a similar texture to the Pygmies' manioc. Lali had spent her day in the forest hacking down sago palms with a hand ax that defines an entire epoch of human existence, the Stone Age. The ax is a chunk of stone sharpened at one end and lashed with vine to a wooden handle. She had pummeled the sago pith to a pulp, and then sluiced it with water to produce a dough molded into bite-size pieces.

After throwing several chunks onto the fire, Agoos eats them with gusto once they are grilled. The Korowai are so wedded to the sago taste that they turn up their noses at the boiled rice and chili sauce Agung offers them. Given a chunk of sago, I find it tastes like warm raw flour. It clogs my throat, releasing its grip only when I wash it down with boiled river water.

Agoos notices my screwed-up face as I force the sago down. "You don't like it?" he asks, smiling. I shake my head. "What strange tastes you ghost demons have."

He tosses on the fire two fish Tinoos had caught in a nearby stream, then wraps a pair of locusts and a large black spider in a banana leaf, placing it on a red-hot rock in the embers. When offered the cooked spider I shake my head, wincing as Agoos pops it into his mouth, crunches it into mash, and swallows it with a gourmand's delight.

Crouched around the fire with us are several men and the child. Using their fingers they wolf down the sago, fish, three lizards, and a lone frog, sharing it equally, just like the Dani and the Pygmies. It occurs to me as I write this that the core commandment of Karl Marx's socialism, "from each according to his ability, to each according to his need" is much closer to the ethos of these Stone Age tribes than the brutal uber-capitalism of many Western countries, including my own, in the 21st century.

The women gather about a second hearth at the far end of the tree house, cooking much the same meal. The sexes stay apart in the tree house, each keeping to their own section of the hut, forbidden to mingle once they make their way up the *yifan* pole.

I ask why. "It's the Korowai way," Agoos shrugs. It's the same answer I get from many of the remote tribes I have been with. Trial and error over a very long period of human existence has taught the tribes what works and what doesn't. They seem to see no need to rationalize what tradition dictates.

The meal gives me the first hint as to why the Korowai might have turned to cannibalism. The Pygmy rainforest is like a Stone Age supermarket packed with all kinds of tasty creatures so that the clan was never short of protein. But Agung tells me that the Korowai rainforest meat is hard to come by and this might have prompted the Korowai to figure out a way to get protein through eating human flesh.

After dinner we sit cross-legged on the verandah to watch the day end. Not long after the sun drifts below the tree line the entire sky bursts into flame, a vast turmoil of red and gold, streaked with clouds of all colors. A velvet cover suddenly drops, plunging the jungle into night. Dozens of fireflies invade the clearing, dancing through the air like wicked fairies, pinpricks of pulsating silver light tracing their zig-zagging paths.

Agoos has a Jew's harp made from bamboo and presses one end against his mouth, strumming a haunting tune on what is a family heirloom. "My father passed it on to me, and his father passed it on to him. When I have a son I will teach it to him."

I stare out into the night, imagining the silhouettes of trees to be massed warriors. "Could the rival clan use the cover of night to attack?"

Agoos shakes his head. "The evil spirits lurking in the jungle are most active and hostile at night. You risk having them kill you with black magic if you leave the tree house while it is dark."

To the Korowai, then, the night forest is a terrifying world, much like that feared by our cave-dwelling ancestors. They must also have crouched over comforting fires in their nighttime sanctuaries, dreading the demons, hobgoblins, witches, banshees, and trolls prowling out there in the dark.

From demons, we switch the conversation to gods. Agoos was told by friends who spoke to the missionaries that *laleo* believe in just the one god. Like Wassse and the Bayaka, he finds this puzzling. "There are spirits in everything–each tree, rock, stream, flower, plant–it's just that we can't see them."

Most powerful is a supreme spirit named Ginol who created the present world, his fifth effort, having destroyed the previous four because they did not please him. Thank goodness our own God was not so hard to please. This will not be the final world, Agoos tells me. Around the fires for as far as the collective tribal memory reaches back, the old people have told the younger ones that white-skinned ghost demons will invade Korowai land. Once the *laleo* arrive, the fifth world will be obliterated.

"The land will split apart, there will be fire, thunder, and mountains will drop from the sky. Our world will shatter and a new one will take its place."

The poignancy and accuracy of the prophecy stuns me. For generations the Korowai have known that we *laleo* were coming, known that we would be bringing with us the cataclysmic means of their destruction. I am at a loss over how to respond. Apologize, leave immediately to try to dilute the curse?

Not all Agoos's clan have welcomed me so warmly into their tree house. Some of the women and the warrior who confronted us in the forest turn away angrily each time our eyes meet. Because I personify the coming apocalypse, I can't condemn their fury. Nor can I blame the Korowai who live beyond what Van Enk calls the pacification line, three days' walk through the rainforest from here, who refuse all contact with outsiders.

These Korowai have sworn to kill any *laleo* who dares set foot on their land, even Van Enk and Veldhuizen, who showed they wanted to help preserve their traditional ways. More likely, golden-skinned ghost demons from Jakarta will be the ones to destroy the Korowai world using chainsaws, bulldozers, and assault rifles. And that time must be drawing near.

We move back to the hearth and for more than two hours the men swap stories or play their Jew's harps around the fire as its reflection colors the bark walls and leafy ceiling a smoky amber. I take a closer look around me, seeing that nothing dates beyond the Stone Age. No mirrors, radio, chairs, tables, cupboards, steel utensils, matches. No books, TV, dishwasher, taps, phone, or even lamps.

Agoos examines my T-shirt as I change to a jumper to ward off the night chill once the fire goes out. "We call this *laleo-khul*, ghost demon skin," he says, grinning. The term is wonderfully apt, the naked

Korowai at first contact unable to imagine the *laleo's* garb as anything but a strange-looking epidermis that can be magically removed and put back on at will.

Because of the taboo, Agoos and Lali can only gaze at each other across the hut. Even married couples are forbidden to sleep together in the tree house and must snatch fleeting moments of love at secret places in the rainforest. There, mosquitoes attack their bare flesh.

"Don't the stings distract you?" I ask.

Agoos smiles as he rests his head against the floor. "I enjoy it so much, I never notice."

After two years of marriage the pair are still childless. When Lali does give birth, it must happen in the jungle. "It is taboo in the tree house," he says.

"Why?"

Agoos shrugs. "Because that's the way we Korowai do it."

Sleep comes swiftly in the tree house and by 9 p.m. I'm curled up by the smoldering hearth on the men's side of the hut, hemmed in by slumbering warriors. Slumped around the other hearth are the women, the fire embers casting a hushed glow across their bodies.

Sometime after midnight I stir, convinced I am still in a wondrous dream. Gathered around me are the silhouettes of naked primeval people. Bows and arrows, stone axes, and bamboo knives glare from the wall, the skulls and skeletons are grisly shadows overhead. Befuddled by sleep, I find it impossible to name the current century, impossible to pinpoint the place where I am. Puzzled but not disturbed by this fuzzy taste of oblivion, I drift back to sleep.

Someone grips my shoulder. My eyes spring open. It is Agoos. *"Manotropo, laleo!"* he says, smiling. "It means, 'Good morning, ghost demon.'"

"Manotropo, Agoos!" I reply, returning the smile.

Agoos watches as I rise from my mat on the tree house floor and remove the jumper. "The sun is here. Do you want to eat sago and spider?"

Dawut has risen early, and a warm odor wafting from below signals that he has boiled some of the rice we brought with us. "Thank you for your kindness, but I'll eat ghost demon food."

There had been a downpour overnight and the rain-speckled forest exudes a giddy odor of dank earth and foliage, just like the rainforest of Wasse and his clan beyond Bayanga. The sun has risen, but has yet to reach the high tree line, and the sky is raw gray, luminescent along the treetops. In the clearing below, women in tiny grass skirts weave through the banana trees on their way to harvest sago in the rainforest. A trio of slender silent dogs accompanies them. This seems more evidence that the Korowai dogs are valued friends. Do they also accompany the Korowai hunt like the basenjis?

"Aren't they in danger if the rival clan attacks now that it's daylight?"

Agoos shakes his head. It seems the women, as well as the men, must gather and hunt each day to feed the clan, and the risk of an ambush is a workaday hazard.

Standing twenty yards above the clearing, I see why the Korowai build these towering leafy fortresses to thwart invaders, but there are many other advantages. Tree hut's inhabitants are safe from the evil spirits that flit about the forest floor at night, and escape the malarial mosquitoes that forever seek human blood below. The air up here is fresher, cooler, breezier. From the verandah the Korowai can shoot arrows at birds flying by and also gain pleasure from contemplating their beloved gardens in the clearing—the many types of banana trees growing in clumps and neat rows of knee-high sweet potato plants.

"Korowai men call themselves 'Lords of the Garden' because they cherish those gardens in the clearing, and the sago fields in the rainforest," Agung explains.

Eager to meet the war chief and learn why the Korowai are cannibals, I scurry down the pole. Once again, it buckles and quivers under my weight. The girl with the dog follows me down to the ground, clutching the pet to her bosom. She is slim-hipped, looks about thirteen, and stares at me with a bold curiosity. Like a Mohawk Indian, a strip of fuzzy black hair runs down the center of her otherwise shiny dark shaven head.

Her name is Fuom. She explains that Agoos's wife regularly scrapes off her frizzy hair, wielding a strip of sharpened bamboo the size of a dinner knife.

"It hurts very much, but it makes me look beautiful," she says with a shy smile.

"We men use the same knife to cut the hair from our faces because our women like us better that way," says Agoos.

Something else is clearly hurting Fuom, because her dark brown eyes look haunted and the natural beauty of her features is shadowed by some inner agony. "She will soon be married against her will to a fierce, powerful man from another clan deeper in the rainforest," Agung explains after asking Agoos.

Fuom gazes in open anguish at me, perhaps hoping that the *laleo* can save her with his unearthly magic. "He saw Fuom at a beetle grub ceremony not long ago and threatened to kill her father unless she became his bride," Agoos says. Reluctantly, Fuom bent to his will even though she does not love the man.

"Would the fierce man have eaten Fuom's father if he killed him?"

"Of course not. He was not a *khakhua*."

"A khakhua?"

"The war chief will explain," Agung says.

Fuom's breasts have barely begun to bud and her hips look incapable of bearing a child. "That's why she's sad, because she fears giving birth while she's still so young," Agoos tells me. "But most Korowai girls marry at her age."

Agung sits at my elbow the entire time, transforming the machine-gun chatter of words into English. "The Korowai call such men, *khen-menng-abul*," he says. "They are born leaders possessing the ferocious spirit needed to lead their clan brothers on successful raids." The *khen-menng-abul* will arrive at the clearing five days from now bearing the bride price, highly desirable chains of densely strung dogs' teeth and cowrie shells, as many as will cover an adult torso, and also two adult pigs. "To guard against inbreeding, Korowai girls like Fuom marry into other clans, while the boys never leave the birth clan," Agung says.

Fuom shrugs when I ask her age. The Korowai do not count the years or the months or the weeks. Each day piles on the one before, and even Agoos has no idea how old he is. When I ask how high he can count, he ticks off the fingers on his left hand, continuing to count as he touches his wrist, forearm, shoulder, neck, forehead, and then moves down the other arm.

The tally comes to twenty. "Anything greater than that the Korowai refer to as 'many'," Agung explains.

Agung, Dawut, and I wash in a fast-flowing creek at the edge of the clearing while Agoos and his friend Tinoos stand guard with bows and arrows. Tinoos is about the same age as Agoos, but stockier and rarely softens his bulldog face with a smile. A pair of holes have been drilled into his nose, but it is bare of decoration.

A Korowai man never takes a step outside the clearing without his bow and arrows. "We might run into a flock of parrots or a cassowary," says Agoos, "but mostly they're for defense if we're attacked."

Now comes the moment I have both wanted and dreaded. Will the mention of cannibalism, such a sensitive subject, anger the Korowai? Will they then force us to leave the tree house, and the village?

A wiry man in his forties, squatting in front of a smaller tree house, shouts, *"Manotropo,"* as we clamber over fallen trees in the clearing. "He's our *khen-menng-abul,"* says Agoos, softly and with great respect. The clan's "fierce, powerful" man is naked, save for a leaf wrapped about the top of his penis, rattan belly strips, and a pig tusk thrust through a hole bored into his septum. Despite his kindly smile, a battle-scarred torso identifies him as a great warrior. More circular scar marks than I can count dot his body, mementoes of arrows cut from his body after battle. Bunched lines of scar tissue scored on his back, chest, and thighs mark the places where he had been hacked with stone axes.

"What is your war chief's name?" I ask.

Agoos shakes his head. For the first time I see fear in his eyes. "I can't tell you. An invisible spirit stays in front of him at all times to protect him. If anyone says his name the spirit will kill that person."

Not wanting to tempt fate in this strangest of places, I don't press the question. For the next two hours the war chief points to each of the scars, telling me in detail where and how he received each wound. They are horrifying tales of murder, mayhem, and black magic. A large patch of scar tissue spreads across much of his stomach and the war chief gazes wistfully at it as he rubs it with his fingers.

"Awar, a warrior from another clan, stole my daughter and I went to his gardens to get her back. We fought and his arrow went deep into my stomach. Agoos and Tinoos helped carry me home." The war chief keeps silent for a few moments, his hard black eyes burning at the memory. "When the wound healed, I led my warriors back to his tree house and we killed him."

It is astonishing that he survived such a terrible wound in a place that swarms with infectious microbes because the Korowai have only a rudimentary knowledge of medicine, using plants and bark to bind the wound or burn in a ritual to spirit away the pain and damage to the body.

At Mbasman, Barnabas had told me that an Indonesian doctor visits the settlement two or three times a year to inoculate the children there. The medico never dares enter the cannibals' jungle. This results in a terrible death rate from accidents, war, and disease. Life for most Korowai is brutally short. The evidence is clear, judging by the scarcity of children and older people here. Agoos counts them. "The two little boys, a sickly girl, Fuom, a baby boy, two old men, and an old woman." That is all in a settlement of thirty people. The children die easiest, and many do not survive their first year. "That's why Korowai children are not named until they are about eighteen months old," says Agung. The Pygmies wait just one year before giving a baby a name.

The children then run a gauntlet of killer tropical diseases and accidents, without medical help, as they grow up. Life is also very dangerous for adult Korowai, prey to the same horrific diseases, as well as the sudden thud of a cassowary bone arrowhead or the fatal swing of a stone ax.

Van Enk observed that most Korowai die before they reach about thirty-five. "Only the very strongest reach their forties," he told me.

The parents of Agoos and Tinoos are already dead. Few children get to know their grandparents. Another killer is cannibalism, the great unspoken in our world, but a way of life for the Korowai. As much as their primeval way of making fire and use of stone tools, this practice of tribal cannibalism links Agoos and his clan with the Stone Age. Like the Korowai, many of our very distant ancestors practiced cannibalism as a form of sorcery or as a magic ritual, and also to satisfy their hunger for protein in jungles where there were no large mammals or fish.

"How do I raise such a delicate matter?" I ask Agung.

"Just ask. To them eating human meat is the same as us eating chicken."

The war chief starts by telling me that all acts of cannibalism are prompted by the need to punish the *khakhua,* male witches who come from the netherworld to haunt the tree houses and who cast the black magic spells that make men die. The victim is never a woman or a child. The *khakhua's* first move is to take possession of the living body of one of the clan's warriors.

"The *khakhua* then shoots invisible arrows into the victim's heart at night while he sleeps and uses magic to scoop out the intestines to eat, putting back in their place ashes from the fireplace so no one notices," he explains. "The victim dies within days."

No one knows the identity of the *khakhua* before a person dies from the spells, but the witch-man must then be quickly hunted down. It could be the victim's father, brother, cousin, uncle, or friend. This causes the clans to shake with fear for days and sometimes even weeks until the *khakhua* is found, killed, and eaten. That is why our porters were so reluctant to bring us from Mbasman to the tree house and scurried back to Mbasman once we got there.

"Sometimes, the dying person whispers the name of the *khakhua* to his family," explains the war chief, "or we find the *khakhua* by using spells and torture."

It seems a horrible way to find the villain, as it must almost always end with murderous injustice, especially as most of the Korowai deaths must occur from disease or accidents. "Wouldn't a dying person be tempted to name a person he hated very much as the *khakhua,* just to punish him?"

"That would never happen because that person, for lying, would then be punished in the land of the dead," the war chief explains.

The witch-man's end is deliberately barbaric. "We take the *khakhua* to the stream near the clearing, tie his arms with twine, and shoot arrows into him," he goes on. "We leave his body there for a nearby clan to eat."

It is a gruesome trade in human flesh that bonds clans to each other with the ritual exchange of human meat. "We tell the other clan where and when to find the body to eat, and when they kill a *khakhua,* they tell us where we can find the body."

The warriors gather around the body, chanting a cannibal

incantation as each man places a foot on the part selected for his family. Using stone axes, they dismember the *khakhua,* chopping off his head, slicing open his chest and back, and hacking off his limbs. The blood-ied portions are individually wrapped in banana leaf and placed in a pit along with burning hot rocks and covered with more banana leaves, forming a giant steamer.

Agoos loops a string of vine tightly around the length of his arm to demonstrate a favorite method of cooking. "The meat between the vine swells during the steaming, making it easier to pull from the bones." The Korowai always eat with their hands.

The war chief grips his stone ax and chops viciously at the air, showing how he gets to the tastiest part. "First, I bash open the skull, and then I scoop out the brains and eat them. They are delicious."

"Are the brains your favorite?" I ask Agoos.

"I prefer the tongue, it's the softest and sweetest meat," he answers. Tinoos, silent as ever, nods agreement.

The war chief tells me that at the cannibal feast, the Korowai eat everything except nails, bones, penis, hair, and teeth. The Dutch missionary Veldhuizen believes this is not cannibalism prompted by a nightmarish lust for human flesh, but logical vengeance, an extreme version of the payback code that is at the core of Melanesian cultures. The *khakhua* had eaten in a magical way the insides of his victim and is punished by being eaten himself. Or should that be itself.

The war chief says that children are never killed and eaten, and do not take part in the cannibal feasts. "There are many powerful evil spirits near when we eat the flesh and the children are vulnerable." For once in my long career as a wandering writer I squib asking a crucial question, unable to inquire from one of the little boys, or even Fuom, whether they look forward to eating humans when they grow up. I think I know the answer, but don't want to hear them confirm it.

I know of no other tribe in the history of cannibalism where the victims are from the same tight-knit clan as the killers, and are even well known to the eaters, a neighboring clan. Cannibalism in warrior societies mostly has involved feasting on the bodies of enemies killed in battle, or strangers who were regarded as sub-human. But even the Korowai are very human in being squeamish about eating their own family members. Even for the fierce war chief, with his hunger for human flesh, it is taboo to eat the body parts of a person with whom he shared so much in life.

In cannibal literature, especially in fiction, the taste of human flesh is often compared to that of pork, "long pig" being a common expression to describe human meat. The war chief, Agoos, and Tinoos disagree. "It tastes like the sweet flesh of young cassowary," says the war chief as the two young warriors nod.

This is one of the most bizarre moments in my life, sitting in a far-off jungle and calmly discussing with primeval tribal cannibals the way you cook human flesh, much as I would talk with friends about the best way to barbecue a steak at home in Sydney.

Conditioned by horror movies, when planning this journey to eaters of human flesh I expected to be confronted by a tribe of monsters, bloodthirsty creatures sprung from the most terrible nightmare. Instead, Agoos, Tinoos, even the war chief strike me as reasonable people, coping as best they can in a culture abandoned by most of humankind thousands of years ago. Although the idea of eating another human sickens me, I realize that if I had been born a Korowai, then I too would be a cannibal.

Agung sat quietly while these thoughts spun around my mind. Then, without warning, he stands up. "These Korowai are not human," he says in English as he walks towards the jungle. "Only demons eat each other."

Later, I find him sitting by the stream, staring moodily into the water. "I know the talk is difficult for you, as it is for me. But please help me because without you I can't talk to the Korowai."

"All this boasting of eating men is inhuman, Paul, and sickens my stomach."

"It's not as inhumane as you think. Archaeologists have excavated caves in France and Croatia where they found evidence that our European ancestors long ago were cannibals. They were fond of scooping out the brains like the war chief and they cracked open human bones to scoop out the marrow."

Agung screws up his face in disgust. "But they lived hundreds of thousands of years ago. I'm talking about humans now."

"Well, the Aztecs in what's now Mexico ate human flesh as a way of communing with the gods just a few hundred years ago, and so did Easter Island warriors. And, up until the nineteenth century, I know from talking with their descendants that Tongan warriors steamed the bodies of enemies they killed in battle in underground ovens and ate the flesh, much like the Korowai."

"But they don't do it now, and that's the big difference. I would not eat human flesh, even if I were dying of hunger. Though I did read in a book that starving German soldiers ate their comrades' flesh during a siege. And air crash survivors ate the remains of their fellow passengers. But they did it to keep alive. The Korowai are different, they eat human flesh because they like it."

"They also do it to punish the witch-men. But, yes, they do seem to enjoy eating human flesh, and that's why I need to talk to them about their cannibalism, because there is no one left on earth like them."

Agung shrugs and walks back with me to the clearing. "I needed to piss," he says to Agoos, explaining his abrupt departure. Once we settle cross-legged on the grass, the talk of cannibalism continues. The most recent cannibal feast Agoos took part in occurred at a tree house a day's walk from here. He arrived near the end. "All that was left was the *khakhua's* arm, so I helped eat it," he says.

Cannibalism is common among the Korowai who live beyond the pacification line, a place Agoos has journeyed to many times to attend beetle grub ceremonies. "Will you take me there?" I ask, noticing Agung's startled expression as he translates the question.

Agoos shakes his head. "No! They'd kill you for breaking their taboo against *laleo*, and they'd kill me for bringing you there."

The warriors tell me gruesome tales for another hour. The war chief, spying my fatigued eyes, offers me his tree house to rest. The *khaim* is seven yards high, the pole a third as long as the one at Agoo's tree house, but as I place my foot on the second notch the pole snaps. If the break had happened at the higher *khaim*, the fall might have killed me.

"You'd better stay in my *khaim* from now on," offers the war chief.

Soon after, Agoos returns from the jungle carrying a stouter pole. This time I scale it successfully and curl up on the lattice floor, exhausted by a leap across an almost impossibly wide culture gap.

"Tell me about your village," Agoos asks.

It is the next morning, and Agoos, Agung, and I sit naked in the stream that winds around the tree house clearing, enjoying the cool clear fresh water swirling over our bodies. Tinoos, silent and solid as a monument, stands guard with bow and arrows at the ready.

This is one of the hardest questions I have ever been asked. We are both human, we have common emotions that well up from hundreds of thousands of years of social evolution, and that is why men of such different upbringing, the Korowai cannibal, the Dani warrior, the Javanese artist, and the Australian writer can so quickly be as brothers.

If I had to tell Agoos of love, hate, jealousy, lust in my land, then it would be easy. Instead, it is a problem of dimension, of bricks and mortar and glass, of summoning images that must be beyond his most fervent imagination. I sit for some minutes thinking about what to say, and Agoos, attuned to the slow and steady rhythms of the rainforest, does not press me for a quick answer.

"Imagine if you begin running when the sun rises and you keep running until night comes, and you do this for several days, then in my land you'll always be in sight of huts. They're pushed together into one very big village, with no jungle in between. You can run for many days and not see a tall tree."

Agoos shakes his head in wonder, or perhaps disbelief "Truly?" he asks.

"Truly."

"It's hard for me to understand such a place. It would be easy to get lost among so many huts. I could never find my way home."

I point to the tallest tree at the edge of the rainforest. "Our huts are many times higher than that tree."

The spell is instantly broken. He snorts in disbelief. "Humans can't climb that high."

I waste my breath trying to explain elevators, cars, trains, even the wheel.

Tiny fish, their silvery scales catching the sun's rays, flash by us. I point again to the tallest tree soaring more than twenty yards into the sky. "In the great waters beyond the rainforest, there are creatures shaped like fish as long as that and as wide as the creek. We call them whales."

He looks at me as if I'm an idiot. "That's impossible, you're joking," he answers with a laugh. "The water would not be deep enough for such fish to swim in."

I ask Agoos why the Korowai have never ventured beyond their rainforest, to explore the world outside. "The Citak, our enemies, live along the rivers by our land," he says quietly. "The people at Mbasman told me that when they kill enemies they cut off their heads and hang them in their huts."

"Do the Citak ever attack you?"

"No. They stay by their rivers and we stay in our jungles. Except for the Korowai at Mbasman. But they are not so much Korowai any-more. They look like us but they live mostly like the strangers. They are drifting away from us."

"Agoos means we Indonesians," Agung explains. "He told me he was at Mbasman once when traders came in pirogues."

"Do the Mbasman Korowai still eat humans?"

"No. Why do you ask me this? We Korowai don't eat humans, we eat *khakhua*."

CHAPTER 9

We return to the war chief's tree house to eat breakfast. Agoos is loyal to the sago from his jungle garden and refuses Dawut's rice, sweet potatoes, and chili sauce. I soon discover that Agoos, Tinoos, the war chief, and three other warriors who have joined us know nothing about the outside world beyond Mbasman. They shake their heads when I ask if they have heard of Jayapura, America, Australia, the Indonesian President. I try to explain movies but neither Agung nor I can find the right words to conjure up in their minds the magic images that appear on the screen but have no substance, no flesh, blood, or soul.

I've brought along a magazine and when I show them a picture of a horse and its rider, they reel back, bug-eyed with terror. "Aiyaaaaa," Agoos cries. He has never seen a mammal bigger than a pig, and to him the horse must be no less astonishing than a live Tyrannosaurus Rex would be to me.

"Does it eat humans?" the war chief asks fearfully.

"No, we sit on such a creature and ride through our jungles."

The war chief snorts in disbelief. Agoos tells him about the whales. The war chief points to the south. "I believe there are such creatures because I know there is a place beyond the land of the dead where the water never ends."

The missionary Van Enk had already told me that the Korowai

universe is made up of three concentric circles." The innermost is the world of the living, the second is the realm of the dead, and the third is the netherworld, what the Korowai call "the endless great water."

The coastline is just one hundred fifty miles from the tree house. "Do you want to see this great water?"

The war chief trembles. "Never! I don't want to go beyond the land of the dead. When I die my spirit will escape through my skull and then it will travel to the jungle, at the edge of our land, where the dead live. There, they hunt, marry, eat pig and cassowary, but they do not eat humans. They can never have children."

"Agoos, would you like to journey to the endless waters beyond the land of the dead?"

He measures me with powerful brown eyes. I see the longing in them.

"Of course he doesn't," the war chief snaps. "Korowai would die of unhappiness or be killed by our enemies if ever we left the safety of our rainforest."

The conversation lulls as we eat breakfast. Flipping through the magazine, I come to a double-page spread showing a big-thighed, big-breasted girl in Patpong, Bangkok's red-light district. The warriors' eyes widen in surprise when I show it to them. Korowai women are lean as whippets and the men must wonder what they might do with all that golden flesh on display.

I try to explain the role of a prostitute and their difficulty in understanding convinces me that it is not the world's oldest profession. I already know that Korowai sex is strictly confined to marriage and that adultery is punished by death. So it takes an enormous leap of the mind for them to comprehend sex for sale.

"Imagine that you are at a beetle grub ceremony and a pretty girl offers to go into the jungle and have sex with you if you'll give her an ax, or food, or a bow. If you agree, even if she doesn't like you, then she'll go with you. And when you've finished she'll go with any other man who gives her something of value."

This sets off a buzz among the men. Agoos tosses his head from side to side in denial. "No woman would do such thing. Her clan would kill her."

I point to the picture. "It's true, this shows a girl offering herself for sex." Agoos holds the magazine to the light to see the girl more clearly. "Is it true what the *laleo* says?" he asks Agung.

"Yes, a woman like that will go to the jungle with you in exchange for something you have that she wants. In my land there are many women like that."

The penny suddenly drops and Agoos, eyes gleaming, whoops with delight. His excitement spreads to the other warriors and for a long time afterwards they ply me with questions about the sex trade.

"How many men does the girl go to the forest with in a day?"

"What does the girl do with so many bows and axes, and so much food? Surely, she'll gather much more than her clan can use?"

"Why would a man marry such a girl when he knows she's done such a terrible thing?"

"If the girl is ugly, does she receive less than a pretty girl?"

Even though they are fascinated by the smallest detail of the sex trade, they still cannot understand why the girls' parents or husbands allow them to sleep with strangers, and why they do not kill them for breaking the taboo. Ultimately, as in other clannish warrior tribes I had journeyed among, such as the Pashtun of Afghanistan, family honor always surmounts an individual's desires. Whoever breaks that inflexible code and stains the family's honor is murdered.

By the porch the war chief sits listening intently to the banter about this custom of girls selling sex, pondering the bizarre habits of the *laleo* beyond the rainforest. "If it were my daughter, I'd feel shame, and if I knew she took men other than her husband to the jungle, then I'd kill her," he says.

Still excited about the Patpong girl, the warriors leave for their gardens of sago in the rainforest because it is already the third period of their day. Using nature as their clock, the Korowai separate each day into seven periods: dawn, sunrise, mid-morning, noon, mid-afternoon, dusk, and the night.

Agung, Dawut, and I sit in the clearing by the tree house as two small boys with toy bows and harmless arrows made from sago palm leaf struts play at war, stalking each other with murderous eyes. They scream in triumph each time an arrow hits its target.

"How many more days must we stay here?" Agung asks.

"Three or four. Why?"

He offers the eloquent shrug I now know so well. "I want to leave as soon as possible. These people are demons."

"It's proper for a man to kill his enemy," Dawut says. "How does eating him make it any worse? Once he's dead, he's not going to know."

"If you eat him, you eat his soul. Not even the worst enemy deserves that," Agung answers

"I've read that other cannibal tribes ate human flesh to possess the dead man's courage and strength," I offer. "The Korowai do eat their enemy, the *khakhua*, but as a kind of payback, and so they can't do it to possess their courage."

"I think it's simply their way to eat meat," says Dawut. "We Dani have many pigs and chickens. But you can see that the Korowai have few pigs and not many large animals. So they eat humans to gain strength from the meat."

"I don't care what the reason," Agung replies. "I'd let you cut my throat before you'd make me eat human flesh."

"You were here before," I venture, "and wanted to come back."

"Yes, I knew that they were cannibals, but I never talked to them much about it then. I enjoyed myself hunting with Agoos and being at a beetle grub feast. Your many questions to them have made the difference—even though I still like Agoos."

After lunch of chili rice I ponder on why the Korowai evolved as a cannibal culture. Was Dawut right? In the Bayaka and Amazon rainforests protein is plentiful from the meat of forest creatures. But the Korowai rainforests are mostly bare of large creatures with the exception of the cassowary, and Agoos had told me they rarely encounter the large flightless birds, which are hard to catch. The Korowai do keep pigs but they are mostly used for ceremonial purposes such as bride price. Could it really be that the cannibalism evolved from their human desire for protein? Probably not. Although eagerly anticipated, it seems cannibal feasts do not happen often; otherwise the Korowai would have disappeared a very long time ago. Over time they seem to have evolved a system where they indulge their taste for human flesh but understand, even subconsciously, that you cannot enjoy it too often.

But the Korowai cannibalism seems to stem more from their gruesome rationalization of death by disease combined with their obsession for payback. Death from an arrow or by falling out of a tree house is easy to understand. But death by invisible microbes? Over the centuries, perhaps even millennia, the Korowai seem to have solved this mystery by evolving a belief in the ghoulish *khakhua*.

In the sixth period of the day the rainforest echoes with the yodels of the warriors and women returning from their gardens. Except when there is a battle or beetle grub feast, the everyday rhythm of Korowai life is relentlessly uniform, and that night we relive the previous evening, eating, exchanging stories around the fire, and sleeping.

I wake with the musty smell of cooked sago warming my nostrils. The war chief and Agoos sit by the hearth eating breakfast.

"What do you most desire in life?" I ask the war chief. His rheumy eyes light up. "To be young and strong again, like Agoos, and to kill my enemies. But that can't be and so I'd most like a *laleo* ax. Korowai from Mbasman have shown me such axes. They possess great magic, they cut through trees many times faster than our stone axes."

"And you, Agoos?"

He looks across at the war chief, as if afraid to say what he is thinking. "To see villages like yours beyond our jungle."

Later that morning, in the third period of the day, Agung and I tag along with Agoos and Tinoos as they head for the rainforest. Keeping pace with us is a hungry-eyed hunting dog and the war chief's son, Limon, about four years of age, who carries a toy bow and several tiny arrows. At the edge of the clearing Agoos sends the unwilling child back to the tree house.

Crossing the creek over a slippery log bridge, we plunge into a rain-soaked thicket and for more than an hour we creep silently through the leafy labyrinth. Even with sneakers protecting my feet I wince as sharp stakes hidden in the soggy ground dig into them, but the Korowai don't flinch. As they pad through the trees, I see that two decades of jungle living have toughened their soles into a thick layer of callus that must be as hard as concrete. Agoos halts and points up at the canopy. A tribe of gossiping cockatoos perches high in a tree. In tandem the warriors yank back their bowstrings and let fly arrows that hurtle at the canopy. With a swish of wings, the cockatoos flee, squawking in fear. A single bird tumbles to the forest floor, skewered by Agoos's arrow, blood splattered across its creamy breast.

By midday they have potted three birds and a green snake, the serpent ferreted out from the undergrowth by the dog who detected its odor. But the greatest prize, a cassowary, has eluded us. The Korowai covet the giant flightless bird's meat for its taste and quantity. "Cassowary are very hard to find and we don't get one very often," says Agoos.

That night I spurn Dawut's rice and eat only Korowai food, manfully downing the charred sago but relishing the jungle parrot though with a twinge of guilt. When I was a boy I had a pet sulphur-crested cockatoo, Cocky, and he was one of my best friends.

Agoos reaches over and grips my arm, his eyes shining with friendship. "*Laleo*, what is your name?"

"Paul!"

"Powl! It's the strangest name I've ever heard. Like the cry of a bird." He smiles at the thought. "Powl! Powl! Powl!"

"Why have you waited several days to ask my name?"

"I thought you were a *khen-menng-abul* of your tribe. How else can you travel for many days to be with us, braving the Citak on the river? So I thought your name would be secret, and that if you told me I would die. But now I know that you're not a man who fights, but a man who talks. Your words are your weapons."

I grin at his acuity. Skewered! Stone Age man summing up with exquisite precision a Computer Age writer. "Tomorrow, we have a surprise for you, Powl. It's the time for a beetle grub feast."

Agung leans across the bamboo floor. "We're lucky. Few outsiders have seen the ceremony. Even I didn't know it was to happen until now."

Soon after sunrise the next day the war chief leads Agoos, Tinoos, and several other warriors to the clan's sago fields deep in the jungle, to collect food Korowai relish—beetle larvae—for the feast. Three months before they had chopped down several stout palms and bored holes in many places along the fallen trunks. Scarab beetles had laid eggs in the holes and now it was a simple matter of pulling out the grubs and wrapping them in banana leaves.

In the fifth period of the day, as the sun drifts towards the tree-line, the Korowai gather at a low hut, on the ground in the clearing about fifty yards long, fifteen wide, used only for beetle larvae ceremonies. Uttering sacred chants, the war chief uses wooden tongs to place river rocks the size of a shot put into a roaring fire, then places the first banana leaf package on top of them.

The pleasure of eating beetle larvae banishes for the moment any thought by Fuom of her tragic fate. The little girl, about to be taken away as a bride by the war chief of a nearby clan, smiles with delight as she plucks a live grub from one of the banana leaves and watches it wriggle. The creamy grub has pinprick black eyes and is about as long, and twice as plump, as her finger. She offers it to me and when I shake my head, looks puzzled. She pops it into her mouth and chews the grub with relish.

Agoos has gathered the naked warriors together, ten in all, and they race up and down the hut, growing more excited by the moment. *"Wa, Wa, Wa,"* they chant, loudly, gutturally, as they rattle their bows and arrows. War saturates every moment of Korowai life, even when they are celebrating at a feast.

A gust of steam rises from a banana leaf as the war chief lays it open to reveal a pile of cooked grubs, now a tangle of melted fawn flesh. He pulls out one and gives it to me. I chew and swallow the grub, keeping it in my mouth just long enough to taste its oily, nutty flavor. One is enough even though I could fill myself with the pile the war chief has collected.

On a low bamboo platform a mother suckles her sleepy-eyed baby as she sings a lullaby. "The grub feast binds us closer as Korowai, makes us strong. Always remember that you're a Korowai, my son. Never abandon our way of life."

The Korowai dance up and down the sacred hut until nightfall, chanting songs, eating grubs, then more grubs, happier than I had seen them at any other time. Later, at the tree house, the women watch from the other side as the warriors boast about their feats in battle and sing war songs. Midnight has long passed when we all fall asleep, nestled against each other for warmth.

Agoos shakes me gently, waking me from a deep sleep. The

smell of warm rice wafts up from below. Dawut is cooking breakfast. "*Manotropo*, Agoos." Agung squats beside me. "Agoos has just told me that the fierce man will come for Fuom this afternoon. He says it's best we're long gone by then because tempers will be red-hot and there might be trouble. Her father is still unhappy that Fuom has to marry, he believes she's too young, but he's afraid the fierce man will carry out his threat and kill him if he refuses."

Poor Fuom, I think as I climb down the pole from the tree house for the final time. She will not give birth for at least nine months, but even then it will be dangerous at her young age. With no doctor or medicine, she could die if anything goes wrong. I can only hope that she falls deeply in love with her fierce suitor and that she lives a long life and has plenty of children, and enjoys many beetle grub feasts.

At the fire I join Agung to squat and eat rice and sardines with a spoon. This time Agoos accepts a bowl of *laleo* food, but spurns the spoon and uses his fingers to scoop up the mixture. "Ghost demon food tastes good," he proclaims. After we finish eating, Fuom, Lali, the war chief, and Tinoos line up below the tree house to receive medical treatment. I had brought simple medication such as antiseptic Betadine and had conducted a clinic each morning, dabbing it onto their cuts and scrapes. This would be my last chance to help them.

I squirt the Betadine onto an ugly raw wound on Fuom's ankle. A simple scratch had become infected, ending as a swollen angry tropical ulcer, and the microbes had been eating into the flesh when I started treatment. Now the wound is healing. Most of the Korowai have ugly scars from tropical ulcers that could have been cured within days with Betadine. Their jungle is a paradise with a lot of nasty thorns.

I hand the last bottle to Fuom. "Put a small amount onto the wound each morning after you wake, and just before the sun sets. The ulcer should be gone in a few days."

"Tuck it under your skirt now, and hide it in the jungle in your new home so your husband doesn't know about it," Agoos advises Fuom. He turns to me. "If he sees that its magic is so powerful, he'll take it from her."

Agoos scurries up the tree house pole and returns with my camera bag. Handing it over, he looks shyly at me, as if he wants to say something but can't summon the courage. The bravest of the brave? What can he be afraid of saying?

"Take me with you to your village, Powl. I want to see how you live."

His soft-spoken request intrigues me. The journey could prove dangerous for him, he might be seduced by the outside world and never return to Lali, the war chief, and his tree house. But I want to get more medicine to his clan and this could be the way.

"If I take you, will you return?"

"Of course. Lali and I long to have children who will tell our names to their children. That way we will live forever. I just want to see what it looks like beyond Korowai land."

"Do you think we should take Agoos to Wamena, to fetch medicine for his people?" I ask Agung.

"Yes, of course. Why not?"

"He might be unhappy to return to the tree house after what he sees there."

"Paul, understand that their traditional life is fast coming to an end. In a few years they'll all be living like the Korowai in huts in Mbasman. So it won't hurt Agoos as long as he comes back. He can stay with me in Wamena and I'll make sure the MAF fly him back."

When Lali and the war chief learn of this epic journey, they accept it without complaint or tears, unlike the Dani who were deeply unhappy when they heard Dawut was travelling far to the south. Perhaps they don't know how far Agoos will travel from the treehouse, or that he must go by plane. Before leaving, I hug little Fuom and then farewell the war chief with a solemn handshake. Then I take a long last look at the tree house, this relic of our primeval past.

Agoos, clutching bow and arrows, leads the way across the clearing and into the jungle, followed by Dawut, Agung, and then me.

"Tinoos and two other warriors have gone ahead to guard us on our journey back to Mbasman, because an enemy clan might ambush us," Agung tells me.

Armed with bows and arrows, Tinoos and his comrades scout the way, keeping about two hundred yards ahead, to our left, right, and center. They stay in contact every ten minutes or so with high-pitched yodels. This time the trek is easier, as I am now practiced in crossing log bridges, waist-deep mud swamps, and other rainforest obstacles.

At the edge of the rainforest, in sight of Mbasman, I clasp each of the warriors in farewell. Tinoos typically remains silent, but he grips my arms and I feel the warmth of his friendship flow into me. The trees close in around the warriors as they trek back into their rainforest fortress. They turn for a final wave and are swallowed by the jungle.

Barnabas is surprised to learn that Agoos is coming with us to Wamena, but does not stop him. "It will be good for a Korowai to see modern life. Maybe he can then persuade the others to leave the jungle and settle here. But dress him properly because you could be in trouble if the police in Wamena see you have a Korowai with you."

Agung barters a few cans of sardines for a pair of pants and a T-shirt from one of the Mbasman-dwelling Korowai. Undressing is easy for Agoos. He unhooks the rattan midriff strips and unpeels the leaf covering his penile glans. He has no idea how to put on the pants and laughs as Agung and Dawut sit him on the ground and guide his legs through the openings.

"How does it feel?" I ask when he is clad in the pants and T-shirt.

"Like I'm covered in mud," he grins.

I feel a pang of ill ease. One moment he is a proud warrior, clad in the timeless regalia of his people, and then in the next moment he wears the cast-off rags of modern man, impoverished and stripped of his jungle manhood. Is this a glimpse of the Korowai future?

At mid-afternoon, after a wash and change of clothes, we walk down to the Ndeirum Kabur River with Barnabas to seek a dugout canoe to take us to Yaniruma, a Citak village like Mbasman with a dirt landing strip, where the Cessna will pick us up in a few days. The village chief hails a passing dugout, a long hollowed-out tree trunk, propelled by four tough-faced boatmen with poles.

"They are Citak," Agoos says in a low voice. His eyes narrow and focus hard on the boatmen, the same way as a cat's when it steadies itself to confront danger. "Headhunters!"

Agoos and the boatmen glare at each other, but the money I offer the Citak quells their malice, or so I believe. The excitement of the journey into the great unknown, and our presence, overcomes Agoos's fear of his tribe's traditional enemy.

"Be careful of the Citak," Barnabas warns. "They can be dangerous, but it's the only way you can get to Yaniruma."

Dawut puts his arm around Agoos. "Don't worry. If they cause trouble, they'll be sorry they did. You and I will fight them together."

The Citak are tall, slim, wiry river dwellers in their twenties. Battling the rain-swollen river, two stand upright at the front of the dugout, while the other two balance the rear as they thrust their poles into the river to push us forward a few yards each time. Agung, Dawut, Agoos, and I sit in the middle with our baggage. My backpack provides a makeshift backrest, lumpy but more comfortable than sitting upright for several hours.

As the dugout bucks and twists in the swirling river, Agoos's eyes widen in fear and he swivels a little from side to side as if seeking a way to escape. But he is surrounded by angry, white-capped water. He sits in front of me and I place a hand on his shoulder to calm him, and understanding the gesture, he smiles in gratitude.

"*Terima kasih, Powl*," he says.

Nearing dusk, we round a bend and see a tree house perched high by the side of the riverbank, the first sign of life since we left. A naked aging Korowai stands on the verandah. "You must be hungry," he shouts. "I have pig meat, come and eat."

His voice echoes eerily across the river. Something about him makes the hairs rise on the back of my neck, but I have not eaten meat for almost a week and relish his offer. "Let's go have some pork."

Agoos shakes his head. "I've never seen him before, but I fear he is a *khakhua*."

The Citak ignore the invitation, staring straight ahead as they swiftly pole by. A few moments later, the hut disappears into the trees as we round another bend. When darkness comes, they steer us to a mudflat edged against the riverbank. Here, I lay out my sleeping bag, and then we eat a dinner of cold rice and beans cooked by Dawut back at Agoos's tree-house clearing. Agoos downs his with gusto.

"I miss my sago, but I can get used to *laleo* food," he says with a grin.

"Why didn't we stop to eat the pork offered by the old Korowai man?" I ask a boatman.

His dark eyes widen in fear. "He's a powerful sorcerer. Anyone who has stopped to eat at his hut has never been seen again."

This is the fate I fear most when in a far-off place—disappearing without a trace, never to return home again. That would leave my family grieving for many years without ever knowing if I was dead or alive.

In eastern Afghanistan I was seriously wounded in a Taliban suicide bombing by a twelve-year-old boy. He was just five paces from me when he blew himself up. Twenty-three policemen and Special Forces with me were murdered, their bodies torn apart. Two soldiers standing by my shoulder were killed. I had three chunks of shrapnel embedded in my brain and ten in my torso and it took me a full year to recover. They are still there. I find it eerie that the Taliban shrapnel will be with me forever, even in the grave.

I have never suffered post traumatic stress disorder, probably because the shrapnel knocked me out so that I did not witness the carnage. I only regained consciousness a day later in the intensive care ward at the American military hospital near Kabul. The American Air Force saved my life, swiftly evacuating me in a zipped-up body bag by medical chopper.

I would much prefer to come home from Afghanistan in a coffin so that my wife and daughter could visit my grave from time to time than disappear along the Ndeirum Kabur River, last seen departing Mbasman in the Citak dugout. But, of course, we are not usually given the choice of how we depart from life and so every time I go out on the road my family and I never know if I will return.

That night Agoos curls up on the mudflat, nestled against Dawut, a few yards from the Citak. "I don't trust them," he whispers. "I know they want to take my head, but dare not because you're with me."

At mid-afternoon the next day, with no village in sight, the Citak nudge the dugout against the riverbank. They put down their poles and one of them snarls something to Agung, his voice rough and threatening. "We're still several hours from Yaniruma," Agung tells me with a frown, "but the boatmen refuse to go any farther until I double their payment. There's no way we can reach the village ourselves. The land is very swampy here."

This is blackmail, but we have no choice. As I reach for my

moneybag, Dawut suddenly grabs a pole and swings it at the head of one of the Citak, deliberately missing by a few inches. "Next time, I'll squash your head like a pumpkin unless you start poling again," our Dani warrior threatens in Bahasa Indonesia.

The Citak murmur angrily in their language. "Keep your mouths shut until we get to Yaniruma, or you'll regret it," Dawut warns. "Now, three of you pick up your poles and get us back on the river."

The fourth boatman sits captive in the middle with us while Dawut stands at the rear of the dugout, holding the pole in the air, ready to carry out his threat. Agoos stares back at the Dani with admiring eyes. "You are truly a man," he says.

We wait three days at Yaniruma, a riverside village of government-built wooden huts settled mostly by Christian Citak. A small airstrip by the side of the river serves the mission. The time passes swiftly as I transcribe our conversations recorded on several tapes and pore over my notes collected in spiral pads stained by the occasional splash of chili sauce and river water.

Because there are so many Citak, Agoos refuses to go outside the hut we are staying in without Dawut to accompany him. The tall Dani and the diminutive Korowai hold hands, highland style, on their walks down to the river and to look at the airstrip. Ours is the only plane scheduled to land there over the following fortnight.

Clearly uncomfortable, Agoos constantly tugs at his shirt and pants and asks to take off the clothes. As I witnessed, a Korowai male is easily dressed, needing just to pluck a leaf from the nearest tree to wrap about his penis. Agung refuses permission. "You must get used to *laleo* clothes for our trip to Wamena," he says.

On the night before our departure, as we eat our by now monotonous dinner of rice, sardines, and chili, I ask Agoos: "Are you afraid of flying in a plane?"

"Yes! When I was a small boy, we were all very frightened when we saw a plane for the first time passing over our tree house. We thought it was a giant bird, and a man jumped out of the tree house thinking it was going to attack us. He died. But, now, we sometimes see planes in the sky and we know people are in them, though we don't understand how they can fly like birds."

"Then why are you willing to come with us in a plane to Wamena tomorrow?"

Agoos fixes me with a look that mingles intelligence with intense curiosity. "To see your village, Powl."

The next day the Cessna arrives on time at mid-morning. Bill Wilson is our pilot once more. "So, my prayers worked," he says. "Welcome back."

"Meet my Korowai friend, Agoos!"

As Dawut and Agung load our gear into the plane, including Agoos's bow and arrows, Bill stares at the diminutive figure standing next to me in long pants and T-shirt.

"A Korowai? You're kidding!"

"It's true. He's coming to Wamena with us to pick up medicine for his tree house. Then I'll arrange for the MAF to fly him back here."

"That is something special. When he's ready, I'll make sure he gets back to Yaniruma and have the headman there get him upriver to his village."

"Thanks, mate. I'll give Agung the money to pay for his fare home."

Like a true warrior, Agoos confronts his fear by bracing his shoulders and glaring at the plane as he enters it. He stacks his bow and arrows behind the back seats. The Cessna roars up from the dirt strip, banks left over the river and heads across Korowai country.

Below, the rainforest canopy looks like a vast field of broccoli. Several minutes into the flight, over unpacified Korowai territory, the jungle parts to reveal a clearing with two tree houses. The village looks deserted.

"They heard us coming and have hidden," says Agoos. "The Korowai here hate *laleo*."

Agoos spends the journey staring out the window, absorbed by a high-flying eagle's eye view of the rainforest at first and then by the giant mountains. He looks calm, but his hands grip the seat all the way to Wamena. As we taxi to the small terminal, he points to a jet loading passengers for Jayapura. "That's the biggest bird I've ever seen," he says with a grin. "And, look, it eats people."

He grasps my hand as we walk across the tarmac. Does he seek to bolster his courage with the help of the *laleo* now that he is about to encounter a way of life that neither he nor any of his people could ever imagine? I had journeyed far back in a time machine to be with Agoos and his village, and it is his turn, only now the machine is about to fast-forward him 10,000 years.

Even though Wamena itself is a village when compared with London or Sydney, it is still millennia beyond the Korowai tree houses. As Agoos tightens his grip on my hand, rarely have I been so moved, and rarely in a lifetime of adventure with meaning have I ever approached such a dramatic moment.

John Wolff has sent the hotel LandCruiser to meet us. Agoos grips his bow and arrows and walks around it, shaking his head and muttering in Korowai. It is the first rime he has seen a car and he cautiously touches the bonnet, then a door, and then a tire. "What is this thing?" he asks.

Agoos jumps back, startled, as Agung opens the passenger door. "It's like the plane, a small hut that moves, only it travels along the ground and much faster than you can run," he says.

This warrior from a far-off time peers at the LandCruiser as if it is a strange and threatening creature. I am surprised because he was less troubled by the plane. Dawut opens the back door, gets in, and leans over to take Agoos's hand. "Trust me, friend," he says, drawing the Korowai into the car. Dawut places the bow and arrows in the back.

Agoos settles uneasily on the seat. "This is like sitting on a rotten tree trunk," he says with an uneasy smile. When the car engine starts with a roar, his eyes widen. Dawut leans across to put his broad arm around the Korowai's slim muscled shoulders. But once the car picks up speed, Agoos begins to smile. "I like this, but it would be no good in the jungle," he says. "Too many trees."

The streets are thronged with naked Dani. Agoos stares in astonishment at the men with their erect *koteka* and at the wide-hipped, big-breasted women who are much plumper than the Korowai females.

"Do you have any of those girls here who trade you sex?" he asks Dawut.

"Yes. A girl might trade a night with her for your bow and arrows. She can sell them in the market for a good price."

"Not my bow and arrows. I wouldn't trade them for anything.

Anyway, I was only asking. Lali would be unhappy if I had sex with another girl."

Agoos points to several Dani men holding hands as they walk along the dirt footpath. "Are they from your people?" he asks Dawut.

"Yes! They're Dani, like me."

"I didn't know you Dani were so big," he says, patting Dawut's thigh. "But why do your warriors cover their penis? Are you ashamed to show it to your women?"

Dawut starts to laugh, his broad chest shaking. "No, my friend. We wear it to show our women how big we wish to be. But they know we're smaller."

"I'm glad to hear that. And I'm happy you didn't wear that thing at my tree house. You'd have frightened our women."

As the LandCruiser passes through town, Agoos turns from side to side, confronted at each moment by miraculous new sights. This is the first time he has seen large buildings, cars, bicycles, glass windows, petrol stations, shops, and yet he does not seem overwhelmed. The distance in his own mind that he must travel between the Stone Age and this twenty-first-century town must be less than I expected.

It could also be that because he doesn't understand what these strange objects are, for the moment he wisely chooses to ignore them. He points to the market as we pass by. "These huts are bigger than any I've ever seen, Powl, but you told me of huts many times taller than the tallest trees. Where are they?"

"They're in my land, far away. You must travel in a big plane from morning until evening to get there. Here, the villages are much smaller."

Agoos snorts in disbelief "I'll believe you, Powl, when I see such huts."

We cross the bridge over the surging Baliem River and head along the valley. Tidy rows of sweet potatoes and clumps of banana trees ripple back to the hills, fed with river water by irrigation ditches. Agoos, a Lord of the Korowai gardens, casts his expert eye over the Dani fields. "Your gardens are well made," he says to Dawut. "You Dani must work very hard."

The LandCruiser roars down the road on the way to Dawut's village with Agoos gripping the door handle as he peers at the mountains.

Until the plane ride he had never seen anything taller than the highest tree in his rainforest. From the air, the mountains looked like bumps in the land, but now they soar over us, nudging the sky, more than a hundred times higher than the jungle giants.

Wispy white clouds float across the valley as the car follows the road, weaving between the well-tended fields. Ahead, a black cow grazes on the sweet grass by the side of the road. "Please stop next to the cow," I ask Agung.

Agung pulls up on the opposite side of the road, and Dawut opens the door to let Agoos out. With the sun blocked from view, a chilly wind sweeps through the valley and this man of the tropical rainforest shivers from the cold. He does not see the cow and smiles broadly at the Dani, grateful to be released from the captivity of the moving hut. Agung takes his shoulders and turns him in the direction of the cow.

"Look at that creature," he says. "We drink its milk and eat its flesh."

I thought Agoos would be fascinated by the cow, but instead his nostrils flare as he peers at it with a stunned expression. He looks as if he is trying to comprehend its enormous size, and then he begins to tremble in alarm. "It will eat me," he cries.

Dawut, standing by him, grips Agoos's hand. "No, my friend, it's harmless. Let's go closer and I'll show you."

Agoos pushes the Dani's hand aside and crouches behind the LandCruiser. "It will eat me," he cries again.

This is by far the largest mammal he has ever seen, far bigger than a forest pig. I would have acted much the same stumbling on a living dinosaur and knowing nothing of its habits. No one could convince me that the enormous creature was harmless. And so I feel ashamed that I didn't think of the powerful emotions such an astonishing sight would evoke in Agoos when I stopped the car.

Dawut grips Agoos's hand again. "It won't hurt you, I promise. It's harmless."

Agoos once again yanks his hand free, but now his eyes are burning and his lips are tight. "I'll get my bow and kill it," he cries.

Dawut smiles at his bravery. "If you kill it, the Dani who owns it will come looking for you, to kill you."

"We'd better leave, this is getting dangerous," I say to Agung.

The LandCruiser pulls away from the cow, still grazing on the roadside grass, with Agoos deliberately looking in the opposite direction, his eyes still dilated with that warrior's fusion of fear and bravado.

We reach Dawut's village twenty minutes later. Agoos reaches for his bow and arrows in the back of the car, but Dawut guides him out of the car without them. "You're safe in my village," he says.

A Dani man sees us striding toward the huts and shouts a greeting. By the time we reach the stockade with its knee-high entry step, Dawut's parents, brother, wife, two sisters, cousins, aunts, and uncles are all gathered in the clearing outside their huts.

His father, Jaja, clasps Dawut tight against his body as tears stream down his face. "You've been gone too long, we thought the Korowai had eaten you. We thought your bones were lost to us forever." The elderly war chief turns to me with arms outstretched. "Thank you, *orang putih*, white man, for bringing my son home safely."

Jaja peers at Agoos in his ragged shirt and pants. At first glance he must look like many of the outsiders who drift about in Wamena's streets, men come from tribes all over the country to do the servile work of the Indonesian masters, tasks too groveling for the proud warrior Dani. But there is something else about him that catches the war chief's attention.

Dawut gestures to Agoos. "This is my friend, Agoos."

Jaja towers over the diminutive Korowai. "Agoos, you are welcome in our village."

"He's a Korowai, father."

The old man pulls back as if he has been slapped in the face. "A Korowai, a man who eats humans?"

Horror throbs in the eyes of this hero of dozens of battles, this man raised to be a war chief in a warriors' society. The word spreads among the Dani. "Korowai!" they murmur in dread as they back away from Agoos.

I had not expected the Dani to show alarm before a lone outsider, especially inside the safety of their own stockade. But the human fear of cannibalism is so vivid, so etched into our minds, that even the bravest of the brave Dani cringe before a man known to eat humans.

Agoos smiles in triumph as he watches Jaja and the Dani retreat, but keeps silent. Despite his friendship with Dawut, he too has been raised to fight to the death and he must enjoy seeing the warriors of a strange tribe, men much bigger than he, tremble before the power of his presence. It is that commanding blend of charisma, machismo, and bravado that another warrior society, the Polynesians, call a war leader's *mana*.

"Father, he's my friend, he won't hurt you, please make him welcome," Dawut pleads.

Jaja snarls something in Dani which Agung cannot understand and then leads the men into the largest hut. The women disappear into their smaller huts. We stand alone in the clearing. I know the men keep their axes and bows and arrows stacked in their communal hut. "Are they going to attack Agoos?" I ask Dawut.

"If l weren't here, they'd kill him, even though they're scared of him for being a cannibal. But he's my friend and he'll be safe. They won't come out until we're gone, and so it's best we leave."

It is mid-afternoon by the time we return to Wamena. Agoos is tired and asks to sleep in my hotel room, much as I had once asked to sleep in his tree house. I offer him one of the twin beds, but he spurns its soft mattress, preferring to curl up on the floor. In a few moments he is asleep, bow and arrows by his side.

Dawut stays with him while Agung and I go to a clinic to buy several cartons of medicine for the tree house clan—large bottles of Betadine, packets of aspirin, boxes of Band-aids, and tubes of ointment for various ailments. "I'll bring Agoos here tomorrow and have the medic show him how to use the medicine," Agung promises. "He'll be the doctor for his people. And next time I go to his tree house I'll take more medicine."

A day later, at the MAF office by the airstrip, I pay for Agoos's return flight to Yaniruma. I also change $200 into rupiah to give to Agung for Agoos's living expenses at Wamena, and for any gifts he wants to take back to his tree house, including a ghost demon ax for the war chief.

At night, before dinner, I call home from this remote valley stronghold through the sorcery of international direct dialing. My daughter, Cathy, answers the phone. I describe my time with the Korowai and tell her how friendly they were, especially Agoos, because without his help my enthralling journey far back in time would not have taken place.

"Cathy, say hello to Agoos, my friend."

Agoos grasps the phone and listens to the strange words that pass the lips of my daughter in distant Sydney, bounce off a satellite in outer space, and reform in Wamena. He has seen so many astonishing miracles on this day, and so the idea that he can speak to another human far away by holding a strangely shaped chunk of black rock-like material, a phone, does not faze him.

I had practiced the greeting with him as we returned from Dawut's village. With a smile, Agoos says, "Gut avning, Karrie!"

Later, we visit the tin-shed cinema and again Agoos accepts without question another miracle, the magic of film, seeing humans several times life-size love, hate, laugh, and kill. "Rambo III" is still playing, and Agoos bounces up and down in the seat with excitement as horses, cars, and helicopters thunder across the screen. Although the idea of guns and bullets baffles him, his eyes shine with delight as Sylvester Stallone, the *khen-menng-abul*, or fierce man of action movies, mows down the villains. It is obvious that Agoos knows who the hero is and who the desperadoes are.

That night, when we return to the hotel, Agoos must be as exhausted mentally as I was after the war chief had talked to me of cannibalism, and he falls asleep on the floor in my room. Agung takes the second bed while Dawut sleeps by Agoos.

The following morning mist drifts across the valley as we drive to the airport. I have given Agoos my jumper to ward off the mountain air, but even in the cold he still prefers to go barefoot. Once again I am flying with Pirate Airlines and the pilot, Tommy, waves as he boards the plane.

Agung and Dawut wish me farewell, and then it is the turn of Agoos. "We've known each other for a short time, but you'll be my friend forever," I tell him.

Agoos grips my arm, and thrusts his bow and arrows at me. I shake my head. "I can't take them. They're too important to you."

"I'll be safe here, because Dawut will protect me. When I return home I'll make another bow and more arrows. I give them to you, Powl, because, far away in your land, each time you look at them you'll think of me." (As I write this I look at the bow and arrows nestled against the wall by the window in my study. My heart warms once more at the fond memory of my cannibal friend.)

Words of thanks catch in my throat. My eyes meet Agoos's and what passes silently between us is an understanding, much like I felt for Wasse in distant Africa, that, though we may never meet again, the friendship bond we have forged across the millennia will never be broken. Tears shine in my eyes and there is a rock in my throat as I cross the tarmac and climb the stairs to the jet.

I turn for a final wave to my companions in high adventure and enter the plane. I am the only passenger once more, but I turn down Tommy's invitation to sit in the cockpit jump seat, preferring to stay in the cabin, alone with my thoughts.

As the jet vaults the high mountains surrounding the Grand Valley and heads across the rainforests for Jayapura, I grapple with a dilemma that has been nagging me since my first day with the tree people. Should the outside world lobby hard to let the Korowai keep their special way of life, with all its cruelty, keeping them bottled up as Stone Age curiosities, a living anthropological museum? Or should we shun the temptation to quarantine the tribe from the twenty-first century?

Ultimately, these are futile questions, because the Korowai's fate will be decided far away in Jakarta. Soon enough, as Ginol, their supreme god, prophesied at the dawn of their time, the bulldozers will rumble through the jungles to tear down their cherished trees, demolish their beloved sago gardens, and destroy their unique world. Expelled from their rainforest home, any daughters that Agoos and Lali might have could be sold by sex slave traders as exotic attractions to brothels in Jayapura, while their sons might scramble for work in Wamena as taxi drivers and pimps. It has happened to countless tribes in Indonesia, and it will be difficult but not impossible for the Korowai to escape such a fate.

If the Lords of the Garden resist with their bows and arrows the ghost demons' invasion, the soldiers will shoot them down, as they have shot down so many other defiant tribes across the archipelago. For the greater glory of the nation, and the bank accounts of the generals and politicians with the timber concessions, some time in the next few years the Indonesians will drag the tree people out of the Stone Age and into this new millennium whether they like it or not.

SECTION THREE:

WITH THE STONE-AGE KORUBO IN THE AMAZON

CHAPTER 10

The Amazon Korubo beckon.

In stark contrast to the Indonesian policy towards the remote Papuan tribes such as the Korowai, the Brazilian government has quarantined their tribes from another time in 11 percent of the country's immense territory, mostly remote rainforests carved up by winding muddy tributaries of the Amazon. The government vigilantly guards these tribes, shielding them from the outside world and even deliberately shunning contact with all but a few of their people so as not to "infect" them with modern ways.

The tribes are said to go about entirely naked, are very aggressive, and live in communal huts in rainforest clearings. Like the Korowai, they make fire by rubbing sticks together, use only rainforest plants for medicine, but they hunt with blowguns as well as bows and arrows. They are warrior tribes, constantly at war with each other, mostly using blowguns armed with poison darts to silently kill enemies and brutally murder outsiders who dare enter their traditional lands.

Because of the extreme violence and a desire to keep their ancient hunter and gatherer cultures pure for as long as possible, the Brazilian government allows very few outsiders to enter this feisty and intriguing Amazon Garden of Eden. The gatekeeper, Sydney Possuelo, is truly the last of history's great explorers, a veteran Indian tracker, director of the isolated Indians department in Funai, *Fondacao Nacional Do Indio*, the Brazilian government's Indian Agency. The UN has honored him for his protection of these tribes, and *Time* magazine declared him a "Hero of the Planet."

When I phone him at his home in Brasilia, the nation's capital, Sydney agrees to take me with him on an expedition, time travelling back thousands of years, but warns to be patient until he contacts me again. Six months later Sydney emails, asking me to be in Tabatinga in far western Brazil at the end of that week. He is making a rare visit to a Stone Age clan in one of the forbidden territories under his control, a tangle of dense rainforest and winding rivers nudging the Peruvian border.

"The other Indians call the clan Korubo, which means head bashers because they use heavy clubs in warfare," he tells me over the phone. "They are the most violent Indians I've ever encountered, and they murdered one of my colleagues. They recently caught three white men by the river, bashed their heads to pulp, and gutted them. Do you still want to come? A trip like this is always risky."

"See you in Tabatinga on Saturday," I reply.

This is what I am always seeking, journeying to a remote place where people have lived for centuries, even millennia, with few outsiders allowed into their rainforests or brave enough to go, whether it be with the Amazon Indians or a mountain fastness shielding a Tibetan hermit kingdom or riding a bull camel through a scorching desert with the nomadic Tuareg. Their ancient lifestyles are largely and sometimes completely unchanged by the outside world. Again and again this gives me glimpses into the enormous diversity by which humans across the globe have evolved.

I tell Sydney that I am intrigued to discover what differences and similarities I will find between the Korowai, Pygmies, and the Korubo, given that they evolved culturally over thousands of years in rainforests cut off from the outside world. Do the Korubo make fire with sticks like the Korowai? Do they go about naked? Do the Korubo have gods and spirits like the Korowai and the Pygmies? Do they use the same weapons? Are the women dominant, equal, or subservient to the men? I hope to answer these and many other questions.

Whenever I pass through Los Angeles, I break my journey to visit a long-time friend, Alvin Toffler. He wrote the classic, *Future Shock*, a multi-million-selling book detailing how humans handled the rapid and extreme technological advancements in the twentieth century, and predicted, so far accurately, the vast changes we can expect in our lives in the twenty-first century. He followed that book with *The Third Wave*, a seminal work that separated human development into the first wave, agricultural revolution; the second wave, industrial revolution; and the current third wave, technological revolution. That places the Korubo a touch this side of the Creation.

He is intrigued by my latest journey to a tribe in the Amazon still living in the Stone Age. "It's wrong, the government should bring these tribes into the twenty-first century as soon as possible so they can share all the advances that humans have made, especially in education and health," Al says. He shakes his handsome leonine head, baffled that Brazil does not see how it is discriminating against the remote tribes by keeping them ignorant of several thousand years of human progress.

"Their children should go to school and they should have the benefit of modern medicine, using modern drugs to fight off disease instead of dying young."

It is not that simple, I explain. "What about the serious problems facing the Australian Aborigines, the Inuit, and even Amazon Indians who've been devastated by alcoholism, poverty, and malnutrition since they were brought into the modern world not so long ago?" I ask Al. "I've seen it firsthand. The clash of vastly different cultures is almost always destructive, especially when one is far superior in technology. The tribes often suffer a morale implosion.

"Imagine that, without warning, Martians arrive on earth. They have vastly superior technology, including astonishingly destructive weapons, and they herd us into concentration camps, keeping us behind barbed wire, and then enslaving us. They force us to abandon forever our languages and speak only theirs, and abandon forever our religions, forced to practice whatever is the Martian religion. I think we would also suffer a morale implosion that would take us generations to get over."

"Good point," says Al. "I know it's not an easy solution I'm suggesting. There's obviously going to be considerable social and cultural disruption but, if nothing else, they'll be eating healthier food, have modern medicine, and so they and their children will live much longer and be happier."

I am not so sure, having spent months in Australia's tribal lands. I became heart-sore at seeing Aboriginal clans still grappling with the immense social and cultural problems caused by the catastrophic collapse in their collective morale when confronted, more than a century ago, by pale-skinned strangers with their magical weapons, technology, and even food.

I have also seen firsthand the same social and cultural chaos, alcoholism, and high murder and suicide rates among the Arctic Circle's Inuit. The culture clash is still destroying their lives a century after the white men entered their icy lands.

The journey from Los Angeles to Manaus, capital of Amazonas State, takes all day and half the night, a milk run down Central America to the top of South America. Brazil is enormous, the world's fifth largest nation, and occupies almost half of South America, from the Andes in the west to the Atlantic in the east. Just after midnight we touch down in Manaus in the far west; I doze for the remainder of the night stretched out on a wooden bench in the waiting lounge with my camera bag as a lumpy pillow. I had been told that it was dangerous to take a taxi from the airport so late at night, as the chances of being robbed by the driver are high.

I am stopping over for a day to see a city that had a massive influence on the future of the Amazon Indians. In the late nineteenth century the rubber barons who lived in Manaus were some of the world's richest people when the Amazon had the world monopoly of rubber. At the time, the Western world was industrializing at a frenzied speed and vulcanized rubber was an essential ingredient in most modern machinery.

It took more than three centuries for Europeans in the Amazon to harness rubber. The Portuguese navigator Pedro Alvares Cabral was the first European to set eyes on what became known as Brazil in 1500 CE. A stampede of explorers followed, hoping to find and exploit the legendary native monarch, El Dorado, the Gilded Man, whose kingdom was so rich in gold that he daily decorated himself with gold dust.

In tow were hordes of "the soldiers of God," the Jesuit missionary priests.

They were confronted by an horrific gauntlet of life-threatening diseases—beri-beri, malaria, fever, and terrifying man-eating creatures—anacondas, crocodiles, piranhas—as well as tribes as ferocious as any on earth. Many newcomers were killed by Indians resisting the invasion of their land. A fifth of the Jesuit missionaries, brave men who ventured to the most remote outposts in what became Brazil, were never seen again.

Manaus, just over 900 miles upriver from the ocean, was first settled by the Portuguese in the sixteenth century, but remained a small river town until the rubber boom exploded in the mid-nineteenth century. Rubber, also known as latex, is the creamy sap from the *Hevea brasiliensis* tree, indigenous to the Amazon and growing wild in the jungle. It was initially of little use because the latex became brittle and thus unusable at high or low temperatures.

Then in 1843 American Charles Goodyear invented a chemical process to produce vulcanized rubber that remained elastic at high and low temperatures. The discovery coincided with the Industrial Revolution, and rubber became an essential material. It was used to seal gaps in machines, as O-rings, conveyor systems, and hundreds more uses. Goodyear made his fortune when he made tires from rubber.

The Manaus rubber barons had a virtual world monopoly on rubber for several decades and the city prospered with them. Author Lucien Bodard described it as: "the Babylon, the Sodom, and the Paris of the borracha (the rubber people), all in one. Manaus was the supreme society of injustice, the city of high life where billionaires behaved in a way that they would never have dared to anywhere else, even in those days."

By 1879, 10,000 tons of high-priced rubber was being exported yearly to the markets of Europe and North America. Historian Robin Furneaux described Manaus and the rubber barons as: "one of the gaudiest cities in the world. If one rubber baron bought a vast yacht, another would install a tame lion in his villa, and a third would water his horse in champagne."

The wealthiest families even sent their linen by steamer to Portugal to be laundered, believing, snobbishly, that the local water was too muddy for them to use the local washerwomen or their servants.

While Manaus lived it up, indigenous tribes in the Amazon suffered horribly. In acknowledging past abuses, including slavery, in 1755 the Portuguese king issued a law that, "restored to the Indians (of the Amazon Basin) the liberty of their persons, goods and commerce."

Far from the king's grasp, the rubber barons took no notice of the law. Gathering rubber is highly labor-intensive. Each rubber tree is tapped daily with a sharp knife, producing a small amount of a milky liquid that solidifies into rubber. So, they needed a vast workforce of tappers. With the feared firepower of his private army, one rubber plantation owner rounded up more than 50,000 Indians to work as virtual slaves for him. Those who rebelled were put in stocks, tortured, castrated, and even murdered as a warning to the other Indians.

Author Wade Davis, in *One River*, wrote: "The horrendous atrocities that were unleashed on the Indian people of the Amazon during the height of the rubber boom were like nothing that had been seen since the first days of the Spanish Conquest." This pushed many tribes to the edge of extinction.

The savage assaults on the Amazon's indigenous people was not confined to the rubber barons and their era. In *Massacre in the Amazon*, Lucien Bodard wrote that in later years "the Brazilian government itself condemned the massacres. Its main accusations: genocide, the liquidation of entire tribes, machine gunning from the air, epidemics touched off by presents of clothing deliberately infected with germs, gifts of poisoned food, candy containing arsenic given to children. There were more accusations of bestial tortures, of the survivors being reduced to slavery, sexual perversions, and prostitution of the women, of theft of Indian territory."

The Indians also perished in huge numbers, having no genetic resistance to European-introduced diseases such as tuberculosis, smallpox, influenza, and measles. The Brazilian naturalist Alexandre Rodrigues Ferreira wrote that "There used to be ample Indians one sees in places on that river that were once inhabited by innumerable heathen but that now show no signs of life beyond the bones of bodies of the dead. And those who escaped the contagion did not escape captivity as slaves of the colonialists."

The rubber boom in the Amazon did not last long. In 1876, Henry Wickham, a British planter, smuggled out of the Amazon 70,000 rubber tree pods and presented them to the Kew Botanical Gardens near London. Botanists there produced a hardy hybrid rubber tree and offered its seeds to planters in the British colonies of Malaya, Singapore, and Sri Lanka (then known as Ceylon), where tappers were paid a pittance. The end of the monopoly devastated the Amazon rubber plantations. In 1910 Brazil still had more than 50 percent of the rubber market, but by 1940 it had plunged to just 1.3 percent.

Despite this, Manaus today remains a thriving city with more than 2.5 million people. In the morning, after stashing my luggage in a hotel in the city center, I walk along the waterside to visit the fish market built in 1883. It has stained glass windows and the framework was designed by Gustave Eiffel and constructed in the same Parisian workshop where his Eiffel Tower was also built. The market stretches along the waterfront and hundreds of traders, calling out their wares, offer a bewildering variety of marine creatures of all shapes, sizes, and colors.

Nearby is the Italian Renaissance-style Teatro Amazonas, a place I longed to visit since reading about it when I was a teenager. Located on a nondescript city street, its curved driveway, lined with rubber to smooth the ride of the city elites in their carriages, leads up to the opera house. Legend has it that the rubber barons financed the building of the opera house to entice Enrico Caruso, the Pavarotti of his time, to make the long sea journey from Italy to sing the lead in *La Gioconda* at the opening in 1896. No solid evidence exists that he accepted.

The interior is impressive. Only the best would do for the rubber barons. The finest Carrara marble was imported from Italy for the columns, stairs, and statues; the steel walls came from Scotland; the roofing tiles from Alsace in Germany; and an Italian artist came to Manaus to paint the ceiling. Italy also provided the theatre's 198 chandeliers, with many made from Venice's famed Murano glass.

The following morning I leave for Tabatinga, where I will meet Sydney Possuelo. My first view of the Amazon from the air comes just after takeoff as the turbo-prop banks over the massive river where it nudges Manaus. A very wide stretch of muddy water split down the middle extends for as far as I can see. On one side is the black River

Negro, its dramatic hue caused by a lack of silt, and on the other is the rust-colored Solimoes. Both are Amazon tributaries that flow together for about eighteen miles downriver without mingling. From the air the Amazon looks sluggish, an enormous black-backed, rusty-bellied sloth crawling slowly across an immense jungle.

This mighty river, four thousand miles long, emerges from a tiny spring about five inches wide in the grasslands of Peru's Andes and cuts its way from headwaters tumbling from snowy mountains into the sea at the Atlantic Coast. It provides about one fifth of all the fresh water discharged into the world's oceans, with its flow twelve times more abundant than the Mississippi's, and five times the Congo's. Its thrust is so powerful that fresh water from the Amazon can be found more than seventy miles out to sea.

This glimpse of the Amazon River is brief, tantalizing. Then we are over the jungle, vast, impenetrable, mysterious, that flows beneath the plane with no hint of habitation until we make our approach over the great river once more, touching down at Tabatinga two hours later. Here, two thousand miles northwest of Rio de Janeiro, a tangle of islands and sloping mud banks shaped by the powerful Amazon form the joined borders of Brazil, Colombia, and Peru.

Tabatinga is the wild west of Brazil, its most western town, and muscled soldiers in tightly cut jungle-green uniforms, barefoot Indians in ragged clothing, long-legged schoolgirls, and sad-eyed skeletal dogs fill a windy, dusty main street. It is dotted with outdoor barbecue cafes, each with a few tattered seats and tables perched by grease-splattered grills. The air smells of rotting fruit and gasoline.

Sydney Possuelo asked me to stay at the small Hotel Tukana, named after the local Indian tribe. To reach the room you walk a gauntlet along a narrow, dark, claustrophobic corridor lined with life-size, life-like carvings of forest creatures in vivid acrylic color. A huge anaconda strikes at prey; a jaguar is ready to pounce; an eagle spreads its wings; a dolphin is in mid leap. Heavy drinkers book a room here at their peril. A guest coming back drunk late at night and confronted by this menagerie might think the world has turned topsy-turvy with wild animals on the loose, and run screaming into the night.

I hail a motorbike taxi outside the hotel, my destination the Funai office, and grit my teeth as the bike bounces over the many potholes, jarring my spine. A couple of mud-splattered LandCruisers are parked outside its headquarters, a warren of poky offices stacked with blow-guns, bows and arrows, and sacks of rice.

Blowguns armed with long poison darts are the most common weapons used by Amazon warriors for millennia in warfare and in hunting monkeys, birds, and other creatures. Famed British naturalist Alfred Russel Wallace had Indians use blowguns to bring down birds he needed for his studies in the Amazon. Wallace was a co-discoverer along with Charles Darwin of the theory of natural selection as the main agent of the evolution of species.

He found the Indians extremely accurate. In his book, *Narrative of Travels in the Amazon and Rio Negro,* published in 1884, Wallace wrote: "One or two of them (Indians) had blowguns and shot numbers of birds for me . . . When I fired, as was often the case, the bird flew away wounded and fell far off in the forest."

Hunched over a computer in the Funai office is regional com-mander, Armando Soares, slim, in his late thirties but already gray-haired. Life on the frontier with warring Indians and settlers is obviously wearing on the body but not on the spirit because his craggy, handsome face sports a wide smile. After graduating from high school, Sydney Possuelo, at the age of twenty, began as a trainee *sertanista*, literally meaning a man of the jungle, an old-style Indian tracker, who learned his trade on the job. Armando, however, is a new-style Indian specialist, having earned a degree in anthropology before he joined Funai.

"Sydney is not an easy man to deal with, he's tempestuous and mercurial, but he knows the Indians much better than anyone else in Brazil," Armando tells me. "He loves them and is deeply committed to saving them and their unique cultures. If not for him, scores of Indian tribes would have been destroyed, disappeared, defeated by disease or guns. He's a legend all over the country and I feel privileged to work with him."

"What impelled you to become a modern-day *sertanista*?"

"Like Sydney, I wanted to be in the rainforests with the Indians. My brother works in a bank and I've seem him begin to grow old and lose his zest for life because of it. One month in every two I'm out in the rainforests with the Indians. It's tough and dangerous but it's exciting and rewarding. I see many things other people will never. Most of all I'm helping the Indians keep their traditional way of life. As you can see in Tabatinga, once they lose that they are lost, unable to return to their old lives and unable to understand ours."

On the walls of Armando's office are photos of the Korubo, a small, stocky people, entirely naked, sitting outside a communal straw hut. "The Korubo are very violent, highly aggressive," Armando explains. "They hate whites because they've been attacked many times over the decades. Before the whites set up a base, the whites would shoot them on sight and burn their huts, treating them as vermin."

This is a frontier region with much history of confrontation between whites and Indians, and between Indians and Indians. "We're visiting a small Korubo clan we've made contact with by necessity, but even though we know them, we never relax our vigilance when we're with them. If something upsets them, they could smash your head in with a war club at the blink of an eye. The trouble is that we know so little about them and so we're not sure what upsets them."

Armando says there is a long history of whites marching into Indian lands across Brazil over the centuries and seizing them for human habitation or pasture with the federal government's full backing. "Wherever there were Indians settled, probably for many centuries, the whites called these lands uninhabited and claimed them for their own. If the Indians resisted, soldiers and settlers killed them or drove them off the land."

"We had something similar in colonial Australia, a law called terra nullius," I say.

"That's Latin and means the land belonged to nobody. How convenient."

"The Aborigines had their own land rights' system, but because they were nomads this gave the colonialists the excuse to seize any land they desired on the basis that no one legally owned it. It was legalized dispossession of the Aborigines' land all across the country."

"Our peoples have committed great crimes against the Aborigines and Indians but then that's the history of the world. Conquest, dispossession, and often the destruction of the cultures of the losers."

Sydney will be arriving the next day and that gives me a few hours to have a nap and then explore the town. The three days of travelling from Sydney on the other side of the world have been tiring and, despite the roar and rattle of an ancient air conditioner jutting from the hotel room window, I fall sleep the moment my head touches the pillow. The rumble of motorbikes rushing by my window wakes me two hours later in the late afternoon.

"There's a big fiesta tonight, you must go," says the girl at the shoebox front desk. "It's called Colombia en Brasil and on this day each year it celebrates the close ties we have with each other."

Those ties are as close as cheek and teeth and have resulted in one of the world's most unusual towns. The borders of Brazil, Colombia, and Peru bump into each other at this riverside town with a population of about 30,000, and with admirable commonsense the trio of governments decided to let it belong to all three. So locals and foreigners move freely between the three without any check on passports in what is called *Tres Fronteras*, or the Three Frontiers.

It is easy to spot the moment you pass from Brazil into Colombia. Outside the hotel I grab the local version of a taxi, a motorbike ridden at breakneck speed by an intrepid young man clad in jeans and T-shirt who charges the fixed rate, fifty cents a ride anywhere in town. On the Brazil side the shops and houses are grimy and run down, the roads potholed, the windows broken and dirty.

Here, poverty mingles with neglect, as if the sullen residents, who mostly wear a uniform of flip-flops and grubby shorts and T-shirts or tattered floral dresses, have lost all hope of improving their lot. They trudge about with leaden feet in the muggy heat as the buildings and their lives crumble about them from indifference.

But the moment you cross into Colombia, signaled only by a small concrete roadside marker, it's like moving from a ghetto in the worst part of town to the splendid streets where the elite live. It is the same town but has a Colombian name, Leticia. The shops and houses are mostly new and have a sparkle and gleam that signals their owners' success, while the people who throng the streets are clad in neat pants and branded polo shirts or fashionable skirts. Rows of shops sell the latest DVD players, plasma HD TVs, expensive hi-fi systems, cars, and ritzy furniture. Late model taxis crowd the streets here and it's obvious there is serious money floating about.

My driver taps his nose when I ask where the money comes from. I must still be spaced out by jetlag because the answer is obvious. "*Cocaina*," he says.

In the dense jungles of Peru, across the river, cocaine destined for the US is grown in commercial quantities and then smuggled out through Colombia via Leticia. The trickle down economic theory obviously works here in the most southern nook of Colombia because everybody seems to get a share of the cocaine profits.

We pass mansions thrown up at the jungle rim by the newly rich, multi-layered ferro-concrete constructions painted in garish pink, green, and yellow like children's birthday cakes. High walls topped with barbed wire and broken glass surround them. The driver taps his nose. "*Cocaina*."

Powerful Marxist rebels, the FARC, the Revolutionary Armed Forces of Colombia, dominate a significant chunk of territory here in the far south, and to combat them the government has stationed a battalion of troops. Along the road, jogging in precise formation, come thirty soldiers in camouflage pants and T-shirts and chanting a song, their boots giving the tune rhythm, a clickety clack on the road. They are mostly Indian boys with broad bronze faces, narrow dark eyes, and shocks of raven hair flopping across their foreheads. Whether it be Washington, London, or Leticia, you don't see many, if any, rich men's sons in the cannon fodder foot-soldier platoons.

The driver waits until they turn down a lane, heading for their base, and then taps his nose once more. "*Cocaina*," he says.

"Do you mean the soldiers grow cocaine?"

"Nah, but their leaders take a cut from the *cocaina* traders for protecting them from the police."

"And the police?"

"Their leaders take a cut from the traders to protect them from the army."

"And the FARC? How do they finance their revolution?"

I know it is coming, the tap on the side of the nose. "*Cocaina*."

By the time I return to Tabatinga, the main road at the midway point between it and Leticia has been transformed into a carnival with most of the town, thousands of people, thronging dozens of canvas stalls manned mostly by Indians selling juicy slabs of barbecued beef, puberty initiation dolls, voodoo-like magic charms, and frothy bottles of beer. This is the Colombia en Brasil festival, a clear reaffirmation of the bond between Tabatinga and Leticia and by extension the two countries.

The sky has darkened and a band of nightclub cowboys in silver-edged sombreros, ponchos, tight black pants, and shiny black Cubana boots has set up on a large stage fronting the stalls. Huge loudspeakers blast their music across the square while a big screen to the side of the stage broadcasts their every movement.

The musical cowboys have harps, guitars, and drums and their music is sharp, tough, and bristling with machismo. The singer has a thrilling voice, and his songs are powerful declarations of love and honor, murder and revenge on the savannah. In every song he begins softly but quickly asserts his manhood, striding to the edge of the stage and loudly, musically, talking directly to his audience about his loves and fights. This stirs the men who have packed the square in front of the stage to shout back their own declarations of macho dominance over their women and their enemies.

"They're a famous band from the north of Colombia and they've come here to sing just for tonight," a girl standing next to me says.

"How can such a small town finance a visit by such a famous band?" It's Dumb Pablo time and all I have in my defense is jetlag.

She taps the side of her nose. "*Cocaina*."

Off to the side, by the beer stalls, several couples are dancing a shameless salsa, their hands groping each other's buttocks and breasts while their lips bite, suck, and lick each other as they move about the small open space in short sharp steps. Colombia and Brazil are deeply religious countries but tonight the priests and nuns have wisely stayed in their presbyteries and convents while the Devil is at play.

Tabatinga has a collective hangover the next morning and on foot I search in vain for a café to take breakfast. The shutters are all pulled down and the streets are deserted. Even the dogs are missing, perhaps sleeping off the street-side banquets of cast-off food left behind by the revellers. A wind stirs the dust so that it seems like the ghosts of better times are drifting down the street searching for the revellers.

Then I hear the singing. At first it seems the keening of the wind but as I draw closer to a barn-like building by the dividing line between Tabatinga and Leticia, I realize that it's a congregation singing hymns.

The church is topped by a cross and a large sign, *Igreja Universal Do Reino De Deus*. It's a fundamentalist Pentecostal sect led by a charismatic preacher, Bishop Edir Macedo, and is notorious in Brazil. He's converted millions with his seductive message that the Kingdom of God is here on earth and the more money each member of his massive flock gives to the church, the more material rewards each will reap in this life.

Bishop Macedo once worked as a humble lottery ticket seller in Rio de Janeiro, a trader of dreams for cash, but realized in 1977 that he could peddle those same fantasies of easily gained wealth in a far more lucrative way by starting his own church and electing himself immediately to high ecclesiastical office.

As his message of sanctified personal greed took hold, more inspired by the hubris of Mammon than the humility of Jesus, he yanked in more than six million devotees in forty-six countries, including the US and Britain. They worship at two thousand temples, their spirits ramped up daily by the church's twenty-two radio stations and sixteen TV stations.

Inevitably, most of his followers in Brazil are from the poor, desperate to improve their lives here on earth, and the fruits of their despair earns the *Igreja Universal Do Reino De Deus*, meaning The Universal Church of the Kingdom of God, about one billion dollars annually.

How tragic then to find this distorted version of Christianity peddling its trade in Tabatinga and flourishing. Every time I pass the church during my stay, there is always a service with the pews filled with about five hundred worshippers. The congregation this day consists of barefoot Tukana Indians, the town's poorest residents, but the men are dressed in clean pants and white shirts while the women are clad in their best cotton dresses.

Here is the first direct evidence that Sydney Possuelo is inspired by a realistic estimation of the dangers in his campaign to shield remote

Indians from the modern world's exploitation of them and destruction of their cultures.

In the late nineteenth century, Alfred Russel Wallace visited a Tukana village, Juquira, along the Rio Negro and was thrilled when they performed a traditional dance for him. He wrote: "The wild and strange appearance of these handsome, naked painted Indians, with their curious ornaments and weapons, the stamp and song and rattle which accompanies the dance, the hum of conversation in a strange language, the music of fifes and flutes and other instruments of reed, bone and turtles' shells, the large calabashes of caxiri [palm-fruit wine, perhaps similar to what the Bantu drink at Bayanga] constantly carried about, and the great smoke-blackened gloomy house produced an effect which description can do no justice."

One hundred and thirty years later, in the last pew, I nudge shoulders with a barefoot Tukana man whose eyes seem dulled by a deep-rooted hopelessness. At another time he would have been a proud warrior, aggressive in the defense of his family, provider of abundant food for them, and loyal to the ancient Tukana culture whose rituals nurtured him from birth to death and through adolescence and marriage.

Now he probably lives at the fringe in a tumbledown hut, bereft of most of his culture. If he is typical of the urbanized Indians Sydney has written about, he will be unable to understand most of the new ways thrust upon him and his family by the conquistadores.

He can't find a steady job, is unable to feed or educate his children properly, is scorned by mulattos a notch or two above him on the totem pole, and hardly noticed by the white-skinned descendants of the Portuguese who colonized Brazil. Perhaps the appeal of Bishop Macedo's church is the open-armed welcome the pastors give him and his family, even if this hospitality is accompanied by a spiritual blackmail that seeks to take from him much of the pittance in his ragged pockets.

With him are his sad-eyed wife, her mouth tugged down by years of despair, and two children, a bone-thin boy and girl who squirm impatiently on the hard seats, knowing that the service will last several hours.

The pastor surprises me by preaching in a monotone as he passively holds up a Bible. I had expected the kind of bible-thumping sermon seen on American religious TV stations. There, the preacher prances and postures, physically fighting the invisible Devil and calling on God to shower the faithful with material blessings. But the Tabatinga pastor's message is much the same: Give generously of what you have to our church and God will return it many times over.

When the collection plate arrives, the Indians reach into their pockets or woven shoulder bags to extract the few cents they probably cannot afford, placing the coins in the trust of the church and hoping Bishop Macedo speaks the truth and that this seed of hope will grow into a mighty tree of money and possessions.

After the lengthy sermon, an assistant takes over prayers while the pastor leads me to a small office at the front of the church. He is middle-aged, slim, with placid eyes that reflect his self-satisfaction. But he pulls back, as if I've uttered one of the Devil's names, when I tell him I am a writer going to the jungle with Sydney Possuelo.

"My name is Pastor Antonio," he says guardedly, his eyes now bristling with suspicion.

"And your family name?"

"We have no family names, that's the way of our church."

Pastor Antonio is open about his church's role in converting Brazil's Indians. "Here in Tabatinga, the bringing of Jesus's message to the Indians is our special role. They have their own gods, their own religions, but these have come from the Devil and we have a sacred duty to convert them, to bring them the Holy Spirit."

"But why take their money? Your Tukana parishioners are very poor people and the money they gave you today would be better spent feeding their children."

Pastor Antonio shakes his head. "What they give now will be multiplied many times over by a grateful God."

"How long have you been in Tabatinga?"

"Twelve years."

"Can you show me any parishioners who've grown wealthy as a reward from God by giving money to your church?"

"A tree doesn't grow overnight. The seed must be planted and watered often so that one day it will grow big and healthy."

"You're avoiding my question."

"I'm answering it in the proper way. Our church needs funds to preach the word of Jesus. You can see I'm not a rich man, we plow the money we get into the church so it will grow even stronger."

"You may live simply but your leader, Bishop Macedo, is a very rich man."

"That proves his message is true because he is much blessed by God."

"You've got the Tukana in your grip. What about the Indians in the Javari Valley, where the government forbids all outsiders to go? Do you want to convert them?"

"Of course, it's our sacred duty. Our government is wrong to block us from going there, and we pray day and night that one day we can go to the Javari to save the Indians' primitive souls. Possuelo is an evil man and he's wrong to stop us. He does the work of the Devil and one day God will punish him for this."

"Would you consider entering the forbidden zone without permission to bring your message to the Indians?"

"It's too risky. The government guards it with police, they'll shoot us, and we have no wish to be martyrs. We have too much work to do here. We came here to convert the Tukana, to baptize them, and we've planted the seed, but we still have a long way to go. There are still many Tukana who resist God's Holy Word."

Good for them, I think, as Pastor Antonio strides back to the pulpit without a farewell handshake. A couple of hours later Sydney Possuelo arrives on the flight from Manaus. Although in his late sixties, he seems twenty years younger if you ignore the white whiskers sprinkling his black beard. He strides across the tarmac, his wiry body humming with energy. Up close his dark eyes burn with the gleam of a true zealot. He is clad in neat khaki pants and an olive-green military-style shirt open at the neck to reveal a brass cylinder the size of a rifle bullet strung on a necklace.

"I've had malaria thirty-nine times and it holds my medicine in case I have a sudden attack," he explains as we drive to the Funai office.

There, Sydney hurls sharp words at a hapless worker who has trouble operating a computer holding Funai statistics he wants to know now, at this moment, immediately, and then sits me in front of a blackboard in an office stacked with blowguns and stone axes. The walls are hung with pictures of Indian communal huts taken from the air.

"The Javari Valley forbidden zone is about the size of South Carolina and is home to about thirteen hundred Indians who still live in the Stone Age," he says. It is one of the most remote and rarely visited parts of the Amazon Basin. "We deliberately shun contact with them, we don't know their exact number, and we don't want to. We don't want to know their languages, customs, even their tribal names. Our aim is to keep outsiders from entering so they can live their lives their own way and know little or nothing about us."

Sometimes, though, the paths of Funai workers and Indian tribes deep within the forbidden zone cross unexpectedly. "On our last expedition into the Javari our steamer came across a group of Korubo men and women who'd come to the river to collect tortoise eggs," Armando reports to Sydney.

The Korubo were naked and it was probably the first time they had ever seen whites. The Funai workers kept their distance, remaining on board during the contact that lasted just a few minutes. "We had a female doctor with us and an old fellow called out for us to hand her over to him because he fancied her."

Sydney smiles knowing that the flames of desire do not always falter with age and that a man of power, influence, and charisma can often attract a much younger woman. He has been married three times, and his current wife is an English woman thirty years younger. They have a one-year-old child.

He points to an aerial photo of a communal hut in a deserted jungle clearing. "We can tell by the shape that it's Korubo and the people probably ran into the jungle or hid in the hut when they heard our plane coming. The Korubo call themselves *Dslala*, but the other Indians call them Korubo and the name has stuck. It means 'head-basher,' because they prefer to use war clubs when fighting."

On the wall is a gruesome photo of the shattered head of Sydney's then right-hand man, a famed Indian tracker murdered by the Korubo when they made first contact with the clan seven years earlier. "Ta'van, the most powerful warrior of the clan we were visiting, crushed his skull with a war club when he turned his back on him."

National Geographic magazine reported secondhand that the killing had something to do with the Korubo religion. "That's not true,"

Sydney says. "Ta'van told me some time later that, 'We killed him because we didn't know you then.'"

His eyes turn sad. "His answer was enough, it explained everything."

"Do you feel angry at Ta'van when you see him face to face."

Sydney shrugs. "I have feelings, but for decades loggers and fishermen from settlements downriver shot the Korubo as if they were animals. If you were a Korubo, would you trust a white, any white? The first chance you got you'd kill them as revenge or to make sure they couldn't kill you."

"What are the chances that the Korubo will attack us? It's not that long ago that they murdered your colleague and the three white men."

Sydney shrugs. "That chance is always present with Indians in the forbidden zone. Murdering enemies is an important part of their lives."

"Do you take any precautions?"

"Of course. Do you think I'm loco? I never stay with the Korubo at night. They could easily kill me while I slept. And I always take two Indian guards armed with rifles with me when I visit them. They know the power of guns. Still, the risk is there. They could ambush us as we walked through the jungle to their hut. They'd know we were coming because they live not far from the river and they'd hear the outboard motor of our canoe."

Sydney pauses, his sharp eyes fixed on me. He may be reading my body language to see how I react. On such an expedition, the last thing he wants is someone he can't trust to act coolly in a crisis.

"Do you still want to go?" he asks. "It's not to late for you to turn back."

"Are you still going?"

"Of course, I visit them twice a year."

"Then I'm happy to come with you."

"I thought you would. I checked you on the Internet and found you've been on many dangerous expeditions. I've never taken a journalist before."

Sydney says it took four expeditions to find the clan once he had been told there were Stone Age Indians living near the edge of the forbidden zone. "I wanted to leave them alone, but they were under attack by loggers and fishermen who threatened to wipe them out and so I stepped in to protect them. When I made first contact, they told me they belonged to a big group of Korubo that I later estimated lived about four hundred kilometers deeper into the jungle.

"But about ten years ago warriors fought over a woman, Maya, and she led twenty Korubo in fleeing through the jungle to the river where they now live. Maya is the clan chieftain and she sends the men out to fight if they are threatened."

So, the legend of the warrior Amazon women may hold some truth. I had never been to a warrior tribe where a woman was the chief. Yet recent archaeological evidence has shown that nomadic tribal women, Scythians in the Caucasus in the eighth century BC, were commonly warriors.

According to *National Geographic,* "Archaeologists have found a skeleton buried with bows and arrows and quivers and spears and horses. At first they assumed that anyone buried with weapons in that region must have been a male warrior. But with the advent of DNA testing and other bioarchaeological scientific analysis, they've found that about one-third of all Scythian women are buried with weapons and have war injuries just like the men. It's overwhelming proof that there were women answering to the description of the ancient Amazons."

The derivation of the word "Amazon" is not clear, though it is known that the ancient Greeks used it to describe a mythical tribe of fierce female warriors who fought by the side of their men. The river was given its name in 1542 by a Spanish soldier, Francisco de Orellana, who was the first European to explore it. He was attacked by Indians with their women fighting alongside the men, and that prompted him to name the river after the warrior women mentioned in Greek mythology.

Sydney uses chalk to draw on a blackboard a map of the forbidden zone, its rainforests hemmed in by rivers and forming the border with Peru. "It's my duty to protect the isolated Indians because they've suffered terribly from their cultures clashing with ours," he tells me. "Once we enter their land and set up towns, the Indians are attracted to them and they quickly lose their culture, suffering ill health, disease, poverty, prostitution, and alcoholism. There used to be many millions of Indians in Brazil when the Portuguese arrived five hundred years ago, but they're now down to about 300,000 and most are like the Tukana here at Tabatinga, living in or near towns. They've largely lost their tribal ways, and so isolated tribes like the Korubo will quickly disappear unless we protect them from the outside world."

He echoes the thoughts of another famed explorer, James Cook, who made the first contact by Europeans with scores of tribes across the vast Polynesian arc of the Pacific. He wrote in his journal: "To our shame (as) civilized Christians, we debauch their Morals already too prone to vice and we interduce among them wants and perhaps diseases which they never before knew and which serves only to disturb that happy tranquillity they and their fore Fathers had injoy'd. If anyone denies the truth of this assertion let him tell me what the Natives of the whole extent of America have gained by the commerce they have had with Europeans."

Sydney enforced his wish to protect the remote Stone Age tribes by creating the department of isolated Indians in Funai, bringing in a strict policy of refusing all contact with the tribes so as to keep their cultures pure. He expelled all the whites from the Javari Valley and will not allow any to return. "I saw what happened to the Indians once I'd made first contact. Even giving them T-shirts destroys them. That's why I changed the department's policy and doubled the territory of the remote tribes in the forbidden zones."

That night we cross into Colombia to eat at an outdoor café: slabs of barbecue beef, pork, and grilled river prawns washed down by beer. Sydney and I swap stories of distant tribes we've visited. "Do you know the haka, the Maori war dance?" he asks. "It's the most ferocious war dance I've ever seen, but only on TV."

"Sure, I've seen Maori tribal warriors do it many times." I punch my chest with both fists, crying out the haka's opening words, *"Ka mate, ka mate, ka ora, ka ora,"* and thrust out my tongue and bulge my eyes, making a ferocious face in the traditional way.

"Bravo," Sydney cries as he punches his own chest. Armando smiles indulgently at two adventurous youngsters who have never grown up.

"Señors!"

We turn to find a stocky Tukana girl, about sixteen years old, with dilated pupils standing outside the café, two paces from our roadside table. Her jet-black hair streams down her back while a white T-shirt strains at her breasts and jeans hug her behind.

Sydney taps his nose. "*Cocaina*."

"Do you like me?" she asks softly in a blurry voice that seems disconnected from her body, as if she's a puppet and the voice is the unseen puppet master's. "Do you want to sleep with me?"

Sydney shakes his head and shrugs. "I feel responsible for thousands of girls like her," he says as the girl staggers across the street to hustle diners at another café.

"When I was a boy my ambition was to be a *sertanista*, an Indian tracker, and make first contact with remote tribes. I joined the department at age twenty, inspired by the adventures of the three Villas-Boas brothers—Orlando, Claudio, and Leonardo—who dedicated their lives to protecting the Indians. They trained me, and over the years I have led hundreds of expeditions into the jungle, making first contact with seven tribes, the most of any *sertanista*."

He pauses a few moments to sip beer, staring at the glass, his eyes misty. "The *sertanista's* role then was to open up Indian land for settlers, loggers, fishermen, and gold miners, and I saw what happened to the Indians who were living in their own Garden of Eden. They ended up like the Tukana, stripped of their cultures, impoverished, poorly educated, malnourished, and with their girls and women selling their bodies. Once we make contact with the Indians, we begin the destruction of their universe and drag them into ours. That's why I brought in the policy in 1987 of forbidding outsiders to enter the territory of the isolated Indians who had little or no contact. Sadly, it was too late for the Tukana."

Sydney's love for the Indians and his urgent efforts to save those still untouched is clearly driven by this immense guilt he feels for his actions. "I was misguided then," he says. "*Sertanistas* have been opening Indian land ever since the first Europeans came to what is now Brazil centuries ago. But at least I realized how wrong I was in time to save some of the tribes. Tomorrow, when we go to the Korubo, you'll see Indians living just as they were when the first colonizers arrived. Very few outsiders have ever seen them."

CHAPTER 11

The Funai pontoon speedboat is anchored in the muddy river at a steep riverbank, and on the following morning I help Sydney and Armando load food and water into the speedboat we'll take to the base at the head of the forbidden zone, about one hundred and twenty miles upriver. Sydney, clad in black shoes, smart jungle green slacks, and dark long-sleeve shirt, is in high spirits, laughing and joking as he maneuvers the six-seat speedboat out into the Amazon. This is the Three Frontiers where Brazil, Colombia, and Peru share this broad stretch of river.

There is no defined point in the swirling waters where the Amazon of Brazil turns into the Amazon of Colombia or Peru and the waterway bustles with river craft from all three nations. Small water taxis scurry about like water beetles; antiquated steamers haul trade goods to riverside settlements; while a pair of double-decker riverboats weave through the river traffic carrying several hundred passengers east along the Amazon to Manaus and west along the Javari, a tributary of the great river, to the Peruvian town of Iquitos.

Although the riverboats have just left port, most passengers are already settled, elbow nudging elbow, in the crowded rows of hammocks strung across the two open decks and at the stern. Hardly a person stirs in the muggy heat, understandable because even drawing breath requires considerable effort, and the riverboats look like funeral craft bearing hundreds of bodies away from some terrible disaster.

Sydney stands at the speedboat's bow, steering it with one hand into the Javari, about one hundred and fifty yards wide here. The river here forms the border with the jungles of Portuguese-speaking Brazil to our left and the jungles of Spanish-speaking Peru on the right, with free passage for all vessels.

This is the result of Vatican realpolitik in the late fifteenth century. Much of South America was carved up in 1493 when Pope Alexander VI calmed a bitter quarrel between Spain and Portugal over their discoveries here by scoring borderlines across South America that divided it between the powerful Catholic nations. Those borders stand to this day, and this arbitrary carve up by a white-capped pontiff in a far-off land centuries earlier has had profound consequences for the Indian tribes and the colonial settlers.

Gunning the throttle, Sydney sends the speedboat charging upriver. He points to the dense rainforests lining each side. "Bandits lurk along the river and they'll shoot to kill if they think we're worth robbing. So duck if you hear rifle shots."

About thirty minutes into the journey, we pass the Brazilian town of Benjamin Constant, named after a nineteenth-century Brazilian soldier and political writer. When I ask Sydney why, he replies with a Latino shrug, all pursed lips, hunched shoulders, "don't know" eyes and raised hands. The town is a straggle of ramshackle shops and huts spread across the sloping riverbank.

At the river's edge is the town's reason for existence, a timber mill where loggers have strung together hundreds of giant rainforest logs to float in the shallows, awaiting their dismemberment by buzzing mechanical saws. The carve-up has produced a mountain of moist sawdust at the back of the mill.

Perched at the top of the slope is an imposing cathedral that seems far too big for the little town. Sydney glares at the cathedral and then at the timber mill. "Bastards!" he shouts, shaking a fist.

"The bishop and mill owner are brothers and represent my biggest enemies, the church and the loggers," he explains. "The church plots to convert the Indians to Christianity, destroying their traditional ways forever, and the loggers cut down their trees, destroying their forests. I spend much of my time battling the church and the loggers to save the Indians."

The two brothers have snagged the town's most important positions, the leading churchman and leading merchant. Now I understand the size of the church. A bishop's glory is given substance by the glory of his cathedral where he holds spiritual court, and Benjamin Constant's senior cleric must have glad-handed his rich brother for the funds to build this monument to his churchly ego. They are two big frogs in a very little pond.

Speeding up the Javari, we pass many more timber mills on both sides of the border river and thousands of valuable hardwood logs strung together into rafts awaiting the saw and export mostly to Asia, Europe, and the US.

The vast jungles along the Javari are beyond Sydney's protection, chunks of them divvied up by corrupt politicians among the loggers in exchange for very large bribes. So, in doubling the nation's forbidden zones to protect the isolated Indian tribes, Sydney has also saved huge swathes of rainforest from destruction.

This is no mean feat, because the Amazon is the world's greatest biological repository hosting about 55,000 plant species, 20 percent of the world's total. It has 20 percent of the world's bird species, totalling 1,622; 10 percent of the mammal species; up to fifteen million insect species; and more than 3,000 species of fish, or about fifteen times that of Europe.

Sydney's crusade has made him saint, hero, and savior to conservationists worldwide because he has shielded tens of millions of acres of virgin rainforest from the hordes of hungry developers greedily eyeing the Amazon, including Benjamin Constant's businessmen. They want to knock down and burn off the vast rainforests to use the land for grazing cattle, growing soybeans, prospecting for gold, tapping rubber, and for logging hardwood. By protecting huge chunks of pristine rainforest, he is also helping to save endangered animals such as jaguars.

"The isolated Indians' land is all virgin rainforest," Sydney tells me after shaking his head in anger as we pass yet another huge raft containing hundreds of hardwood logs roped together and perhaps slated to be torn apart and reshaped into expensive furniture in some far–off Asian factory. "Many politicians in the pockets of the developers oppose me, plenty of them hate me, but I don't care because I know I'm right."

I am beginning to understand why Sydney can be insufferable to the politicians, public servants, and business people he tackles in Brazil's cities, hectoring them. "Oh God, here comes that madman again," they must say as they duck for cover.

To them he must seem a devil, but to me Sydney has right on his side and they are usually wrong. I admire his willingness to battle his enemies to conserve what is left of the Amazon wilderness. The Amazon's rainforests are being reduced each year by seventy-eight million acres, threatening their many thousands of unique bird, mammal, and fish species as well as the Indian tribes who still live in a traditional way. Already 20 percent of the Amazon rainforests have been destroyed.

After two more hours we reach another riverside town on the Brazilian side, Atalaia do Norte. It is a twin of Benjamin Constant, with a timber mill and huts and shops crammed along the muddy riverbank slope, but without the cathedral. "Some of my worst enemies live here," Sydney says, eyeing the town guardedly.

The three whites massacred by warriors from the Korubo clan we are visiting came from here. "It's a close-knit town, and they've never forgiven me for enforcing the law so Ta'van and the other two warriors were not prosecuted for the murders. But mostly they hate me because the loggers and fishermen were exploiting the Javari Valley and killing any Indians they came across. When I declared it a forbidden zone and expelled them, they lost a lot of money and the obscene pleasure they got from hunting Korubo."

Two years earlier the Atalaia men, tough merciless frontiersmen, hit back, organizing a raid on the same base we're heading for in the forbidden zone. "The sawmill owners and fishermen put together a raiding party of three hundred men and they sailed up the river armed with guns and Molotov cocktails, determined to kill me and burn the base. I called in the federal police, who buzzed the attackers in helicopters and threatened to blast them out of the water."

After an uneasy standoff, the raiders turned back. "They'd still like to destroy the base and kill me," he says. "They've told me that one day they'll try again and promise that next time they'll succeed."

It wasn't the first time Sydney's life was threatened by opponents of his enforcement of the forbidden zone. "Settlers pistol-whipped me because I was stopping them from invading Indian territory, and one even threw a Molotov cocktail into my boat."

Indians have also targeted Sydney countless times during his four decades as a *sertanista*. Deep in the jungle, fellow Indian trackers have fallen at his feet riddled with arrows when their expeditions were ambushed by tribesmen as they attempted to make first contact. But he is more forgiving of them. "We were the intruders, they were guarding their rainforests, and so I don't blame them," he says.

The Funai honor roll is grim, with one hundred and twenty Indian trackers murdered in the jungles by Indians over the past two decades. When attacked by Indians, Sydney's men and women are under strict orders to fire back only to scare off their attackers. "We live by the *sertanistas* motto, '*Morrer se precisa for, matar, nunca,*'" Sydney tells me. "It means, 'Die if you must, but never kill.'"

The slogan was coined by one of Sydney's heroes, the explorer Candido Rondon who preached love for the Indians and reconciliation at the beginning of the twentieth century. As a military engineer he explored much of the remote regions of Brazil and, like Sydney, was appalled at the mistreatment and exploitation of the Indians by settlers.

In 1910, Rondon set up the government's Indian Protection Agency, Funai's forerunner. Like Sydney, he was shot at by remote Indians and his saddle was skewered with arrows. He forgave them, understanding their need like people the world over to protect their lands from an often cruel and barbaric invader.

Rondon wrote: "I assure you that the Indian, no matter what the tribe, are as susceptible as the most civilized Westerner to love and goodness . . . not to mention their intelligence, so commonly recognized since colonial times."

Rondon set up the agency with the most important condition being that Indians should not be forced into rapid acceptance of Christian civilization. Over time corruption weakened Rondon's benevolent policy and in 1987 Sydney, having witnessed government missions provoking death and disease among the remote Indians, yanked Funai back to carry out Rondon's original philosophy. He set up within Funai the department for isolated and uncontacted Indians.

Funai's website states that Sydney changed the federal government policy of eventual integration of the uncontacted tribes with, "'one of protection and respect for the Indians' right to remain isolated." As Sydney had told me, "contact is only sought if isolated groups are thought to be under serious threat." The department "is responsible for protecting fourteen million hectares of isolated Indians' territory, more than three times the size of Switzerland."

Sydney knows better than most the savage nature of many uncontacted tribes, but prefers not to recount the attacks he experienced. They must have been similar to an attack witnessed by Algot Lange, a Swedish explorer, in his book *The Amazon Jungle: Adventures in Remote Parts of the Upper Amazon River,* published in 1912.

Lange was with twelve Mayoruna warriors on the Itui river, where Sydney and I are going, when they spied a dozen Peruvian *caucheros* (rubber plantation workers) in search of rubber trees or Mayoruna women or both. The warriors were armed with long war poles, much like the Korubo's, but studded with jaguar teeth. They also had three-pronged poison spears. Using the juice of a jungle berry, *urucu*, they had painted their faces scarlet.

The chief carefully planned an ambush and the warriors struck without warning. Lange wrote: "I heard great shouts of anger from them (the Peruvians). The warriors let loose a volley of poison arrows. The bow and arrow men charging with their stingray arrows poisoned with *curare* rushed down like breakers on a stormy night. Several of the Peruvians managed to fire their large-calibre bullets into the backs of our charging bow and arrow men but in their turn they were picked off by the blow pipe men who kept firing their poisoned darts from a distance.

"The club men broke into action. With fierce war cries of *YOB-HEE-HEE* they launched themselves into the fight, swinging their strong clubs above their heads and crushing skulls from left to right. By this time the huge black clubs of the Mayoruna fell again and again, with sickening thuds, piercing the heads and brains with the pointed jaguar teeth."

224

Lange had not joined in the battle but when a Peruvian rushed at him with a bloodied machete he fought back: "I fired point blank, sending three bullets through his head. Another Peruvian had an arrow through his upper abdomen, the broken shaft projecting behind his back. Four Indians were killed by rifle bullets. But the dozen Mayoruna had wiped out the entire party of twenty *caucheros.*"

The massacre happened on the Itui River, not far from where Sydney has his base. Within a day I would be with those three Korubo warriors who murdered the three white men just as savagely with their war clubs. As we near the forbidden zone and the Korubo, Sydney's smile grows wider. An hour later, as dusk nears, we swing left into the smaller coffee-hued Itui river, snaking upstream through dense jungle and hemmed in on both sides by sloping banks and the towering rain-forest trees lusted after by the loggers.

About sixty miles along the river Sydney's base is marked by large signs on poles dug into the riverbank banning outsiders from going on. "Prohibited. Identify yourself," they read in Portuguese. We are at the very edge of the Vale do Javari, the Javari Valley, one of the world's last great wilderness areas. It is one of the forbidden zones set aside by the Brazilian government exclusively for Stone Age Indians.

Its dense pristine jungles, with a perimeter of two thousand miles, cover more than forty-nine million acres and form part of the frontier with Peru. There are no roads, only narrow tribal tracks, and the clans live amid misty swamps, twisting rivers, and sweltering rainforests, bristling with anacondas, alligators, piranhas, and jaguars. They have little or no knowledge of the outside world and face off against each other in relentless, unceasing warfare.

The river splits into two here, with the Itui and the Itaquai running off at right angles. The triangle of land at this watery apex has been cleared by Sydney for his base, which consists of a wooden bungalow perched on poles on the slope and topped by a ten-yard-high radio aerial. A Brazilian flag hangs limply atop a tall mast outside the bunga-low. At the river is a pontoon with the base's one-room medical clinic. Waiting for us is Maria das Gracias Sobras, a small, dark-haired nurse in her thirties hired by Sydney to look after the health of the Korubo clan we're visiting.

"Call me Magna," she says as she helps me onto the pontoon.

With her are two short wiry Matis Indian warriors, Juma and Jemi, who have creamy, crescent-shaped river snail shells pushed through their septums and large circular shells plugged into their ear lobes. They have thrust twigs into holes bored into their nostrils and six straight lines have been tattooed across their cheeks.

"The tattoos are magic, they look like jaguar's whiskers, and they turn them into jaguar men and help them move through the jungle at night and creep silently up on their enemies," Sydney explains as he hugs the warriors. "Their dialect is similar to the Korubo's and I use them as trackers and guards. We never visit the Korubo without at least two guards armed with rifles and never stay at night. It's too dangerous."

The bare-board bungalow has a dining room with wooden benches and tables hemmed in on three sides by small spartan bedrooms with no furniture except the bed and a kitchen. On the fourth side, a veranda opens to a view of the river below. Sydney disappears inside his bedroom but soon emerges stripped of his senior bureaucrat's Funai uniform. Now clad in his jungle gear, he is barefoot and wears ragged shorts and a tattered khaki short-sleeved shirt open to the waist. It reveals a dragon tattooed near his neck.

"I feel like a *sertanista* again," he says, smiling.

A broken thermometer on the wall forever reads 43°C, and a two-way radio in the dining room constantly crackles with static or blurry faraway voices, our only contact with the outside world. That is the way I like it, although if we come under attack by the Korubo or another tribe, it reminds me that we are too far away from swift help.

Sydney checks a room stacked with rifles and ammunition while I watch pink-skinned dolphins chasing fish in the river. Because the river water is so murky, the dolphins have evolved to be almost blind but find their way about using the peerless sonar echo-locating equipment in the fat-filled bulge on their foreheads.

Dinner is delicious, jungle vegetables, pasta, and chunks of juicy wild boar shot by Juma, one of the Matis warriors, in the jungle earlier in the day. Pigs reared commercially have never tasted a quarter as good as the species' rainforest version, having a strong gamey flavor that pleasures the tongue long after the meal is finished.

Darkness comes swiftly and, with clouds casting a shroud across the moon and stars, the slope and river below disappear into a black void. The jungle is deeply silent, the only sounds coming from the bungalow, the sounds of our muted conversation, and the short-wave-radio chatter. As we drink coffee, a stern-faced Juma stands at the balcony railing sweeping a powerful searchlight back and forth across the river junction, searching for any outsiders, illegal loggers and fishermen, attempting to slip past the bungalow in small boats and disappear into the forbidden zone's vast jungles.

"We watch the river twenty-four hours a day to make sure no intruders enter," Sydney says. "No one gets past the Matis."

Armando is with us but defers always to Sydney, not so much because he's the boss, or because he doesn't want to tempt an explosion of Sydney's fragile temper, but because he knows he is the apprentice in the presence of a grand master. The old style *sertanista* is a dying breed and both Sydney and Armando are thankful for it.

When the Portuguese explorer, Pedro Alvares Cabral, strode ashore on the northeastern coastline in 1500 CE and claimed the land to be known as Brazil for his far-off king, up to eleven million Indians lived in the Amazon Basin. During the following centuries, battle-toughened *sertanistas* led countless white settlers into the wilderness to seize Indian lands and enslave and slaughter the tribespeople.

Thousands of clans were wiped out as rubber tappers, gold miners, loggers, farmers, cattle ranchers, and fishermen swarmed over the pristine jungles. In the first seventy years of the twentieth century alone, one tribe disappeared each year, according to Brazilian anthropologist Darcy Ribeiro, down to one hundred and forty three from two hundred and thirty tribes.

Millions more Indians died from strange new diseases such as tuberculosis, the flu, chickenpox, and measles, for which they had no immunity. Sydney himself was seduced by the thrill of the dangerous chase, like a real-life Indiana Jones, leading hundreds of dangerous search parties into Indian territory. But by the early 1980s he felt increasingly disillusioned, saddened, as development and deforestation relentlessly followed in his footsteps and he saw that the clash of cultures was destroying the tribes.

"We are very arrogant, we arrived in this land with cross and sword and demanded that the Indians be like us," he says as we stare out into the darkness, broken every half minute by the stab of Juma's searchlight. "We think there are no problems we can't sort out. We have the power to decide whether we have contact or no contact with the Indians and so we play God with them. We should be more humble."

Sydney can be among the least humble men among his own race, and so I am intrigued to see how he will act with the Korubo. He fixes me with fierce eyes. "I've come to understand that our two cultures, as different as any on earth, can't exist side by side. The history on this frontier has been one of bitter and bloody conflict, and many whites have died as well as Indians who lost countless dead and who killed hundreds of whites. But the Indians will always lose, blow pipes and war clubs against guns and bombs, and that's why I expelled all whites from here a decade ago and won't let any back.

"Before we came here the whites from Atalaia, loggers and fishermen, persecuted the Indians, shot them on sight, burned their huts. I've seen Korubo warriors fished out of the river, shot and dumped by whites, their flesh rotting away. That's why the Korubo have a historic hatred of all whites."

This fierce hatred of whites has lasted for centuries. I have with me a quote from Rosa, a Bororo Indian in 1913, and read it to Sydney. "Do not trust the whites. They are the men who control the lightning, who live without a homeland, who wander to satisfy their thirst for gold. They are kind to us when they need us, for the land they tread and the rivers they assault are ours. Once they have achieved their goals they are false and treacherous."

The fighting on both sides was relentless and savage. In 1874 an expedition sent by steamer to explore the Itui was attacked. John Hemming wrote in *Amazon Frontier*: "The silence was suddenly broken by great shouting from a crowd of Mayoruna. The Indians appeared on a sandbank, brandishing their weapons, firing a cloud of arrows, shouting defiance with their brilliant feather ornaments sparkling in the sun."

The Brazilian commander returned fire. "The beach full of Mayoruna was raked by gunfire, the chief and others were killed and the rest put to flight. The Brazilian commander boasted: 'Without losing a single man, we asserted through today's victory our supremacy in this region of indomitable natives.'"

Children were not spared the barbaric treatment. A revenge attack on a tribe for killing a rubber worker wiped out most of the villagers. "With cries of alarm the Indians came running from the two doors and at that moment the deadly shots of the attackers knocked them to the ground. There was great mortality, but many ran off. Approaching the hut the raiders managed to catch some fifteen children aged from eight to ten years; they left the younger ones. On the return journey, the prisoners began to cry too much. It was necessary to abandon them, leaving them lost and tied to a rope."

A burst of light above signals that the heavens' searchlight, the moon, has broken through the cloud cover and sparkles the water. Silvery ripples show that the dolphins are still at play or catching fish.

Sydney glances at the dolphins for a few moments and then turns back to me. "There are still at least twenty-one tribes living deep in the Amazon that have no contact with the outside world, and if I have my way they'll stay like that. Maybe I can't stop the modern world from eventually reaching here, destroying the tribes in the Javari Valley, but if I can give them thirty or forty more years to be themselves, to live in their own special universes, then that makes all the effort and pain worth it."

I am intrigued by this curious profession of *sertanista*, found only in Brazil, and the amazing transformation of the greatest among them, Sydney, from a man of war to a man of peace, at least for the Indians.

"When I was a boy I wanted to walk in the jungles in big expeditions, observing rivers and jungles, to be with the Indians, to know them, eat their food, sleep in their huts," Sydney continues as we sip bitter black coffee. "That's why I became a *sertanista*, a man who is a non-conformist, who does not want to live in the city, but in the jungle. He is a jack-of-all-trades, able to give an injection, help in giving birth, fix an engine, pilot a plane, deal with a snake bite, hunt to feed himself, and defend himself if attacked.

"When I joined, the classic image of a *sertanista* was a man who made contact with tribal people in the jungle. *Sertao* in Portuguese means 'backwoods.' Man has an adventurous spirit and it was then believed important that we widen the frontiers of Brazil. So, the *sertanistas* led many big expeditions to the most remote jungles to seize the land while taking Indians as prisoners and making them slaves. They were monsters. The man who showed Brazil a new way was Candido Rondon, a soldier and explorer who formed the forerunner of Funai, the Indian Protection service, to protect the Indians against massacres and their land being stolen. He began the transformation of the *sertanista* from an Indian killer to what we are today, a protector and friend of the Indians."

Sydney's "Road to Tarsus" transformation came in the 1970s and 1980s when the Brazilian government began carving a complex of roads through remote Amazon jungle. *Sertanistas* headed the teams, pacifying the Indian tribes in territory marked out for the roads. Under Brazilian law, remote Indians are regarded as minors and cannot own land.

Countless Indians and many *sertanistas* died in the battles as the Indians fought to protect their sacred territory, held by them for thousands of years. In 1987, Sydney established the department of isolated Indians within Funai to effect the change from aggressor to defender.

"Most *sertanistas* opposed me, as well as the church, government, and the academics whose job it was to study tribal Indians. The *sertanistas'* glory was to make first contact with a tribe, to become a father to these Indians, in a way to give birth to the tribe's entry into our world. But I enforced a policy where *sertanistas* would do the opposite, to shun contact while protecting the tribes. At the time there were around twenty-five of us, but now there are just four or five."

He points to the dragon tattoo on his neck as a sign that he's still a non-conformist. "I was always in love with tattoos because I was raised with the idea that they were only for sailors and prisoners. I got this tattoo at the age of sixty-one, when I was visiting Spain. It was a sign of my freedom."

Sydney puts an arm fondly around my shoulder. "If you were born in Brazil, I think you'd have become a *sertanista*.'" I smile in gratitude at this compliment from one of history's great explorers. "*Obrigado camarada*." It means "Thanks comrade."

The rooms have no lights, and at 10 p.m. I find my way into bed with the help of moonbeams from the open window overlooking the river. Sydney's suggestion that I was born to be a man of the jungle has given me a warm glow and I fall asleep quickly and dream of anacondas grappling with dolphins in the river below the bungalow.

Suddenly a gut-shaking scream wakes me. Am I having a nightmare? No, my eyes are wide open and there's the terrible sound again clawing the night. Is it a war cry? Surely I must be dreaming? No. Someone is running barefoot up the bungalow steps. Thump, thump, thump.

I peer out the window. A naked Indian gripping a tall wooden club is racing towards me up the stairs and screaming at the top of his lungs. No one has yet stirred in the bungalow. Am I alone? Are we being attacked by Korubo warriors? I crouch by the door and open it a little. As the Indian reaches the balcony, Juma hurries from a room and strides over to the warrior, who falls to his knees and starts to sob.

He keeps repeating the same word, "Maya," followed by a heart-shaking moan. Juma sits him on a bench but the warrior refuses to let go his war club. Moments later Sydney comes into the darkened room, kneels by the warrior, puts his arm around him and talks softly to calm him, his words translated by Juma.

I edge into the dining room drawn by one of the most extraordinary encounters in my four decades of roaming some of the world's most remote places. This warrior from the beginning of time is short and stocky, and his hair is cut in Amazon Indian style, basin-shaped with a crescent shaved across the crown. Blood-red markings decorate his body, which is totally naked except for a vine string that encircles his waist and is tied to the foreskin of his penis, jerking it into an upright position.

This could be sexual display, a way of preventing the penis from jiggling as the warrior runs through the jungle, or both. He is hard-muscled and looks as fit as an Olympic athlete. The war club is a few inches taller than the warrior and is stained blood-red.

The warrior looks at me warily and angles the club so that it points at my head. His unspoken message is clear. Don't come too close or I'll split your head in half.

"This is Shishu, a Korubo," Sydney explains. "He's run all the way through the jungle to tell us that Maya, his wife, is dying. This is very serious. She's the clan chieftain, and if she dies the Korubo might disappear into the jungle and we'll never see them again."

So, the timeless legend is at least partially correct, with an Amazonian woman leading this clan of born warriors. Shishu is emotionally exhausted and Sydney and Juma grip his arms as they lead him back down the slope to the pontoon. Armando has readied a motorized canoe and a grim-faced Sydney, Magna, and Shishu climb aboard. Juma and Jemi, carrying rifles, join them, their eyes hard as rock.

"The clan's communal hut is about forty five minutes up river," Armando tells me. Sydney guns the outboard motor as the canoe heads upstream, disappearing into the darkness. "This is very bad. We never go to the village at night because it's too dangerous. It could be an ambush, an attempt by the Korubo to kill Sydney. We've put so much effort into knowing this one clan and if Maya dies we'll probably never see them again. Her successor is her daughter, Washman, a very tough woman in her early twenties. Fishermen shot dead her father a few years ago, and she hates whites."

CHAPTER 12

The pontoon's flood lamps color the river golden for just a few yards and then we are faced with a deep dark void, a terrifying blackness, as if a shroud has dropped over the river and jungle, denying us even a glimpse of what nightmares lie beyond. As they disappeared into the blackness Sydney, Magna, the Matis guards, and the Korubo warrior seemed to have gone time traveling in the motorized canoe, slipping in an eye-blink from this millennia back to another, thousands of years earlier.

Armando, grim-faced, paces up and down near the pontoon at the river's edge. "We can now only wait and see if Sydney and the others come back alive," he says to me. "If Maya dies while they're at the village, in their grief the warriors might murder them. We know so little about their ways that we just don't know what happens when a Korubo dies." He lets a tiny smile slip onto his lips. "We're hoping Maya lives to be one hundred."

He stares into the darkness. "If Maya dies we'll probably lose contact with the clan. As I said, Washman, her daughter, hates us."

"That's no surprise with the Atalaia whites murdering her father."

Armando nods. "It's the reason why we set up this base. We'd rather leave them alone, to live their lives without any interference from us, like the main body of the tribe deeper into the jungle. As

Sydney told you, warriors fought over Maya about ten years ago and she fled through the jungle with twenty others to a spot near here that just happened to be at the edge of the forbidden zone. That put them in danger from the *gampeiros*, the illegal loggers and fishermen, who used to go on Indian hunts. It was like a turkey shoot. They carried shotguns and murdered any Indian they came across—man, woman, or child. After a fight where two whites and ten Korubo were killed, Sydney stepped in to make contact with the clan to protect them."

"Did it take long to find them?"

"Yes, it was difficult. Sydney led one of our seven *frente de vigilinca*, or squads specializing in seeking evidence of isolated Indians. The Korubo are semi-nomadic, they move between four widely dispersed *maloca*, communal huts, as their crops come into season, and so it took Sydney four lengthy expeditions over several months to find them in the jungle not far from here. Once he came across evidence of their presence, he left aluminum pots and knives on one of their jungle pathways. When the Korubo took them over the next few days, Sydney slowly gained their confidence with more gifts. Once Maya saw we wouldn't harm them she sent Shishu, Ta'van, and some other men to make contact with us. Now we treat their illnesses but keep contact at a bare minimum so they can live as true Korubo, and not as some pale imitation."

"But surely by giving them aluminium pots Sydney broke his own rule."

Armando shrugs. "Sometimes you have to compromise and we had to use gifts to show them we came as friends. If Sydney had not made contact, all the clan would probably be dead by now, killed by whites. The pots and knives don't change their lifestyle much. Their clay pots are heavy to carry as they move from hut to hut and so lightweight pots make their lives a little easier."

As each hour passes the tension tightens. We ignore the many mosquitoes buzzing around our faces, wondering whether Sydney and his crew will make it back alive. The canoe left just before midnight, and it is now 4 a.m.

"They should have been back long ago," Armando says as worry lines furrow his forehead. "I'm very afraid something terrible has happened."

About ten minutes later, Tepi, another Matis, turns towards the river and points at the darkness. "They're coming back," he tells Armando. I hear nothing, nor can Armando, but he and I are veterans of journeys among tribes cut off from the blare and blast of modern city life and we have long ago learned to trust their far superior hearing.

The canoe's prow nudges through the dark curtain as Sydney steers towards the pontoon. With him are seven Korubo sitting in the canoe, staring straight ahead. Armando lets slip an audible sigh of relief as he grabs a rope from the canoe and ties it to the pontoon. Sydney and Magna help a middle-aged woman from the boat. She is entirely naked and her stocky body and face are streaked with blood-red stripes as if she has just survived a massacre. She looks very ill and her eyes are turned inwards as she absorbs the pain in silence.

"It's Maya, the clan chieftain," Armando says. Shishu, her husband, follows, still gripping his war club, followed by a warrior in his mid-teens carrying a club, a grim-faced young woman, a boy nearing puberty, and two little girls. One girl has a spider monkey baby nestled on her back, clinging to her neck. The other cradles a baby sloth, not much bigger than her hand, with a narrow head and very sleepy eyes. Western children might have more comfortable lives but Korubo family pets look more interesting.

As Sydney and Magna help Maya into the one-room clinic on the pontoon and ease her onto the sick bed, leaving the door open to soften the Korubo's suspicions, Shishu and the others squat together by the water's edge. They stare at the stranger, me, with hard suspicious eyes that show no hint of friendship or even friendly curiosity.

The younger woman's glare, especially, throbs with hatred and suspicion. It must be Washman. Like Shishu earlier, the Korubo seem to be warning me to stay my distance or one of the warriors will smash in my head. It's a grim admonition. At this very place, just across the river, a Korubo warrior split the head of Sydney's colleague, another *sertanista*, who relaxed his caution for just for a few moments while with the clan and paid with his life.

These people, from what archaeologists call the Neolithic Era, clearly are very healthy and well fed. In the most remote New Guinea jungle I had been to, about the only other place on earth where you can still find Stone Age people with little or no contact with the outside world, the Korowai rainforest clan were skinny, sharp-faced, and puny looking. Not these Korubo. They remind me that the early Portuguese settlers were impressed by the Indians' looks. One writer noted: "Their bodies are so clean and so plump and so beautiful, they could not be more so."

Where our shirts are soaked in sweat and pants splattered with mud, and we have yet to leave the base, the bronze-skin Korubo look as if they have just stepped out of a bath, their bodies shining with cleanliness. The little girls have dark-eyed angelic faces while the teenage warrior is movie-star handsome with a Beatle-style mop of thick raven hair flopping over his brow.

Perhaps to string-bean Portuguese settlers the Indians were plump but the Korubo, though well padded, carry no visible fat. Maya and the younger woman are stocky and firm-skinned while Shishu and the teenager have lithe, hard-muscled bodies toughened by countless journeys through the jungle on hunting expeditions or war parties. Like Shishu, the teenager has tied his foreskin with vine circling his waist and even the boy, though he must be too young for sexual display, has a foreskin string in place, yanking his penis into prominence, as if he is a man in training.

I sit cross-legged about three paces in front of the Korubo and smile a greeting. I have not the slightest idea what they are thinking as they stare back at me, and am sure they have no idea what I'm thinking. There is a cultural gap between us thousands of times wider than the distance that separates us and neither of us will ever bridge it while Sydney's policies of exclusion remain in force. The minutes flow swiftly as we face off, me trying to win their confidence with smiles and they having none of it. Now and then Shishu and the younger woman glance through the clinic's open door to see if Maya is still there.

Suddenly Shishu shoves his war club at me and thumps the deck, missing me by a few inches. I jerk back in surprise. The warrior in Shishu recognizes this look and laughs mockingly at me. He says something to the others and they join his merriment, even the little girls. His voice is lilting, high-pitched, and he seems to separate each Korubo word from the other, rather than let them flow freely, as if he is taking an elocution test.

Armando beckons. "It's best we all go back to bed and leave them here while Magna and Sydney find out what's ailing Maya. They're probably nervous seeing a strange white man. You'll get a better look when Sydney takes you to their village later this morning."

At breakfast, two hours later, as the sun climbs over the leafy rim of the jungle trees on the far side of the river, Sydney introduces me to a Brazilian delicacy, chunks of sugary quince jam spread on top of slices of processed yellow cheese and eaten in a gulp.

"You like it?" he asks with an amused smile, reacting to my puzzled expression.

"I don't think so but I could get used to it. I'm sorry I didn't bring you any Vegemite, which Australians love even more than prawns on the barbie."

"What is this Vagamut and this berby?"

"A barbie is our slang for a barbecue and Vegemite is a spread you put on bread at breakfast. It's black, looks like sump oil, and tastes like the meat from a cow three days dead. But we begin eating it as soon as we're weaned and love it to death."

He pulls a face, mingling horror with distaste. Like most Brazilians he is a great, if often unrestrained and undisciplined, actor in life. His gestures, exaggerated to an Australian, seem aimed at an audience in the back rows. "It sounds like a present I should give to my three mothers-in-law."

Magna slides along the bench to be beside Sydney. "How is Maya?" he asks.

"She's fine. Armando took them back to the village just before sunrise and she seemed okay when she left. It's probably osteoporosis and I gave her an injection and some tablets. I think she's on the edge of menopause and she's using her illness to seek attention."

"But Shishu was extremely distressed when he arrived last night. He really seemed to think Maya was dying."

"The Korubo, like other isolated Indians, have little or no knowledge of disease, or conditions like osteoporosis, and so when they suffer severe pain it must seem to them as if they are dying," Sydney explains.

"I've been with a tribe in New Guinea, the last cannibal tribe on earth, where they seem to rationalize death by disease, knowing nothing of microbes, by claiming it's caused by a devil sorcerer in their midst. They seek him out, sometimes using torture to get him to confess, then kill and eat him."

"Hah!" Sydney laughs. "I know many devils in Atalaia, Benjamin Constant, and even Brasilia that I'd like to send to New Guinea as gifts to the cannibals."

At mid-morning, as Sydney, Magna, Jumi, Jema, and I clamber into the canoe and head upstream to the Korubo village, the heat and humidity are intense, like hands gripping my neck, making it difficult to breathe. The rush of wind as we gather speed gives momentary comfort but I know that once we alight at the riverbank we'll be thrown back into the sauna bath with its dial on full heat.

The muddy river winds in tight loops and I trail my hand in the cool water as we pass sandbanks where caiman, a kind of alligator, and tortoises are sunning. Huge rotting logs settle at strange angles in the shallows where they've tumbled, with spindly white cranes perched on them, as still as statues. Flocks of rainbow-hued parrots fly overhead.

"The river is teeming with fish, including piranhas, and the Korubo eat as much as they want as well as plenty of meat from the jungle animals," Sydney says as we turn another bend in the river, to glimpse yet another turn just ahead, and knowing there is another just beyond that. "In fact they eat better than most people on earth and you can see the result. They are very healthy and have long lives unless they die in battle, and that's an ever-present risk."

Strike one against Alvin Toffler's theory that the Korubo would be underfed and so prey to all kinds of diseases spurred on by bodies weakened by malnutrition so that they die at an early age. But though it may seem Paradise at first sight, the Korubo world is crawling with many kinds of devilish creatures.

Giant anacondas, said to be up to thirty feet long and weighing as much as twelve hundred pounds, lurk in this and other Amazon rivers, an unseen daily menace to the tribes. "A few years ago Maya took her five-year-old daughter to the river to wash at the same place we'll go ashore," Sydney says. "An enormous anaconda shot up out of the water and grabbed the girl by the ankle, dragging her under. She disappeared and was never seen again, a big meal for the anaconda. The clan built a hut by the spot where she was taken and stayed there for seven days and nights, crying and wailing."

The poor little girl would have been squeezed to death by the giant snake's coils, caught head first in the anaconda's gullet and inched down into its stomach. In a grisly way the little girl's life was sacrificed for new life, the anaconda ensuring that it had plenty of protein to survive a months-long fast before giving birth to her own young.

"Life goes on," Sydney says with a shrug. "The beautiful little girl you saw with the pet sloth is Manis, daughter of Maya and Shishu, and she was born after her sister was taken by the anaconda."

Merciless warfare using blowguns, bows and arrows, and clubs is another day-by-day hazard for the tribes within the Javari Valley forbidden zone. Most of the thirteen hundred Stone Age tribespeople live deep within the rainforest, and so don't have to fear marauding raids by the whites from Atalaia and Benjamin Constant. Sydney's keen-eyed Matis guards at the base ensure that none get past the warning signs on the riverbank. But Maya's clan lives at the edge of the forbidden zone and, because they don't understand lines on maps, the warriors sometimes leave their sanctuary to go on raiding parties downriver.

Sydney was at Tabatinga when Ta'van, the clan's most powerful warrior, led two other warriors including the teenage boy the previous night on a war party downriver in search of whites. Maya sent them to avenge the killing of her then husband.

"They found three white men by the river cutting trees," says Sydney as our canoe edges closer to the Korubo village. "Each of the Korubo targeted a white and split their skulls with war clubs. By the time I arrived they'd returned to their *maloca*, mission accomplished. But they left a ghastly scene with the whites' canoe awash with blood and littered with pieces of skull. The warriors had flung the three bodies onto the riverbank and then bashed their heads so many times that they were just pulp. The Korubo then gutted them."

Sydney raced to Atalaia to alert the police, not to arrest the warriors but to protect them from vengeful relatives. "Because they have no knowledge of our law, they can't be prosecuted," he explains. "But

I had to go before a magistrate at Atalaia to prove they were innocent because as Stone Age people they were ignorant of the law."

In a ghoulish and yet logical response, Sydney welcomed news of the massacre spreading to Atalaia, Benjamin Constant, and Tabatinga because it spotlighted the Korubo's terrifying violence. "I prefer them to be violent because that's their natural way, it frightens away intruders and keeps the Korubo safe."

Sydney puts a hand on my shoulder. "Be careful at all times while we're with the Korubo. Ta'van, especially, has an unpredictable nature, he doesn't laugh very much, he's the strong silent type. I've seen him suddenly get very angry and in a fighting mood because we did something wrong even though we didn't understand what or why."

Up ahead I spy a pair of dugouts pulled up on the slope of the sand bank. "Korubo?" I ask.

Sydney has come barefoot and nods as he steers the canoe towards the riverbank. Gripping their rifles, Juma and Jemi, the Matis guards, nimbly hop from the canoe as it nudges the bank. Just before our breakfast there had been a tropical downpour that turned the slope into a mud pit. I sink into the mud up to my calves at every step, and yank each leg out in turn as I head slowly up the steep slope.

A pathway worn into the jungle floor by the Korubo leads into a dense thicket of trees as gloomy as a cathedral nave. The jungle's deep silence is intensified by the shrill scream of millions of insects. Juma heads along the slippery pathway in the lead, followed by Sydney with a rifle on his shoulder, Magna with her medical bag, me, and then Jemi guarding our rear. The sweat pours from me forming puddles on my forehead that tumble into my eyes, stinging them.

Suddenly Jemi shouts a warning. A yellow-headed cobra lurking by a tree had struck at Magna but its deadly fangs bounced off her rubber boots. Jemi rushes forward and crushes the snake's head with his rifle butt. I shiver, despite the heat, because I'm wearing running shoes without socks and was a couple of steps behind Magna. Had I been ahead of her the highly poisonous snake would have struck my bare ankle and then only a rapid injection of anti-venom would have saved me from an extremely painful death.

"That cobra causes more deaths than any other snake in the

Amazon," Sydney says. Warring Korubo, deadly cobras, monster ana-condas, ferocious piranhas—where do the hazards end? But it would be an anti-climax if the Stone Age people we are about to encounter lived in a land without danger.

The Korubo have thrown a log across a stream with steeply sloping muddy banks, and my companions nimbly step across it like high-wire balancers. I pause, deciding whether to risk breaking a leg if I fall from the slippery log or choose the easier alternative. Caution wins and I slip down the bank, ease into the murky water, up to my waist, and then climb the other side by crawling on my belly, slathering my pants and shirt with mud. At this moment the Korubo's nakedness seems per-fectly logical for living in a jungle inundated by rainfall on about two hundred and fifty days each year.

The mud dries quickly. A mile in from the riverbank Sydney cups his hands and shouts a melodious "Eh-heh."

"We're near the village," he explains, "and only enemies come in silence." The hairs on my neck stand up when we hear a faint, "Eh-heh," returning his call from somewhere ahead in the jungle. Sydney calls once more and again is echoed by someone up ahead.

We trudge along the muddy path keeping our gaze fixed to the ground, wary of cobras, and soon sunlight stabbing through the trees signals a clearing. We halt as we reach it because there's no sense in barging into the abode of a warrior tribe even with the calls signal-ing our peaceful approach. The sun-dappled clearing is the size of two football fields and scattered with fallen trees, with rows of maize and plantain planted between them. At the top of a slope, by the rain-forest rim, are twenty naked Indians. The women and children have painted their bodies blood red and the men grip formidable clubs. All are grim-faced.

"Korubo," Sydney whispers. "The head bashers. I warn you again, Paul. Do not relax your vigilance because they are very violent and can be your best friends or your worst enemies. We know hardly anything about them and so we can never predict what they'll do next—hug you or murder you."

Juma and Jemi grip their rifles, their eyes fixed on the warriors with their war clubs. The Korubo stand outside a *maloca*, a long, narrow, communal straw hut built on a framework of poles, about five yards wide, four yards high, and ten yards long. Sydney points to a man, a little taller than the others, with a wolfish face and glowering eyes. "That's Ta'van," he says.

Ta'van's sturdy war club is a few inches longer than he and stained red. Could it signify the bloodshed it has caused? Sydney shrugs. We approach slowly, carefully, and when I lock eyes with Ta'van he glares back defiantly.

It was Ta'van who murdered Sydney's close friend, Raimundo Batista Magalhaes, across the river from the base, crushing his skull with a war club when the *sertanista* turned his back on him. Sydney told me Maya had ordered the killing and held the *sertanista's* arms to prevent him from escaping. The clan then fled into the jungle, fearing revenge, but returned to the *maloca* after several months.

While the men wield the war clubs, Sydney told me earlier that the women rule the clan, so it doesn't surprise me when the first person to speak is Maya, who seems to have made a miraculous recovery. She has a matronly face and speaks in a girlish voice, but her hard black eyes suggest an unyielding, ruthless nature. "She makes all the decisions," Sydney told me. By her side is her daughter, Washman, her expression as truculent and unfriendly as at our first meeting a few hours earlier.

Women were equal to men in the egalitarian Pygmy society, while the Korowai women were subservient, but here in the Amazon it seems the women, true to legend, are dominant. The peaceful nature of the Pygmies might explain the gender equality there, just as the warlike nature of the Korowai could explain why the men, stronger than the women, are dominant. But what could have led to the Amazon women lording it over the warriors?

Could it be that their society is a relic of a form of human society, matriarchy, where women were the rulers? Matriarchy was common among humans in very ancient times across Europe and Asia, and there are glimmers of it today in Central America, Burma, Vietnam, and northwest India. Years ago I had witnessed another form of female power still existing in full bloom in the Trobriand Islands, east of the New Guinea mainland. There, the tribal men hold the power but all inheritance, including selection of the chieftain, flows through the female line.

Sydney approaches Maya with hands held out to show he carries no weapon, the Korubo knowing from horrific experience the destructive power of the white man's guns. He sits down with her on a log by the *maloca*, speaking softly to her, using Jemi as his translator. The other Korubo gather around to listen.

Their stark nakedness is unsettling at first and I don't know which way to look, hoping not to embarrass anyone by staring at them. But this is a reflex action of a Westerner because naked bodies are the norm to the Korubo. Within a few minutes any slight sense I had of sensuality with this display of naked flesh is gone and their bare bodies provoke not even a hint of a sexual association. I imagine this is what it must be like in nudist colonies in the West.

The Pygmy men and women traditionally wore grass skirts, while the Korowai men went about naked and the women wore very short grass skirts but left their breasts uncovered. Why the difference? Dawut provided the answer: sexual exclusivity. A man was free to flaunt his naked body but demanded that his wife, or future wife, keep the sight of her naked body just for him. But then that leaves the riddle of both the Korubo men and women going about totally naked. Here, the answer escapes me.

The conversation lasts half an hour with Maya doing most of the talking, telling Sydney about the crops, the hunting, and their health. Answering Sydney's question, she says that no whites have gone beyond the guard post at the junction of the two rivers. So, the Korubo have been undisturbed by outsiders since his last visit several months earlier.

Smiling, Maya invites Sydney and Magna into the *maloca* but pointedly leaves me out of the invitation. Sydney, with his hand patting the air, signals me to be patient. Juma stays behind to protect me from a surprise assault. I sit on the log but he stands alert with his rifle. As I brush away giant ants and mosquitoes, I constantly glance around the clearing, not trusting the head bashers.

Maya's five-year-old daughter, Manis, decides to stay outside and sits on the log staring up at me with a shy smile. Her pet baby sloth nestles against her neck, its tiny black eyes blurred by constant sleep. It turns its head away from the sun. Manis and I are unable talk to each other because Juma, guard and translator, can't speak English and I can't speak Portuguese. But the little girl and I ignore the vast culture gap between us in this very rare encounter, me as strange and intriguing to her as she and her pet are to me.

After half an hour Maya leads Shishu and the other Korubo out from the *maloca,* followed by Sydney and Magna. There is no door, just a narrow waist-high opening in the straw wall, forcing them to bend low. This seems a safeguard so enemies can't easily storm into the *maloca* in a surprise attack. All the men still grip their war clubs, wisely I expect. Sydney had told me they are ever vigilant for an ambush from their clansmen, whose leader had sparked their exodus by attempting to seize Maya from her then husband.

I smile seeing Sydney stripped to his underpants. His ghostly white legs, belly, and chest contrast with the bronzed skin of the Korubo. They look in the full flush of health while Sydney's leached flesh resembles that of a dead fish. "Being like this makes me feel more comfortable with them," he explains.

Magna opens her medical bag and the Korubo line up as if they know what to expect. She withdraws syringes and vials and Maya bends to receive, without a sound or a wince, a shot in her buttock. Shishu follows, then Ta'van and the other Korubo.

"We whites brought malaria to the Amazon and now it's common among the tribes, including the Korubo," Magna tells me. "It's easily treated with an injection once a month. Apart from malaria, the most serious health risks they suffer are battle wounds."

The carrier of malaria is the blood-sucking female anopheles mosquito that injects the plasmodium parasite into the bloodstream of an uninfected person. An attack begins between ten and fifteen days after a victim has been stung. A chain effect can occur among a community.

In his book *Amazon Journal,* Geoffrey O'Connor described the symptoms of a malaria attack. "The gold miners I've met in the Amazon describe the initial symptoms as a loss of appetite and pounding headaches 'that feel as if someone is taking an axe to the back of your skull.' Waves of fever interspersed with chills can last for several hours and attack the body over the course of three or four days. Then the face goes pale, the fingers turn white, and the nails become blue. There are two more stages. One is characterised by dry heat and burning skin with the body's urine turning strange colors. Then there is stage three: the killer. That's when the body is drenched in sweat and the urine turns into a thick blood-red liquid. These are signs that the untreated illness has attacked the spleen and the liver, enlarging them, blowing them out of shape, shutting down their vital functions. Malaria can also go for the brain, invading the cerebral tissues, driving people crazy."

Malaria is endemic in the jungles of the Amazon and I can imagine the fear and panic whenever it struck at the Korubo and other Indian tribes. The World Health Organization estimates that 480,000 people die from malaria each year, the majority of them in Africa.

When Magna finishes injecting the Korubo, Sydney beckons me. "You know how to do the Maori war dance, the haka. If you perform it for the Korubo, it may help them accept you. As you can see they're still suspicious of you and that could prove dangerous."

The Korubo stand beside the *maloca* with puzzled expressions as I tell them I'm about to challenge one of their warriors to a fight to the death, but I stress, only in fun. I hope Juma can explain that difference to them. Sydney tells them that this is a far-off tribe's ritual challenge to an enemy tribe immediately before battle and that one of their warriors must accept the challenge, signifying that his clan is ready to fight. Shishu steps forward, thrusts his hands against hips, and glares at me.

I strip off my shirt and gulp nervously. Then I punch my chest as hard as I can with both fists, stamp my feet and scream out the beginning of the bellicose chant in Maori. *"Ka mate, ka mate, ka ora, ka ora."* Jumi translates the words. "I die, I die, I live, I live." I stomp to within a few inches of Shishu's face, poke out my tongue in Maori style, and twist my face into the traditional grotesque mask that is supposed to terrify the enemy.

He stares hard at me and stands his ground, refusing to be bullied. As I shout louder, my emotions are in a tangle. I want to impress the warriors with my ferocity but worry that if I stir them up they'll attack me with their clubs.

Oh, what the hell, I think. In Maori warrior style I'm going to let it rip and give them the full force of the haka. Banging my chest, slapping my thighs, and stomping my feet again and again, I shout that I'm going to burn down their hut, ravish their women, slaughter their men, and drag off their children as slaves.

I end the haka by jumping into the air with arms held high and shouting "Hee!" To my relief the Korubo are smiling, too practiced in real warfare to feel threatened by an unarmed outsider shouting threats and pounding his flabby chest. Only Ta'van remains grim-faced. He strides up to me and bangs his war club against the ground. Oh God, here's trouble, I think. Then he surprises me by punching his chest repeatedly.

This peerless warrior is paying me a high compliment. He wants a repeat of the haka and wants to take the challenge. One by one, the Korubo men take it in turn to have me challenge them in a haka and none take a backward step. By the time I finish five haka, I'm in more danger of perishing from a heart attack than from having my head caved in.

Ta'van strides up to me again and says he wants to show me the Korubo ritual before battle. "Do not move," Sydney warns me. "I've only seen this once before and Ta'van went close to losing control and bashing my head in with his club. I truly feared for my life."

Gripping his club, Ta'van begins deliberately to hyperventilate, sucking in deep breaths, blowing out his cheeks, and expelling the air explosively. It's just like the Maori warriors I'd seen hyperventilating before performing an authentic haka in New Zealand. All warriors are brothers under the skin.

His breathing comes faster and faster, louder and louder, and he bellows like a bull. Suddenly, he whacks the ground with the war club a few inches to my left. This doesn't look like play-acting. He raises it in the air and whacks the ground again. Just as close. The blows come faster and faster so that the war club is a blur. His aim is precise and each time the club shakes the ground around me but misses my body by a hand span. His face is flushed with angry blood and his eyes are wide and wild.

Maya shouts something and he immediately stops. Still holding the club, he stares at me with a look that I can't decipher. It's not hatred or anger, but it's also not welcoming. His emotions have been fired up to boiling point by the battle ritual and at this moment he might not know if I'm friend or foe. Sydney puts his arm around my shoulder. "We'd better leave now. It's best not to stay too long on the first visit."

On the way back in the canoe, he says, "You impressed them with the haka. They'll talk about it in their *maloca* for many years to come."

The sky is darkening as we head back to the base. I hardly glance at the flocks of parrots that fly overhead on their way home to roost because my mind is humming with excitement from our visit to the Korubo. Even with that brief visit, I've spent more time with them than any other reporter, but there is so much more I hope to know about their lifestyle.

After another dinner of wild boar washed down with coffee, Sydney, Magna, and I sit at the table to chat about the Korubo. Outside, Juma sweeps the searchlight back and forth over the junction of the twin rivers in search of intruders from Atalaia and further downstream.

Remembering Al Toffler's warning that the Korubo, deprived of modern medicine, would be riddled with disease and die young, I was surprised to see them looking so healthy. The warriors had fit, taut bodies as muscled as champion athletes. "They eat very well and their diet includes many kinds of fish, wild pig, spider monkeys, birds, sloth, fruit, manioc, and maize," Magna says. "Despite their lusty appetites, there is not an ounce of fat on any of them. The men and women work hard for up to five hours a day, hunting and gathering, and have a healthier diet than most Brazilians.

"Because they eat little fat or sugar and drink only water they have very good skin and seem to have long lives. After work they have many hours free to sit on the log or inside the *maloca* chatting and eating. Theirs would be an enviable life except for the constant tension they feel, ever alert for a surprise attack by enemies."

I noticed that even the middle-aged Korubo had few lines marring their faces. "I go from the base once a month to treat them and I've never seen them quarrel or hit their children. The partnerships between the men and women are usually constant, they're monogamous, but if partners can't get along then they tell me they can remarry."

Is it possible that physical punishment of children, which the Korubo, like the Pygmies and the Korowai, find abhorrent, is a later evolution in human history? But the Korubo paradise has an abundance of thorns and they practice at least one chilling custom. Like many other Amazon tribes, they sometimes mysteriously kill babies born disabled. "We've never seen it actually happen but they've told me they do it," Magna says. "I know of a case where they killed the baby two weeks after birth. They wouldn't tell me why. It might have had a cleft palate, which is common among babies in the Amazon, or it might have been born with another disability that would have made life tough in the jungle."

The clan has five couples, a bachelor, four boys, and five girls, and Magna believes murdering newborns could also be a way to balance the sexes. But they don't count the actual number in their clan. "They use the word, 'many' for anything beyond a few digits," she explains.

I was intrigued to see there were no religious carvings or rainforest altars that the Korubo might use to pray for successful hunts or other godly boons such as an afterlife. In their jungle haunted by nightmarish predators, animal and human, the Korubo surely must need some form of religious or spiritual practice to feed their souls as well as their bellies. Do they have their own gods?

Like much of Korubo ways, this is a mystery. "I've never seen them practicing any kind of ritual that looked as if it were spiritual in the two years I've been with them," Magna says, "but we know too little about them to be sure."

"I refuse to allow anthropologists to study the clan firsthand because it's too dangerous to live with them," Sydney explains. "I won't let anyone stay overnight with them, even myself, even if I were protected by Jemi and Juma, unless we have an emergency like last night. So, we may never uncover many of their mysteries because one day Maya's clan must leave the *maloca* and return to the tribe's main group deep in the jungle."

If and when anthropologists gain permission to live with and study the Korubo, they may find similarities with other tribes including the Marubo, with just six hundred members and who live at the Javari Valley's southern edge. In *Vanishing Amazon*, Mirella Ricciardi wrote: "The Marubo all trace their origins back to nine mythological heroes, each of whom gave his name to the clans of descendants who came after him." During collective rituals the Marubo recount lengthy myths which recall the past, establishing the ancestry of the clans and their separate identities. "The myths are sung out line by line, by an older member of the community and repeated in chorus by all the others gathered there."

But there is one Korubo custom common to most humans that Sydney and his team know about. "As you saw, some of the children are approaching puberty, and the Korubo know the dangers of inbreeding," Magna tells me. "They've told me they'll have to go back to the main group one day to get husbands and wives for the youngsters, but they keep away for now because they're still afraid of being attacked and killed if they return. We'd miss them very much but we know it will eventually be for the best."

"I've never tried to make contact with the main group of Korubo," Sydney says, "because their *maloca* are so deep in the forbidden zone that settlers from Atalaia and Benjamin Constant pose no threat to them. The only times I've ever seen their presence is when I've made aerial surveys over the forbidden zone in a light plane looking for huts of uncontacted tribes, often in impenetrable jungle. Even then they usually flee into the jungle when they hear the plane coming."

Sydney shows me a stack of aerial pictures he has taken of the communal huts of the uncontacted tribes. They look much like the Korubo *maloca*. He says each tribe has about thirty to four hundred people. "We've identified seventy-one sites in the forbidden zone where uncontacted tribes live but there may be more. We don't know the tribes' names or languages, and we don't want to know, because I feel content to leave them be. They're happy hunting, fishing, farming, and living their own way. They don't want to know us, they want to be left alone with their unique vision of the world, and my primary task is to respect their isolation and protect them."

I tell Sydney about the Korowai, explaining that they build their huts high in the trees as protection because the clans constantly fight each other with bows and arrows and because it keeps them away from the deadly malaria-carrying mosquitoes.

"I was the third white man the clan had ever seen, they called me *laleo* or ghost demon, but small planes sometimes passed overhead even if the Korowai had no sense of their meaning. When told they carried humans hurtling through the air, they laughed in disbelief. When they first saw them overhead, they told me some of the Korowai were so afraid, believing they were giant birds coming to eat them, that in panic they leaped from their lofty huts and perished."

"You never know how a tribe is going to react at first contact with whites," Sydney remarks. "Mostly, they'll try to kill you. But the Korubo, for all their ferocity, were peaceful, apart from Ta'van murdering poor Raimundo and those three whites along the river. We left gifts such as aluminium cooking pots by their *maloca* once we found where they were. They'd run away each time, fearing we'd come to kill them. It took months for the warriors to come guardedly out of the jungle, almost certainly ordered to by Maya, and meet us. Shishu was captivated by the lens of the cameraman with us who was documenting the first contact. He peered into the lens, saw his reflection, and asked me in great wonder, 'Who is that little man in there?'"

With the Matis translating, the Korubo men asked these pale-skinned aliens from another world whether they had the same sexual organs. "I had to take down my pants and they were happy to see I was built the same as them, truly a human. We had a woman on a later expedition and the Korubo women took her aside and examined her private parts. The men asked me how we performed sex and yelled with delight when they realized there was no difference."

Back in my room, I examine the photos I took at the *maloca* and am astonished to see that Ta'van's bellicose charisma had created an optical illusion I had never experienced before, even though I've journeyed to warrior tribes on several continents. The top of his head barely came up to my shoulder but he bristled with so much presence that until I saw the photos I was certain he was a few inches taller than me.

CHAPTER 13

The next morning our motorized canoe makes the half-hour journey to the Korubo *maloca* on a river swarming with animals but no sign of human habitation. The sun has lured a dozen caiman, similar to alligators, onto the riverbank to soak up its rays and so gather warming strength for the day. Hundreds of vividly colored parrots must be nesting in the jungle by the river, because great flocks pass overhead once more, their bright red and blue feathers glinting in the sunlight.

I have on three sets of thick socks in case a cobra strikes on the path to the *maloca* and this time summon courage and tread across the log that spans the creek, holding my hands outstretched for balance. Sydney lets me call out "Eh-heh" to signal our approach and moments later comes a faint echoing call from deeper in the jungle.

We're greeted by a sight that amazes Sydney. The warriors have painted their bodies scarlet or slathered themselves with white clay and wear headbands and long streaming armbands made from jungle raffia. "I've never seen them do this before," he tells me. "I think they've done it to honor your haka," he adds with a grin.

This time Shishu beckons me to enter the *maloca*. Jumi, rifle at the ready, follows with Sydney and Magna. The Korubo are sprawled in vine hammocks strung low between poles holding up the roof or squatting by small hearths scattered with ash.

Stacked overhead on poles running the length of the hut are long slender blowguns; stone axes and woven baskets lean against the walls. Circular holes dug a few inches into the dirt floor hold the war clubs upright, at the ready. There are six fireplaces, one for each family.

Maya, the hut's dominant presence, sits by a fireplace husking corn, which she then grinds into mash. She hands me a cob she has grilled in the fireplace and it's delicious. Even the warriors are cooking and cleaning. The young muscular Teun sweeps the hut's earthen floor with a switch of tree leaves while Washman, his wife, supervises. Tatchipan, the handsome young warrior who took part in the massacre of the three white men, squats over a pot cooking the skinned carcass of a spider monkey. Ta'van helps his wife Mona, plump and pleasant, boil a string of fish he caught in the river that morning.

The men then squat in a circle and wolf down the fish, monkey, and corn. Ta'van breaks off one of the monkey's arms, complete with hand, and gives it to Tatchipan, who gnaws the skimpy meat from the bone. Even as they eat, I remain tense, wary that they could erupt into violence at any moment despite the honor they have paid me by donning their finery.

After the warriors finish eating, Shishu grips my arm. "You're a *nowa*, a white man," he says. "Some *nowa* are good, but most are bad." I glance at Ta'van, who stares at me without expression while cradling his war club. Does he consider me one of the good whites?

Shishu provides the answer when he crushes a handful of *urucu* berries between his palms, spits into them, and slathers the bloody-looking liquid on my face and arms. "Now you're not a *nowa*, you're a Korubo," he says with a grin. Hunching over a wooden slab studded in rows with small sharp monkey teeth, he grinds a dry root into a powder, mixes it with water, squeezes it into a half-coconut shell, and invites me to drink.

I smile my thanks. The muddy liquid has an herbal taste and I share several cups with Shishu and Sydney. I expect it to be a narcotic like kava, the South Pacific concoction made from a potent pepper root mixed with water. I've drunk kava many times in Tonga, Samoa, and Fiji and enjoyed the blurry peaceful buzz it gives. But the Korubo drink has no noticeable effect. Sydney tells me that the men drink the gritty liquid before they go into battle.

Other Korubo potions are not as benign. By the hut's entrance Tatchipan kneels, places a stick vertically on a slab of wood with a notch in it, and twirls it vigorously between his palms for a couple of minutes, much as a caveman might have done 100,000 years ago. The friction produces sparks that set alight the tinder, a small bundle of dry grass that Tatchipan blows on vigorously to ignite a flickering flame. He then inserts the burning grass into a bundle of twigs stacked in a hearth, setting them on fire.

Halfway across the globe, in a remote New Guinea jungle, I have seen naked tribesmen make fire in exactly the same manner. Trial and error over a very long time must have led the ancients to make parallel discoveries of how to make fire. Tatchipan places a clay bowl brimming with *curare*, a black syrup he's made by pulping a woody wine, onto the fire. After stirring the bubbling liquid, he dips the sharp tips of dozens of slender blowgun darts into it.

The *curare*, Shishu says, is used to hunt small prey such as birds and monkeys. It's not used on humans. Why not? He points to his war club nestled against his thigh, and then to my head. I get the message, confirmed by Sydney. The Korubo are the only Brazilian Indians who now brandish war clubs in their fights, the other tribes using blowguns and bows and arrows.

Perhaps the drink I have just taken is used not only when they are about to go to war but also before the men go hunting Soon after, Shishu invites Sydney and me to come with him on a hunt. He says good-bye to the women, who head for the manioc and maize fields. Then, he hoists a twelve-foot-long blowgun on his shoulder and strings a bamboo quiver containing a dozen *curare* darts around his neck. We leave the clearing with me struggling to keep up as he and Sydney lope through the shadowy jungle, alert for prey.

Hour slips into hour. Then Shishu stops and shades his eyes while peering up into the jungle canopy. I can't see anything except tangled leaves and branches but he's spotted a monkey almost hidden by the leaves. He takes a dab of gooey red ochre from a holder bound to the quiver and shapes it around the end of the dart as a counterweight. Then he takes the petals of a white flower from another holder and packs them around the sticky ochre to smooth the dart's path through the blowgun.

He raises the blowgun to his mouth, aims at the monkey, puffs his cheeks and blows, seemingly with little effort. The dart hits the monkey in the chest. The *curare* is a muscle relaxant that causes death by asphyxiation and several minutes later the monkey, unable to breathe, tumbles to the forest floor at our feet.

Shishu swiftly fashions a jungle basket from leaves and vine around us, pushes the monkey inside, and slings the basket over his shoulder. He kills another monkey and a big black bird, and then with hunting ended, Shishu leads us back to the *maloca*. He stops at a stream near the hut to wash away the mud, and I plunge in, still in pants and shirt, to get rid of some of the muck. The jungle heat soon dries me out.

I reenter the *maloca* with Shishu, Maya, Ta'van, Mona, and Sydney. The Korubo's voices tinkle like music as we men sip the herbal drink and the women weave baskets. Suddenly Shishu shouts a warning and leaps to his feet. He's heard a noise in the jungle. It could be an attack. He and Ta'van grab their war clubs and race outside followed by Sydney and me. From the forest we hear the familiar password, "Eh-heh," and moments later Tatchipan and another young warrior, Marebo, stride into the clearing. Sydney sighs with relief. "False alarm," he says.

Once again the men entreat me to perform a haka and this time I give them the full works, ending the war dance as is customary by dragging down my pants at the back and baring my bum at them. They scream with laughter. I did not tell them that this gesture is the Maori supreme insult to their enemy before battle. I had decided not to tell Sydney in case he passed it on to them. Three encores follow.

Marebo, who was also in the war party that massacred the three whites, places my hand on his chest to feel small bumps just under the flesh, buckshot from a shotgun. "*Nowa,*" he says and grimaces.

"He was caught in an ambush not far from here before we'd set up the base, and whites from Atalaia shot dead two of the clan's warriors," Sydney tells me. "Marebo was lucky to escape alive. The murderers were never punished."

This moves me to tears. I'm clearly a *nowa*, one of the hated tribe that has caused so much death and misery to this Korubo clan. Yet, they have welcomed me to their jungle home and shared their life with me.

We return to the base at sunset but are back by mid-morning the next day. Sydney and I relax in hammocks inside the *maloca* as the Korubo sit cross-legged around the fireplaces or sway gently in hammocks. Maya hushes the warriors when they grow too noisy, boasting about past fights, and sends them out to fish in dugouts, canoes made from large logs hacked into shape with stone axes.

Ta'van guides his canoe with a paddle to a riverbank about an hour upstream and strides along it, clearly with a purpose I can't fathom. He laughs with delight and digs with his bare hands to uncover a cache of about fifty cream-colored eggs. They're a Korubo delicacy, buried by a mother tortoise. "Somehow he felt them under the sand beneath his bare toes," Sydney says.

Back on the river, the warriors cast their vine nets and haul up twenty struggling fish, some shaded green with stumpy tails, others silvery with razor-sharp teeth. Piranha.

The nutritious fish with the bloodthirsty reputation is a macabre but apt metaphor for the circle of life in this combative paradise where hunter and hunted often must eat and be eaten by each other to survive.

When we arrive back at the *maloca* Maya is cutting Washman's wet hair using a long reed with an edge sharp as a razor. She shapes the hair into two segments, shaving to the bone a two-inch-wide arc across the middle of the skull from ear to ear. Washman's thick black hair flops over her eyebrows but Maya cuts it close to the skin at her neck.

Each day we go hunting with the warriors or relax in the *maloca* but always return to the safety of the base each night. The week we have with the clan goes much too fast and my heart aches as we join them on our last day.

Sydney will not bring photos of the outside world to the Korubo because he is afraid the images, shimmering with magic to these Stone Age people, will encourage them to try and visit the white settlements downriver. That would obviously be very dangerous for them. As I sit with Ta'van on the log, I ponder whether Sydney is right to isolate these remote tribes, keeping them bottled up in their rainforests as prehistoric curiosities.

Is ignorance really bliss? Or should Brazil's government throw open for them the doors to the twenty-first century, bringing them extensive medical care, modern technology, and education?

I remember Pastor Antonio at Tabatinga declaring that his church had been commanded by Jesus to go out into the world and bring His teachings to all peoples. He had declared that Sydney had no right to stop the pastors from entering the Javari Valley forbidden zone to "save the primitive Indians' souls."

His view is echoed by many church leaders across Brazil. The resources of the forbidden zones are coveted by people with more worldly concerns, and not just entrepreneurs salivating over the timber and mineral resources worth billions of dollars. Not long after my visit, five thousand armed men from Brazil's landless workers' movement marched into one of the tribal forbidden zones southeast of the Javari Valley, demanding to be given the land. Funai officials feared they would massacre the Indians there and so they forced the marchers to retreat by threatening to call in the military.

Sydney remains unmoved by criticism of him isolating the uncontacted tribes. "People say I'm crazy, unpatriotic, a Don Quixote," he tells me as we sit with the clan by their hut. "Well, Quixote is my favorite hero because he was constantly trying to transform bad things he saw into good."

As we get ready to leave, Sydney gives the clan a glimpse of the outside world by trying to describe an automobile. "They're like small huts that have legs and run very fast." Maya smiles and shakes her head in disbelief.

Ta'van punches his chest, imitating the haka, asking me to perform the war dance one last time. I throw all my energy into this performance as thanks for the unique gift the Korubo have given me. Ta'van grips my arm and smiles in farewell. Shishu remains in the hut and wails, anguished that Sydney is leaving. Tatchipan and Marebo, lugging war clubs, escort us down to the river.

As the canoe begins its journey across the millennia, Sydney looks back at the warriors, a wistful expression on his face. "I just want the Korubo and other isolated Indians to go on being happy," he says. "They have not yet been born into our world, and I hope they never will."

Bibliography

Addison, Jo. *The Battle of the Pygmies and the Crane.* NSW State Library Collection, 1774.

Arens, William. *The Man-Eating Myth: Anthropology and Anthropophagy.* Oxford University Press: New York, 1974.

Ashkenasy, Hans. *Cannibalism: From Sacrifice to Survival.* Prometheus: Amherst, New York: 1994.

Ballif, Noel. *Dancers of God: Pygmies.* Sedgwick and Jackson: London, 1955.

Bjerre, Jens. *The Last Cannibals.* M. Joseph: London, 1956.

Bodard, Lucien. *Massacre in the Amazon.* Tom Stacey Ltd: London, 1971.

Chinnery, Ernest. *Cannibalism.* Gilbert Murray Papers: National Library of Australia.

Cavalli-Sforza, Luca: *Genes, Peoples and Languages.* University of California Press: Berkeley and Los Angeles, 2000.

Collier, Richard: *The River that God Forgot: The Amazon Rubber Boom.* Collins: London, 1968.

Conrad, Joseph. *The Heart of Darkness.* Penguin English Library: Middlesex, 1983.

Conklin, Beth: *Consuming Grief: Compassionate Cannibalism in an Amazonian Society.* University of Texas Press: Austin, 2001.

Central African Republic: Country Profile. The Economist Intelligence Unit: London, 2008.

Davis, Wade. *One River.* Simon and Schuster: New York, 1996.

Decalo, Samuel: *Psychoses of Power: Africa's Personal Dictatorships.* Westview Press: Boulder, Colorado, 1989.

du Chaillu, Paul. *Adventures in the Great Forests of Equatorial Africa and the Country of the Dwarfs.* Harper and Brothers: New York, 1890.

Elmslie, Jim. *Irian Jaya under the Gun.* University of Hawai'i Press: Honolulu, 2002.

Furneux, Robin. *The Story of a Great River.* Putnam: New York, 1967.

Hemming, John. *Amazon Frontier: The Defeat of the Brazilian Indians.* Macmillan: London, 1987.

Gardner, Robert and Karl G. Heider *Gardens of War.* Andre Deutsch: London, 1969.

Haskins, Cheryl Parker. *The Life and History of a Mighty River.* Doubleday: Doran, 1945.

Kalck, Pierre. *Historical Dictionary of the Central African Republic.* Scarecrow Press: New Jersey, 1980.

Kalck, Pierre. *CAR: The Failure of Colonization.* Pall Mall: London, 1990.

Lange, Algot. *The Amazon Jungle.* Echo Library: Middlesex, 2007.

Levine, Robert M. *History of Brazil.* Palgrave: New York, 2003.

Law, Diane. *A Secret History of the Great Dictators: Idi Amin and Emperor Bokassa.* Constable and Robinson: London, 2011.

Matthiessen, Peter: *Under the Mountain Wall.* Penguin: New York, 1987.

Lewis, Jerome. "Pygmy hunter-gatherer egalitarian social organization: the case of the Mbendjele BaYaka." In Hewlett, B., (ed) *Congo Basin Hunter-Gatherers.* Pp. 219-244.

Millard, Candice: The *River of Doubt: Theodore Roosevelt's Darkest Journey.* Doubleday: New York, 2005.

Newkirk, Paula. *The Astonishing Life of Ota Benga.* Amistad Press: New York, 2015.

O'Connor, Geoffrey. *Amazon Journal: Dispatches from a Vanishing Frontier.* Dutton: New York, 1997.

Osbourne, Robin. *Indonesia's Secret War: the Guerilla Struggle in Irian Jaya.* Allen and Unwin: Sydney, 1985.

BIBLIOGRAPHY

Ricciardi, Mirella. *Vanishing Amazon*. Harry N. Abrams Inc.: New York, 1991.

Restoration of Irian Jaya into the Republic of Indonesia. The Indonesian Mission at the UN: NSW State Library, 2001.

Sarno, Louis. *Song from the Forest*. Houghton Mifflin: Boston, 1993.

Stanley, Henry M. *In Darkest Africa*. Henry Morton: London, 1890.

Swann, Alfred J. *Fighting the Slave Hunters of Central Africa*. Steeley Co: London, 1928.

Stone, Linda and Paul F. Lurquin. *A Genetic and Cultural Odyssey*. Columbia University Press: New York, 2005.

Thompson, Liz. *The Dani of Irian Jaya*. Collection of Port Melbourne Library: Melbourne, 1997.

Turnbull Colin M. *The Forest People*. Simon and Schuster: New York, 1961.

———. *Wayward Servants: The Two Worlds of the African Pygmies*. Eyre and Spotswoode: London, 1966.

Trompf, G. W. *Melanesian Religions*. Cambridge University Press: London, 1991.

UN Human Development Index for the Central African Republic. http://hdr.undp.org/en/countries/profiles/CAF

van Enk, Gerritt and Lourens de Vries. *The Korowai of Irian Jaya*. Oxford University Press: Oxford, 1997.

Vogel, Alfred. *Papuans and Pygmies*. Arthur Baker: London, 1953.

Wallace, Alfred R. *Narrative of Travels in the Amazon and Rio Negro*. Reeve and Co.: London, 1853.

Wallechinsky, David. *Tyrants: The World's 20 Worst Dictators*. HarperCollins: New York, 2009.

Williams, Glyndwr. *Captain Cook's Voyages, 1768-1779*. The Folio Society: London 1997.